TODAY'S DESTRUCTIVE CULTS AND MOVEMENTS

5/20/93

God's Blessings
Father Larry Gesy

TODAY'S DESTRUCTIVE CULTS AND MOVEMENTS

Rev. Lawrence J. Gesy

Foreword by Mother Teresa of Calcutta

Contributing Authors: Carol Giambalvo, Daniel H. Green, Maggie Moulton, Jane Petrie, Michael Summers, Donald H. Thompson

Our Sunday Visitor Publishing Division
Our Sunday Visitor, Inc.
Huntington, Indiana 46750

Chapter 9 of this book includes excerpts from *The Devil: "alive and active in our world"* by Msgr. Corrado Balducci, © 1990 by Alba House and reprinted by permission. All rights reserved. Council documents quoted in this book are reprinted with permission from *Vatican Council II: the Conciliar and Postconciliar Documents,* © 1975 by Costello Publishing Company, Inc., and Rev. Austin Flannery, O.P. All rights reserved.

Our Sunday Visitor Publishing Division
Our Sunday Visitor, Inc.
200 Noll Plaza
Huntington, Indiana 46750

International Standard Book Number: 0-87973-498-1
Library of Congress Catalog Card Number: 92-83995

Cover design by Rebecca J. Heaston;
back cover photo by Denise Walker, photographer, *The Catholic Review*;
illustrations on pp. 127 and 184 by Fay Brown Steele;
symbols in Appendix VIII courtesy National Cult Awareness Office

PRINTED IN THE UNITED STATES OF AMERICA

498

*This book is dedicated
in memory of my deceased parents,
Joseph and Alvina Gesy,
to my brothers and sisters,
and to the priests and parishioners
under the powerful protection
of Our Lady of Victory*

ACKNOWLEDGMENTS

I wish to express my gratitude to my co-worker Doris Quelet, to the co-authors of this book, and to the staff of Our Sunday Visitor Books, especially Jackie Murphy and John Laughlin, the acquisition and project editors. Thanks to Msgr. Satterfield, censor for the book, and to Msgr. Malooly, Vicar General of the Archdiocese of Baltimore, who granted the imprimatur; also for the support of the priests and the people of the Archdiocese of Baltimore and of Our Lady of Victory parish, especially Fathers John Kelmartin and Frank Ernst, as well as Father Ronald Pytel, pastor of Holy Rosary Church in Baltimore. I express my gratitude to Denise Walker, photographer for the *Catholic Review*, for the back cover photograph.

Special thanks to Most Rev. William Keller, Archbishop of Baltimore, for his encouragement and pastoral support. In the same way I thank Mother Teresa for taking the time to personally write the Foreword to the book. May God and the Blessed Mother bless you for the great love that you have for His people.

Thanks to Doubleday & Co., Inc., for texts from *The Jerusalem Bible* (JB), © 1966-67-68; to the Confraternity of Christian Doctrine for excerpts from *The New American Bible* (NAB), © 1969-70, 1986; and to the Division of Christian Education for the National Council of the Churches of Christ in the United States of America for verses from *The New Revised Standard Version* of the Holy Bible (NRSV), © 1989 (all rights reserved).

Finally, gratitude to many expert sources. If any materials have been used inadvertently without proper credit, please notify Our Sunday Visitor Publishing Division in writing so that future printings can be corrected.

— Father Larry Gesy

CONTENTS

FOREWORD

Mother Teresa of Calcutta

54-A, AJC Bose Road, Calcutta - 700 016

(facsimile)

July 27,'92

"As long as you did it to one of these My least brethren. You did it to Me"

Dear Fr.Larry Gesy and co-authors,

This brings the readers of your book my prayer that it may lead.them from despair to hope; error to Truth and captivity to freedom.

Jesus not only came to preach GoodNews to the poor. He became the Poor One - the hungry one, the homeless one. And He said:" What you do to the least of My brothers, that you do to Me." Jesus in the least of our brothers is not only hungry for bread but He is also hungry for love. This hunger for love is in fact hunger for God, for God is Love. The nakedness in today's world isnot only for clothes. The real nakedness in our world today is the need for our human dignity. The greatest poverty today is the poverty of not knowing who we are - of not knowing that we are the Children of God - that we have a Father in heaven Who cares for us tenderly. The poorest of the poor today are those who do not know they are created for greater things - to love and to be loved and to share the joy of loving with one another. They seek to nourish their souls on the falsehood found in destructive religious movements.

If we really centre our lives on Jesus, if we really understand the Eucharist and nourish our souls with the Bread of Life and the word of God, we would not only be able to recognise the likeness of God in ourselves and others but we would also be able to restore it to those who seem to have lost it. My prayer is with you that all who read this book may realise that: Jesus is the Truth to tell; the Word to speak; the way to walk; the Love to share and the Life to live - the fullness of life which Jesus Himself came to give us.

Let us pray.

God bless you
lu Teresa mc

Mother Teresa, Missionaries of Charity

1.

Contemporary Destructive Religious Movements

Father Lawrence J. Gesy

EVERYONE is familiar with a yardstick, which is three feet, or thirty-six inches, long. This standard of measurement is universal in the United States, although many other nations use different standards of measurement, such as the metric system; every society, however, depends on some standard of measurement.

In our contemporary civil society and in our Judeo-Christian faith communities, we also have standards by which we measure right and wrong, good and evil. These laws of God and of the state protect the peace and harmony of civilized nations.

Our beliefs provide the yardstick by which we can measure and then judge what is right or wrong in contemporary religious movements. If a religious movement does not measure up to or violates natural law, the Sacred Scriptures, the Traditions of the Church, the Constitution of the United States and the civil laws implementing it, our personal conscience, and our freedom of will to choose in accordance with that conscience, that movement is destructive.

As believers in God, our yardstick is the Scriptures, inspired by the Holy Spirit, and the Traditions of the Church, guided by the Holy Spirit, which traditions include the beliefs, laws, forms of worship, and customs by which Christian people have lived and do live out their faith through the centuries. We respond to God's revelation by our acts of faith, and this belief is expressed in action: in worship, both private, personal prayer and public liturgy; and in moral life, private, personal moral acts and those actions by which we bring our moral principles into the public arena of civil affairs, the workplace, and society in general.

The following beliefs, which we may call "orthodox principles," are commonly held by "mainstream churches":

> *The Trinity*: In God there are three Persons, the Father, the Son, and the Holy Spirit. The three Persons are equal in nature yet distinct in Person (John 1:1-3).
>
> *The Son*: The Son of God is the second Person of the Blessed Trinity. He is God and man. He is the Incarnate Word of the Father who came to earth as the image of the Father and as our Redeemer. (Philippians 2:5-11, Hebrews 4:14-15, John 1).
>
> *Humankind*: We are created in the image and likeness of God. We were created to serve God on this earth and in eternal life (Genesis 1:26, Psalms 8:5, John 1:11-13).
>
> *Salvation*: Jesus Christ as God and man died on the cross to redeem us from our sins. He won eternal life for us (Romans 10:4-17).
>
> *Revelation*: God reveals Himself to us in Sacred Scriptures. Jesus Christ is the fulfillment of the Word of God (John 14).

The measuring stick which determines the rightness or wrongness of our actions as citizens is the Constitution, composed by our Founding Fathers to safeguard freedom or liberty and justice. As our society grew strong on that Constitutional foundation, our legislative and judicial bodies continued to be guided by it to ensure a democratic society.

The First Amendment to the Constitution assures freedom of religion, of speech, and of the press:

> "Congress shall make no law respecting an establishment of religion, or prohibiting the free exercise thereof; or abridging the freedom of speech, or of the press; or of the right of the people peaceably to assemble, and to petition the Government for a redress of grievance."

Evil enters the world through the actions of persons who have distorted ideas about God or who act on their own disorderly desires. Destructive religious movements teach or show their followers and others distorted ideas about God. They claim religious status under the First Amendment to the Constitution, and thus are protected unless or until they break the law.

These movements deceive innocent persons, causing those persons to believe the movements have and teach the truth, often saying that "mainstream" Churches teach untruths about God but that the movements alone are the way to God and salvation.

The First Commandment tells us: "I am the Lord your God. You shall not have other Gods before me." The "mainstream" Judeo-Christian religions are based on that teaching and law. To put our trust in anything other than God, or to worship a different god, violates our covenant with Him as His creatures, citizens of earth called to become citizens of Heaven.

This book is the result of years of experience which have helped us to understand Contemporary Destructive Religious Movements (CDRMs) and their belief systems. Each writer is an expert in some area of CDRM. Our yardsticks are the natural law, the Divine Law of the Commandments recognized by mainstream religions, and the Constitution of the United States. It is to these that we refer for comparing CDRMs.

The purpose of this book is to share our combined knowledge with the public, to educate people, since all of us have heard "but it could never happen to me." Most individuals — not only youth, but the middle-aged who are seeking, and the elderly who may be lonely or who have other needs — believe they could never become involved in a destructive religious movement. Yet it *did* happen to me.

The title of the lecture was *Cults — Promises and Perils of Alternative Religions*. It was delivered by James McCarthy of the Archdiocese of Denver to approximately three hundred fifty youths, adults, and clergy leaders attending the National Catholic Youth Organization Convention in Kansas City, November 16, 1979.

Jim McCarthy told us that one fourth to one third of those present would become involved in a destructive cult or sect within the next ten years, adding that cults use sophisticated techniques of mind control in recruitment, in conducting their group meetings, in their practices. No age group is exempt, no occupation, no profession, even clergy and religious, is exempt from their attraction.

In Kansas City on Nov. 16, 1979, I, a priest of the Archdiocese of Baltimore, was sure that no cult could recruit me . . . Not me! . . . Never! Yet a year later I became a member of "est" (Erhard Seminar Training), now called the *Forum*. My experience of membership in a cult and as "an exit" from this cult has led me to a sharp awareness that anyone can be vulnerable to the deceptive recruitment practices of destructive religious movements.

What do we mean by "destructive cults"?

The American Family Foundation, a Boston-based organization for studying and promoting cult awareness, defines destructive cults and sects as follows:

"A destructive cult or sect is a highly manipulative group which exploits and sometimes physically and/or psychologically damages members and recruits.
"A destructive cult:
a) dictates — sometimes in great detail — how members should think, feel, and act;
b) claims a special exalted status (e.g. occult powers; a mission to save humanity) for itself and/or its leaders — which usually sets it in opposition to mainline society and/or the family;
c) exploits its members psychologically, financially, and/or physically;
d) utilizes manipulative or "mind-control" techniques, especially the denigration of independent critical thinking, to recruit prospects and make members loyal, obedient, and subservient; and
e) causes considerable psychological harm to many of its members and to its members' families.
"Although some people deem a group destructive merely because it is deviant or 'heretical,' the point of view advanced here reserves the label for groups that tend to be exploitive, manipulative, psychologically damaging, exclusive, and totalist. According to this perspective, a group may be deviant and 'heretical' without being destructive."

Destructive cults have been in existence for many generations but have become more noticeable since the '40s and are becoming increasingly successful and influential. It is conservatively estimated

14

that there are more than five thousand destructive cults or sects in this country, *with three to five million members.* At least thirty-five to fifty percent of their members are former Catholics, a few of whom retain their ties to the Church.

A statement by J. Gordon Melton, in *Christianity Today* for March 16, 1984 (p. 14), reveals the difficulty faced by researchers attempting to write about contemporary destructive religious movements:

> "I no longer break groups into cults, sects, and denominations. I find myself saying, 'This is a New Thought religion,' 'This is an occult religion,' and 'These are Hindu-type religions.' In lumping them together, we assume that all cults have similar characteristics, and they don't."

At a meeting of the College of Cardinals in the Vatican on April 5, 1991, Cardinal Francis Arinze appears to have faced the same problem of how best to designate what he finally calls "New Religious Movements" or "NRMs" in an address printed in *Origins*, April 25, 1991 (p. 749):

> "The term *new religious movements* is more neutral than that of *sects* when referring to these groups. They are called new not only because they showed themselves in their present form after the Second World War, but also because they present themselves as alternatives to the institutional official religions and the prevailing culture. They are called religious because they profess to offer a vision of the religious or sacred world, or means to reach other objectives such as transcendental knowledge, spiritual illumination, or self-realization, or because they offer to members the answers to fundamental questions."

Cardinal Arinze identifies four main types:

1. ". . . movements based on holy Scripture . . . therefore Christian or . . . derived from Christianity."
2. ". . . those derived from other religions, such as Hinduism, Buddhism or traditional religions. Some of them assume in a syncretistic way elements coming from Christianity."

3. "A third group of sects shows signs of a decomposition of the genuine idea of religion and of a return of paganism."
4. ". . . a fourth set of sects are gnostic" (ibid. p. 749).

With regard to the first group, Cardinal Arinze expands: "With reference to Christianity we can distinguish new movements coming from the Protestant reform, sects with Christian roots but with considerable doctrinal differences." Although he does not name specific NRMs in each category, to aid in understanding these types we may be justified in pointing out that the Jehovah's Witnesses and Seventh Day Adventists could fit within this first type.

Movements ". . . derived from other religions such as Hinduism, Buddhism. . ." would undoubtedly include such groups as followers of the philosophy of Zen, Hare Krishnas, practitioners of TM (Transcendental Meditation), followers of Sri Aurobindo, etc.

Cardinal Arinze does not explain what he means by "traditional religions," but it is probable that Shintoism, the religious customs of the American Indians, and the religions of the various African peoples could be subsumed under that title. The Santeria and Voodoo practices of the Caribbean and Mexican peoples and Macumba in Brazil also are a mixture of American Indian religions with African practices and a few terms or names taken from Catholic Christianity, for example, names of saints given to Voodoo (West African) or American Indian gods or goddesses (hence the name "Santeria").

A somewhat less obvious form of syncretizing (mixing) pagan beliefs and practices with Christian beliefs and customs shows up among Hispanics of southern Colorado and northern New Mexico, called the Penitentes, who practice extreme, even torturous rituals, simulating the crucifixion during Holy Week. Also in this category of new religious movements derived from religions other than Christianity, yet at times infusing elements of Christianity into their beliefs or practices, we can include Bahaism and the Unification Church of the Rev. Sun Myung Moon.

The third group of new religious movements are those which Cardinal Arinze remarks as evidencing a "decomposition of the genuine idea of religion and of a return of paganism," and which

". . . maintain a sense of the sacred, but manipulated by man to acquire power over others or the cosmos" (op. cit. p. 750). This category would include Wicca, or witchcraft, which is called "the Old Religion" by many of its followers, meaning the religion of the people of Europe before the coming of Christianity, through rituals honoring the earth, the trees, etc., and through which rituals the practitioners of Wicca attempt to control things or people for good purposes (what is called "White Witchcraft") or for selfish or evil purposes (called "Black Witchcraft").

In addition, there are many groups who do much good, and their large membership and stable organization have earned them a respected place in society, but although they profess belief in the Bible, their belief system — which replaces the Christian teaching about the Trinity, three Divine Persons in One God, with the concept of three gods and other concepts foreign to mainstream Christianity — nevertheless requires that we (as do all mainstream Christian Churches) place them in the category of non-Christian.

Into what category do we fit Satanism? We may find the answer in Cardinal Arinze's analysis of NRMs "from the doctrinal point of view," i.e.: "insofar as they distance themselves from the Christian vision of the world: Those that reject the Church, those that reject Christ, those that reject the role of God [and yet maintain a generic sense of 'religion'], and those that reject the role of religion [and maintain a sense of the sacred, but manipulated by man to acquire power over others or the cosmos]" (op. cit., p. 750).

The belief system and the motivation of the Satanist provides the basis for the category into which individual Satanists belong: Does the person believe in a Creator God, and is that person rejecting the authority and teachings of that God? Does the person accept that Jesus Christ is the Son of God, yet choose not to follow Him? In that case the Satanism believed and practiced is derived from and a form of rebellion against Christianity (category 1). Does the Satanist see Satan as a being with power equal to God's power, a kind of competitor, an opponent? In that case, Satanism belongs in the category of NRMs derived from other religions (in many oriental religions the concept of God includes what we would term good and

17

evil as two different, even contradictory, aspects) or in the third category, that of a decomposition of the genuine idea of religion and of a return to paganism.

Many of the groups, movements, sects, cults, even recognized churches categorized in these pages contain recognizable elements of Gnosticism, Cardinal Arinze's fourth category. In that category also belong the groups stemming from humanitarian, "human potential" backgrounds, such as "est" (now called the Forum), Esalen Institute, or from "divine potential" movements (to use Cardinal Arinze's terms) include New Age and what he calls "religious therapeutic groups," which would include Christian Science, which is based on the principle that the material world is both illusory and evil, and "healing" through use of crystals, diagnosis of physical conditions through observations of a person's "aura." All of these could also be characterized as Gnostic.

We must ask "What does he mean by *Gnostic*?" and "Why does he apply that term to some new religious movements?"

Hans Jonas, in *The Gnostic Religion* (Boston, Beacon Press, 1963, p. 25) states:

> ". . .the Gnostic systems compounded everything — oriental mythologies, astrological doctrines, Iranian theology, elements of Jewish tradition, whether Biblical, rabbinical, or occult, Christian salvation-eschatology, Platonic terms and concepts. . . ."

St. Irenaeus, who wrote the five books of *Adversus haereses* (Against Heresies) between A.D. 180 and 199, writing of the Gnosticism of his time, might have been commenting on the people who start new religious movements today: "Every day one of them invents something new" (*Adv. haer.* 1.18.1).

There are certain basic teachings which underlie all of the varieties of ancient Gnosticism:

The first is that we are divine, or at least godlike, beings, unfortunately living in a cruel and senseless world, which "has cramped our godly style," according to Wolfgang Smith, writing in *Homiletic and Pastoral Review*, March 1988. This teaching is directly opposed to the Judeo-Christian belief that God created everything good, and whatever evil, suffering, trouble, or ignorance there is in this world has come about through original sin and the continuing sins of humankind.

The second basic element of Gnosticism is that the aim of the disciple was to escape imprisonment in this world to the higher world, the Gnostic paradise.

Finally, the means of achieving the desired flight out of the "imprisonment" in the world was some special kind of knowledge (*gnosis* in Greek, from which these cults or devotées derived their name). The gnosis in question was secret, unknown or "unappreciated" by the generality of humans, to be shared only with certain initiates, sometimes carefully guarded bits of knowledge given to members of the cult or, as they were often called, "mystery religions," as the initiates progressed through stages.

Obviously there are major differences between ancient Gnosticism and what contemporary scholars see as a growing influence of new forms of Gnosticism in contemporary thought. How did this come about?

Most of ancient Gnosticism posited some form of creation or emanation of persons into this world from outside of this present world, even though some ancient thinkers said the world itself was eternal. The "knowledgeable" (Gnostics, therefore) desired, and aimed, to escape to a "world" outside of this present one. Most modern Gnostics have adopted the notion of a "closed universe": no "creation," no beginning outside of itself, and an end also within itself, no "paradise" in other words, a perfection which humankind can bring about by itself: *knowledge can solve all of the world's problems*, perfect health (medical science can conquer X, Y, or Z in so many years, and then go on to conquer the next problem), perfect conduct (with better schools we can improve our neighborhoods and our standard of living and end crime).

Notice, in the new forms of Gnosticism, the evil world in which humanity is imprisoned is overcome, "escaped from," by gnosis, knowledge, but the "paradise" is now the "new, improved" world. Just as in the ancient Gnosticism, however, the new Gnosticism continues to accept the pseudo-divinity of humankind and an attitude of "I can do it all myself" instead of recognizing the Judeo-Christian God.

These elements of Gnosticism appear in destructive religious movements in different ways, but it will be evident that they are found in greater or lesser degree in each movement.

Obviously there are many kinds, if we are thinking about more than five thousand destructive cults or sects, but cult-watchers are most concerned at present about the shepherding/discipleship groups, the Satanic and occult groups, and the New Age Movement (sometimes abbreviated as NAM).

Shepherding/Discipleship Groups

Although their stated theology is Christian, many of the leading shepherding/discipleship groups recruit members through deception and use mind-control techniques to indoctrinate their members and to maintain their members' allegiance.

Most shepherding/discipleship groups are ultra-fundamentalist and use the Bible as their only source of teaching about Christian values. These groups frequently engage in "Scripture-twisting," which is a distortion of God's Word to suit the needs or objectives of the group.

Most shepherding/discipleship groups criticize Catholic teaching, ritual, doctrine, creeds, and devotional traditions; considering the Church a man-made organization held together by rules, totally disregarding the historical roots of the Church. Potential recruits receive "disinformation" about the Catholic Church and speak of legitimate churches and church members in such negative terms as "lukewarm," "hypocritical," "deceived," or "dead" to make the potential recruits more receptive to the efforts of the recruiters. Once they have joined the cult, the leaders control the new members by abusing their positions of authority to create the responses of guilt and fear and to exploit their members.

Doris Quelet, who works with me as an associate cult consultant for the Archdiocese of Baltimore, describes typical operations of the shepherding/discipleship movement in this way:

> "The 'Shepherd' claims to provide his sheep with a 'covering' which is a protection from sin and the demonic realm. 'Sheep' must act in obedience to the 'shepherd,' who takes responsibility from God for their actions. Even if one willfully and knowingly commits sin in obedience to his 'shepherd,' his action becomes righteous, because he

has submitted to the authority of his 'shepherd.' To question or challenge a 'shepherd's' advice or direction is considered rebellion. Those who cannot or will not submit are forced out."

Occult and Satanic Activity

Another area of intense concern for the Church in the United States is the increasing number of Satanic and occult groups and their increasingly overt activity. Occult activities include a belief in astrology, in fortune telling, in psychic abilities, in reincarnation, practice of witchcraft, worship of pagan deities, and worship of Satan. It is important to point out that not all who hold occult beliefs belong to groups; nor do all subscribe to the same beliefs; and adherence to Satanism is confined only to a few.

Satanists frequently attempt to recruit, and all too often succeed in recruiting, young people who are attracted by "heavy metal" rock groups, who may dabble in Satanism, and their music, which often includes descriptions of Satanic practices or praise of Satan. They offer drugs (and often praise drugs) to break down the inhibitions of those who are drawn to that environment; they encourage sexual activity in their young followers, and then introduce them to Satanism. Many teen suicides are attributed to Satanic activity, as are also many cases of child abuse.

The New Age Movement

The New Age Movement is a mixture of Eastern mysticism, Western occultism, and some, though very little, Christian thinking. (A marginal issue, but not unimportant, is the New Age use — and abuse — of the term "metaphysical" for their thinking and teaching. "Metaphysics" and "metaphysical" have been used legitimately for many centuries to denote an authentic branch of philosophy, which is quite different in content from the teachings of New Age.) Shirley MacLaine is probably the most active promoter of New Age in the media. But not all practitioners of New Age thinking hold views identical with hers, nor with one another.

Some New Age teachings include the concept that everything is an aspect of divinity (including each human person as divine), reincarnation (including "past-life rebirthing"), auras (including attempted healings based on "aura reading"), "crystal healing," and such psychic phenomena as "channeling" and astral travel. Many groups, apparently less involved with those extreme practices, come nevertheless within the New Age periphery, such as groups promoting "expansion of awareness." The common denominator in all New Age thinking is a degrading of rational, critical thinking, even a negation of objective reality, and an almost exclusive emphasis on "feelings" and emotion.

Why do so many people join cults?

Many idealistic people hope to find a supportive community of people whom they can trust who share their idealistic values, away from the difficult world they experience every day. Many hurting, vulnerable individuals, not only from the eighteen-to-twenty-five age group, but also increasingly from among the well-educated and economically comfortable middle-aged and from the elderly, believe that the religious groups which are now often identified as "destructive" will provide them with acceptance, concern, love, and friendship. It is a harsh fact that the mainline churches, leaders and members, are not making sufficiently vigorous efforts to meet the needs of these people.

In their book *Snapping: American's Epidemic of Sudden Personality Change* (New York: J.B. Lippincott Company, 1978), Flo Conway and Jim Siegelman state:

> "To us, it seemed that people in every walk of life across the country were edging toward a confrontation with the mounting pressure and conflicting emotions of modern life: individual awareness versus social responsibility; immediate pleasure and sensations versus long-range planning and much larger and less tangible form of happiness. People today will pursue any avenue in search of the experience of feeling fulfilled" (op. cit., pp. 186-187).

What do people seek in cults? What characteristics of destructive religious groups appear to be the solutions for which they are seeking? And what can we do about this problem?

Who join cults? Young people who are idealistic, and who find "the world out there" full of compromises, too many people seemingly too interested in "the bottom line," even discovering that

22

some of their erstwhile heroes and heroines have done shoddy things. Young people who are hurting from a broken love affair. High school or college students who have tried too hard for "success" and are suffering from serious fatigue, even to the point of "burnout." Teenagers and young adults who feel misunderstood by their families, or whose trusted parents are going through a divorce, so that the young people feel unbearably stretched in two or more directions.

Who join cults? Middle-aged people and elderly people who perhaps expected too much of life in this world. They thought they would "get ahead" further, make more money, have more security, or they trusted certain friends or relatives, or spent too much of themselves on children who are now grown and have their own lives to live, their own way to make in the world, and the parent or parents are now left with a feeling of emptiness not only in their homes but in themselves.

Who join cults? People of any age who are trying to find out about themselves, to find the meaning of life, to discover what happens after death, and most of all to question whether there is a God and "Does God care about me?"

Who join cults? People who ask, "Do I count for anything or am I only a cypher?" People who think they are or should be something special.

Who join cults? People who find the world a very messy place, people who want some order in their own lives even if it is difficult to find order anywhere else, sometimes people who go around thinking, "Decisions, decisions, I'm tired of having to make decisions."

Almost everyone we know has or has had some of these characteristics at one time or another. Does this mean that such persons are in danger of being recruited by a cult? By no means. But loneliness and stress can bring almost anyone to the point of being vulnerable. Family and friends, teachers and clergy need to reach out in love and not be reluctant to express concern for any person, young or old, who seems to be hurting or to have some need. We, the Church, the People of God, are the hands and feet and tongue and heart of Christ today, called to be friend and healer to our vulnerable neighbors.

We have all heard or read the public service announcements: FRIENDS DON'T LET FRIENDS DRIVE DRUNK. Real friends care about their friends' interests and about what their friends are involved with.

Be aware of the activities of the young people around you. Don't underestimate the dangers of destructive, mind-controlling groups.

Don't allow a family member or a young friend to be pulled into a destructive group because you are afraid to ask questions.

Ask friendly questions with your love and interest showing, so that the young people don't see your questions as an attempt to control them.

Nevertheless, *ask questions*: Who is sponsoring a retreat, a lecture, a workshop, or a Bible-study series? *Ask to see the materials being used.* Ask to meet the leaders of the group. Ask the name of the group and with what larger group or organization it is affiliated. Is the Catholic Church being attacked?

Parents, teachers and clergy need to become more knowledgeable about cult recruitment techniques. Recruiters for destructive cults are personable, friendly, charming, hence arouse little suspicion. Their eye contact is extraordinary, very flattering. They make an individual feel very special and important. Young people should avoid dinner invitations or invitations to go away for a weekend with persons who claim to be instant friends, or with persons who seem to have all the answers to life's questions. This is sometimes termed "love bombing," the purpose of which is to bond the new recruits to the movement. Young people who may suspect they are being "love bombed" should ask point-blank questions about the name of the recruiter's group, and then beware.

But what if someone has slipped through your net of love, concern, caring, and *is being influenced or even recruited by a cult*, but that someone does not speak about it? *Are there signs* which might indicate that is happening?

If the person suddenly begins to speak in a very enthusiastic manner about a new religion (or a new group, or perhaps new "friends");
if the person talks as if infatuated with a new, *unnamed* group of friends;
talks about going away with unnamed new friends, or with an unnamed group;
or, conversely, becomes very evasive, even secretive, about his/her activities or acquaintances;
shows sudden changes toward family members, old friends, responding

24

to concerns or news of family members or friends in ways which are "different," no longer showing friendly happiness or sadness at appropriate times;

expresses inordinately idealistic attitudes;

expresses hostility toward education as if it were a stumbling block to serving mankind;

or perhaps uses stilted language.

The *first response* of someone who suspects that a friend or a family member may be involved with a destructive group is to *keep communications open*. Destructive groups want to isolate a recruit from family, friends, and church. So ask questions gently. Do not become defensive or angry if questions bring a hostile reaction. If the family member or friend is away from home, continue your phone calls and letters, showing respect, love, and acceptance of the person, and avoiding the temptation to attack the cult.

Catholicism and Fundamentalism, by Karl Keating (Ignatius Press, 15 Oakland Ave., Harrison, N.Y. 10528) is an excellent source of information with which to counter the misinformation about the Catholic Church which many destructive cults promote.

If a family member becomes involved in a cult, it is important to get help quickly.

Sometimes one or two sessions with someone who understands how these groups function will be enough to steer a new recruit away from a group. Note "*someone who understands how these groups function*." The parish priest and the Church will already have been discredited by the cult; but in addition, most parish priests have little knowledge of the mind-control techniques used by cults, so they are unable to effectively counsel cult members.

Ignorance of how destructive groups function is producing an immense harvest for these groups. Educational programs for parents, teachers and clergy are desperately needed.

When a person has become deeply committed to a group, it is sometimes impossible for parents to discuss the group or its belief system with their son or daughter without a high level of stress and ill-feeling developing between them. Some of the reasons for this can be discovered within the behavior modification or mind-control techniques used by cults:

Following upon the "love bombing" which draws them, the new recruits

- find themselves in a kind of controlled environment or milieu.
- The group probably has its own "jargon," catch phrases or words (sometimes Scripture verses), which have special meanings for group members different from their meanings in ordinary speech.
- Thought-stopping mottoes or cliches are used to discourage critical thinking and discussion.

These techniques foster bonding of the recruit to the group, giving the recruit a feeling of "specialness," a kind of spiritual elitism, a superior attitude toward other religions, organizations, even government.

- Leaders of destructive religious groups exercise absolute authority, generally based on self-proclaimed special or divine status.
- Following on that, total obedience, blind obedience without recourse, is required.
- Related to that, many believe that there is no salvation outside of their group.
- This builds fear into the recruit, fear of divine retribution or loss of salvation if one should leave, and guilt feelings if one should begin to doubt the teachings of the leaders.
- In addition, there is fear of losing newfound "friends," and the fear of the humiliation and shunning by the group of those who have the courage to leave.

These aspects of cult life directly answer the needs of some hurting people who seek relief from making decisions or are looking for simple answers to life's questions, and those who want discipline in their lives, with new leaders, new purpose.

According to Flo Conway and Jim Siegelman writing in *Science Digest* for January, 1982 ("Information Disease — Have Cults Created a New Mental Illness?" on pp. 88-92), on leaving such a cult, individuals may experience such post-cult symptoms as nightmares, depressions, inability to make decisions, sexual and social adjustments, and in some cases memory loss and diminishment of mental capabilities.

Because of the need to counteract the deep problems created by mind-control processes, some parents hire an exit counselor to present information to the family member which the group might have withheld. That would include information on mind-control, the group's belief system or theology, and the history and/or reputation of the group in the larger community. The exit counselor encourages the person to ask questions, to challenge the information presented, and to repress his/her feelings after receiving the information. This process usually takes three to seven days, depending on the strength and depth of the group's previous control over the family member. That person then *freely* chooses whether or not to remain in the group.

Many families are reluctant to have adult family members exit-counseled, although almost all former cult members who have been exit-counseled express gratitude that their families made that decision. Most have said that they feel they could not have left on their own. The exit-counseling period can also be a time for families to express their love for the member and a time to deal with any cult-related problems which have arisen between them.

Cults and the Church

It is my considered opinion that as inactive and unchurched persons seek a personal relationship with God, the first religious group they encounter will get their attention and possibly their commitment. The late Father Alvin Illig, former director of the Paulist National Catholic Evangelization Association, stated that ninety million Americans are unchurched, sixteen million of whom are baptized-but-inactive Catholics. But in addition to the unchurched baptized Catholics, many Catholics leave the Church permanently because they looked for Bible study and found it outside the Church. The Catholic Church must step up its outreach, its educational program for persons of all ages, and its desire to relate pastorally to these serious concerns.

The Vatican report "Sects or New Religious Movements — Pastoral Challenge" (May 2, 1986) states:

"There is a vacuum crying out to be filled, which is indeed the context in which we can understand not only the criticism toward the Church which many responses contain but foremost the pastoral concerns and proposed approaches. . . . We will mainly emphasize the positive pastoral approaches acted upon, the challenge of the sects may prove to have been a useful stimulus for spiritual and ecclesial renewal."

Suggested Reading: New Religious Movements

The following books are valuable references which supplement one another and, while not for casual reading, are very important for anyone who finds himself or herself confused by current trends in religious thought outside, and, even to a greater extent than might be expected, inside mainline churches.

Larson, Bob, *Larson's New Book of Cults*, Wheaton, Ill., Tyndale House Publishers, Inc., 1989 [After a general introduction to cults, cult concepts, and the roots of cults in world religions, this book provides an alphabetically arranged encyclopedia of cults, with an index in which it is possible to find cults through their alternate names. It has an appendix of cult information resources and a very good bibliography.]

Martin, Walter, *The Kingdom of the Cults*, Minneapolis, Minn., Bethany House Publishers, 1985 [Dr. Martin has compiled very complete documentation on the history and the belief systems of the main classes or divisions of cults. It complements rather than duplicates *Larson's New Book of Cults*.]

Tucker, Ruth A., *Another Gospel, Alternative Religions and the New Age Movement*, Grand Rapids, Mich., Academic Books (division of Zondervan Publishing House), 1989 [". . . pinpoints how the doctrines and practices of a dozen contemporary groups, as well as the New Age Movement, deviate from orthodox Christianity." Dr. Tucker teaches at Northern Illinois University.]

A solidly Catholic approach to the issues raised by the cults treated in the books listed above:

LeBar, Rev. James J., *Cults, Sects, and the New Age* (introductory comments by Cardinals John J. O'Connor and John J. Krol, contributing authors: Rev. Wm. Kent Burtner, O.P., Rev. Walter

DeBold, and Rev. James E. McGuire), Huntington, Ind., Our Sunday Visitor, 1989 [Excellent source material for talks, lesson plans, where to find help, and above all for official statements, pastoral statements by the U.S. Catholic Bishops, individual bishops, and Vatican officials.]

2.

Contemporary Destructive Religious Movements and the Law

Daniel H. Green

A. *Historical Background*

THE courts have been a major focus of societal responses to certain activities of cultic groups during the recent decade. The legal arena has likewise been a major forum for the defense of some of these activities. One might ask, then, "Why, in a country whose Christian founders were able to create such a magnificently enduring document as the U. S. Constitution, which is certainly acknowledged worldwide as the guidepost of constitutional democracy, is this same document so easily used as a shield for oppressive, destructive, and harmful entities like the contemporary destructive religious movements, which are known as *destructive cults*?"

An answer to this puzzle may be found in those very documents which all Americans revere so highly:

> We hold these truths to be self evident, that all men are created equal, that they are *endowed by their Creator* with certain inalienable Rights; that among these rights are Life, Liberty, and the Pursuit of Happiness (From the Preamble to the Declaration of Independence).

Thus our fundamental rights as American citizens are God-given directly to all citizens and are not derived from the law of man nor are they diluted by flowing from God through a monarch or from a so-called prophet whose revealed wisdom is interpreted by him alone. These principles were derived from the very broad and time-tested Judeo-Christian heritage of our Founding Fathers from which we learn that "The purpose of law is to restrain evil; it is not a device to restructure man or human institutions."

Using this wisdom, our Founding Fathers wrote the Bill of Rights, whose very first statement of principle articulated that:

> Congress shall make no law respecting an establishment of religion, or prohibiting the free exercise thereof; or abridging the freedom of speech, or of the press; or the right of the people peaceably to assemble, and to petition the government for a redress of grievances (First Amendment, U.S. Constitution).

So important were the inalienable rights of Americans that their government was prohibited from making any law ". . .*respecting an establishment of religion, or prohibiting the free exercise thereof. . . .*" Thus it is not the role of government to decide what religious beliefs are proper, or improper. It is not the role of government to establish a "politically correct" religion, nor is it the role of government to sanction those beliefs which are nontraditional or deviant. Rather, it is the purpose of law in our society to restrain evil through the articulation of the criminal and civil law and not to restructure man or his institutions.

"How is this generally accomplished?" one might ask. Our constitutionally based legal system reserves to the "sovereign" state or national government the right to maintain public order in order to "establish Justice, insure domestic Tranquility, provide for the common defense, promote the general Welfare, and [to] secure the Blessings of Liberty to ourselves and our Posterity. . . ." This sovereign right is usually referred to as the police power of the government, which then permits the government to define a crime as an act committed or omitted in violation of public law, or an offense against the sovereignty of the State; thus punishment for a crime is done through a judicial proceeding in the name of the State. This same act may be both a crime against the people and a civil wrong or tort, which is a wrong to a private individual and may be pursued in the form of a law suit.

31

Thus we find both criminal and civil litigation involving destructive cults, but the issues addressed in this diverse litigation concern only those *actions* taken by cults and their members which may be characterized as either a criminal or civil wrong and not the system of beliefs held by their membership.

Most litigation begins with an attempt to define the words or actions that are in dispute between the parties to that dispute. The *Random House College Dictionary* (unabridged edition) defines *"Cult"* as:

1) A particular system of *religious worship*, especially with reference to its rites and ceremonies. 2) An instance of great veneration of a person, ideal or thing especially as manifested by a body of admirers: "a cult of Napoleon." 3) The object of such devotion. 4) A group or sect bound together by devotion to or veneration of the same thing, person, ideal, etc. 5) *Sociological.* A group having sacred ideology and a set of rites centering around their sacred symbols. 6) A religion that is considered or held to be false or unorthodox or its members.

The focus of this article is solely upon those groups which have come to be known as and classified as "destructive cults," which may be a contemporary or an ancient religious, political, or similar organization which seems to have a destructive effect upon its members, or one that practices "mind control" upon its members in such a way as to have a damaging effect upon them.

The paradox of the law involving "destructive cults" is that they seek and receive the "equal protection of the law" because they are usually self-defined religious movements which can claim the same cherished protection of the First Amendment of our Constitution as the more traditional religions beliefs held by our Founding Fathers. Thus we see the IRS granting tax exempt status to the Wiccan (or witchcraft) Church, we see the incorporation of the *Church of Satan* as a legal entity, the former *People's Temple* (Jonestown) group being courted by politicians, and groups like the *Rajneesh*, which teach that the family is anathema, gaining enormous economic power through their alleged misappropriation of members' assets through "mind control" techniques and then applying that power to political, personal, and other nonreligious purposes.

One might speculate that the primary motive of the contemporary phenomena of destructive cults is simply to gain money and power through the manipulation of the constitutional protections afforded to them by our legal system. It is certainly not speculation that many of these contemporary destructive religious movements have gained disproportionate monetary and political power far in excess of the number of their members in the society at large. Cases of the abuse of this power by destructive cults are legion and, if nothing else, prove the old maxim that "Power corrupts, and absolute power corrupts absolutely."

It is urged that courts recognize that certain cult behavior appears to result in substantial harm to individuals and to society in general, and that this harmful behavior will be deemed to outweigh the protection that is offered by the First Amendment.

B. Categories of Cult-Related Litigation

Cult-related litigation falls into nine basic categories, which are: 1) suits brought by ex-members and their families; 2) criminal cases; 3) custody cases; 4) deprogramming cases; 5) suits by Cults against critics; 6) tax cases; 7) solicitation cases; 8) zoning/community relations issues; and 9) legislative initiatives. (See "Cultism and the Law," American Family Foundation, October 1987.)

Category 1, civil suits, is very broad and usually involves people who have been harmed by cult activities and have sued for fraud or for various kinds of physical and psychological damage, defamation, sexual servitude, and even wrongful death. Plaintiffs have won some of these cases, but cults frequently are able to outspend their opponents and most of these cases, even the promising ones, are dropped before the issues could be decided in court. A noted exception to this rule is the case of *Molko v. Holy Spirit Ass'n for Unification*, 109 S. Ct. 2110 (1989), wherein the Supreme Court held that ex-members could sue for fraud against the *Unification Church of Sun Myung Moon* for their deceptive recruitment practices.

Juries tend to favor the plaintiff in litigation against destructive cults; however, several extremely large awards of civil damages have been overturned upon appeal because of technicalities and sometimes because of constitutional protections afforded to these religious groups. The monetary leverage of powerful cult groups in appellate litigation frequently gives them an advantage.

A very recent trend has seen some "New Age" litigation, particularly in the workplace where some employers may require membership in the parent cult group as a condition of employment. These cases ask the question: To what degree can an employee be compelled to become involved in a religious, quasi-religious, or psychological "self-help" or motivational program sponsored by the employer? One recent case, not yet concluded, poses the question whether it is unlawful sex discrimination for an employer to require a female employee to participate in "ritual prayers" as a condition of employment but to prohibit her participation in same during those "unclean" days of the month.

Criminal cases have not seen as much frequent prosecution as have civil cases in the last decade. Some noted examples of criminal cases that have proceeded through the courts include: the 1979 conviction of top Scientologists for breaking into government offices; Rev. Moon's 1982 conviction for tax fraud; the 1980 conviction of Senator Eagleton's Scientologist niece and colleagues in the group; a 1982 conviction of a Coptic leader for smuggling marijuana which he claimed was a sacrament; the 1979 conviction of a Hare Krishna leader for distributing heroin; and the 1980 conviction of Synanon members for putting a rattlesnake in an opposition lawyer's mailbox.

Custody cases involving cults have made some dramatic headlines in recent years, particularly those where severe child abuse, both physical and sexual, has been alleged. Kidnapping has become a commonplace tactic in custody disputes when severe abuse is alleged by one or both parents. Unfortunately, courts have uncovered many instances where the allegation of child abuse by the "cult member" parent is but a tactic designed to gain leverage in the domestic proceeding and has little validity. The unsuccessful prosecution of the *McMartin* case in California, the most expensive in history, did much to damage the credibility of the already fragile "child witness" in court proceedings where proof of physical as well as psychological or emotional harm to the child is usually necessary to win a contest with a cult-involved parent. The typical case here involves a non-member parent arguing to the court that any contact with the spouse's cult will harm the children. Expert witnesses are common in these cases and will be called upon to testify that the cult has caused emotional harm to the child. A difficulty in the analysis of these types of cases is the fact that records from custody proceedings are frequently difficult to obtain for reasons of privacy, public access to these proceedings is restricted, and precedents are not readily obtained.

The individual who finds himself or herself in such a proceeding should be cautioned that it is not the *beliefs* of the cult group that are on trial but rather the detrimental consequences of the *conduct* of that group which will hopefully lead an informed court to conclude what is in the best interest of the child.

Deprogramming suits and prosecutions are a highly publicized category of cult law. Some cult members whose deprogramming failed after being kidnapped by their parents from their cult group have sued their parents for such things as false imprisonment and psychological harm. Some parents and deprogrammers have been found guilty by courts and made to pay large fines or damages to the "victims." Criminal sentences are rare in these cases. When a criminal conviction is successful against a deprogrammer or a parent, a suspended sentence is the rule, with the occasional addition of an injunctive "no contact" order between parents or deprogrammer and the child.

Juries are universally sympathetic to the efforts of parents in such cases because they consider these deprogrammings to be family affairs in which parental intervention is a necessary evil. Professionals in this area, now called "exit counselors," need to exercise caution. Civil law suits against professionals are becoming more common, and some cult groups overtly bombard professionals who aid cult victims with civil law suits. Other groups have been known to hire "private investigators" whose sole purpose it is to discredit these professionals.

Suits against critics and against professionals are a deliberate tactic of many of the larger and richer cults. They are called strategic lawsuits because they are designed to intimidate, harass, or silence critics. The 1981 dismissal with costs of a Scientology suit against Clearwater, Florida, ex-mayor Gabriel Cazares is a case in point, as is the 1986 malicious prosecution conviction of Synanon. Legal delay is the rule in any suit with a cult group. Again, financial leverage is the group's trump card, and by delaying a case, some say unethically, the cults can gain a legal advantage and often wear down their opposition.

Another recent legal tactic of cult groups has been to settle cases with their critics by actually paying monetary damages or agreeing to the forbearance of costly law suits on the condition that the critic promises never again to become involved in any action against the cult group.

Tax cases have long been a battleground for all types of religious groups, not just the destructive cults. Most of these groups win tax-exempt status and by doing so score big money. All but the most egregious cases of tax evasion escape prosecution; the mail order ministry of the Universal Life Church was a noted exception. The Ohio Supreme Court ruled in January 1990 that The Way International is a church and does not have to pay sales tax on goods that it buys, nor on the books and tapes that it sells for profit. The Church of Scientology had tax cases in all eleven federal circuit courts, and Scientology was denied tax-exempt status in California because of its extensive commercial operations (*Dianetics*). Much valuable property and real estate is held by so-called cultic churches (e.g., Hare Krishna temples), as tax-exempt property, and the staggering numbers of potential tax dollars that government could collect insures that these tax battles between government and cults will continue.

Solicitation cases are an especially interesting area of involvement between the cults and the law. The often aggressive and deceptive solicitation practices of cultic groups like the Unification Church, the Hare Krishnas, Scientology, and the LaRouche political organization have caused scrutiny from various state and local administrative authorities. Management officials of airports, stations, guasi-governmental public facilities and shopping malls have frequently sought to ban or closely regulate the solicitation of their patrons by cultic and even non-cultic religious groups. It is in this area that we run head first (and especially hard) into the First Amendment. The trend in the courts has been to allow access by these cult groups to the public, usually applying a balancing test between the needs of the merchants or managers of public facilities to be able to control access to their facilities and to "safeguard" their patrons from harassment with the First Amendment "free speech" rights of the cults and the need for them to have access to their intended audience in order to exercise that right. Most such solicitations by groups like the Krishnas, "Moonies," Scientologists, and the LaRoucheites, as long as they are peaceful and non-obstructive, have been upheld as constitutional. Recently the Supreme Court has backed away somewhat from this very broad "hands off" approach, but it remains to be seen how much further case law will limit the rights of the cults.

Zoning cases arise when a cult group arrives in your neighborhood and suddenly there are complaints from neighbors and former members about the group's activities in the community and about how they use their property. Community land usage or zoning has been held to be a proper, albeit modern, function of local governments. "Zoning" has been defined as the legislative division of a community into areas in each of which only certain designated uses of land are permitted so that the community may develop in an orderly manner in accordance with a comprehensive plan. The "not in my back yard" argument is raised when, as actually happened, the Rajneeshpuram commune moves into your town, takes over, outvotes all the former local residents and then incorporates a new town. Fortunately the residents of Antelope, Oregon, took their case to the Oregon Court of Appeals and finally the Oregon Supreme Court, which found (somewhat ironically) that the Rajneeshpuram commune was unconstitutional because the bizarre commune violated the separation-of-Church-and-State principle. Since there is no "common law" history for zoning cases, each zoning case involving a cult group must be handled on a case-by-case basis. If the land-use ordinance at issue has been able to withstand previous court challenges, its application to a nonconforming use by a cult group will likely be successful — for instance, the case of the Unification church facility in New Castle, N.Y., which has been denied approval to be used as a training center for recruits since 1983. But then again the Minnesota Supreme Court ruled in 1984 that a house run by the Church Universal and Triumphant could be used as a monastery, and in 1986 a Virginia Court said that the LaRouche organization could open a children's camp on a restricted basis. The only conclusion that can be drawn from this "mixed bag" of decisions is that you should not overlook zoning ordinances as a means to combat destructive religious movements whose improper actions in a local community seem to violate the conditions of use for which their property was designated.

Legislative initiatives from state and federal legislatures in the cult issue have been sparse. There have been limited congressional debates concerning the Unification Church, but these discussions by the House Subcommittee on Internal organizations focused more upon the political power and intrigue of this group than upon the cult phenomenon itself.

Several states have had some legislative lobbying activity by both pro- and anti-cult groups for legislative changes, all of which fell on deaf ears. The long tradition of separation of Church and State in this country has kept legislative intervention into the cult issue at a minimum and has instead left interpretation of the law for the courts to define.

C. Legal Remedies for Actions of Destructive Religious Groups

The most common situation that this writer has seen which involves individuals who are aggrieved by actions of destructive religious groups is the scenario where a phone call, usually from a network of referral sources, comes to the attorney and is made on behalf of the individual who is cult-involved by a friend or family member. Cult-involved individuals frequently do not have the ability to call for help on their own. This presents the immediate problem of consulting with a person who may or may not represent the best interest of the aggrieved individual. The next fact that the attorney is likely to learn is that there is a large amount of money involved in the case somewhere, or a minor child is involved and the real contest is between the interested relatives and the cult and not the "aggrieved" individual and the cult. Attorneys are trained to identify and categorize the issues that appear in their client's cases according to the subject-matter area of the law that is involved. The categories of cult cases contained in Section B of this article is not all-inclusive but does conform generally to the most prevalent interfaces between cults and the law.

Unfortunately the cult victim is not so easy to deal with. The first reaction of most legally trained professionals when they encounter a cult victim is "So what? You were a consenting adult." Query: Is a person whose will has been overcome by deception and mind-controlling totalist methods possessed of sufficient capacity to make a contract or to make an informed decision about his or her own well-being? Thus, a special sensitivity to the individual's emotional needs must be developed by the attorney because the victim is usually in need of substantial psychological counseling and/or psychiatric care before being able to help the attorney with the case. Patience, compassion, perseverance, and inner strength are qualities that the attorney and indeed all who would help any cult victim must possess, for the road to recovery is long and winding.

3.

Destructive Cults, Intervention, Exit Counseling

Carol Giambalvo

(Portions of this chapter are taken from *Exit
Counseling: A Family Intervention* by Carol Giambalvo)

Introduction

WHEN Father requested that I write this chapter, he asked
that I let the readers know something of my own story.
One of the things he said to me in our conversation was,
"Sometimes God leads us to places we don't intend to go." I never
dreamed I would end up being a cult information specialist, doing
family interventions with persons affected by destructive cults. In
1978, during a particularly trying transition stage in my life, I took
the "est" training. It was marketed as a way to improve
communications, clear up past patterns in your life, and improve
your living. That is why I took the training. What I got was
something quite different. My husband, Noel, and I took every
seminar offered by Werner Erhard's network for the next five years.
I gave up my job and became a full-time volunteer for The Hunger
Project, also founded by Werner Erhard. Eventually, all five of our
children were involved.

Back in 1977, our daughter Terri joined the Hare Krishna
movement. When we saw drastic personality changes in Terri, I
began doing research on destructive cults. At the same time I was
lecturing in high schools for The Hunger Project, I would return to
lecture on cults. I was blinded to how the organization in which I

was participating was similar and found many ways it did not meet the characteristics I saw in most groups classified as cults: communal living, giving up your job and all your money, estrangement from family. I did see some mind-control techniques, but "look at the wonderful results I got from the training!" The ends justify the means? It wasn't until I moved up into a leadership position in The Hunger Project as an Ending Hunger briefing leader that I began to see the social, psychological, and emotional manipulation, and the contrast between the public story and the inside story of the organization became painfully obvious. This happened at a time when I was also further researching hypnosis and mind control and, simultaneously, was in a crisis of faith.

As the good "workshop junkies" we had become, Noel and I also each made a Cursillo toward the end of our involvement. My faith had always been important to me. I thought nothing or no one could come between me and my relationship with God. I had not been looking for a new religion or philosophy. I simply took a self-improvement seminar. On the Cursillo, however, I was able to take a good look at my relationship with God. I had stopped going to church. I had stopped praying. Whom do you pray to when you are in charge of your life, when you create it all just the way you want it? How had this happened? Why? Those questions led me to other observations about my behavior and further questions about how I had been affected by the group. My research into mind control and hypnosis answered those questions eventually, but not until I fully embraced my relationship with God again and left both "est" and The Hunger Project. Helping others discover how they have been affected by a destructive cult and a mind-control environment and to recover from their experiences is the result of my own recovery process, and it is what I feel I need to do out of my response to a loving God who has called me back to Him and loves me unconditionally.

What Is a Destructive Cult?

When we look at the characteristics of a cult, we are not addressing beliefs, doctrine, or ideology. We are addressing behavior and the methods used to recruit and keep members.

Characteristics of a Cult

Pyramidal structure with a leader at the top who has absolute authority (the leader may be charismatic or messianic).

Deception in recruiting (often using front names). Deception about the group's purpose, beliefs, leaders, and history.

Use of thought-stopping techniques to still critical thinking skills of members (chanting, meditation, trance induction, sensory overload or deprivation, repetition, and confusion).

Methods which elicit in members a sense of fear of leaving the group (fear of losing one's salvation or transformation, suggesting that bad things happen to people who leave) and a sense that the group has the only answers; it's "us against the world" or "we must transform the world."

Polarization from the rest of society. Many cult members live together. Those that do not encourage communal living manage to polarize their members in their world view.

Use of mind-control techniques. (We look to Dr. Robert Jay Lifton's eight criteria of thought reform as published in *Thought Reform and the Psychology of Totalism*, Chapter 22, and Dr. Margaret T. Singer's six conditions for mind control to define these.) Mind control is a *system* of social and psychological manipulation designed to produce a deployable agent for the group and/or to maintain a person's involvement.

There are several different types of cults:

Religious	Political	Therapy	Business
Occult	New Age	Human Potential/Self Awareness	
		(Large group awareness)	

Who Joins Cults?

Involvement in a destructive cult is not a reflection on the intelligence or the family background of a person. By far, most of my clients are extremely bright and come from functional families. Most grew up within a religious faith. Dr. Margaret T. Singer, psychologist and professor emeritus of psychology at the University of California, Berkeley, states that cult involvement has more to do with timing. A person is usually in a transition stage in life such as:

leaving high school to attend college (one needs to make new friends, become more independent of one's family, find new romantic relationships);
leaving college and entering a career field;
a mid-life crisis;
loss of a loved one through death or divorce;
loss of a job;
a move to a new location or a new country;
retirement.

At these and other transition periods, we humans are more vulnerable to a group that may look as though it has all the answers for us, provides a structure, and allows us to feel like we are part of something special. We all need to belong. We all need to feel accepted and loved. In transition stages, we are much more vulnerable to groups that actively seek to recruit people who appear to be vulnerable.

People do not go out looking for a cult to join. If they were looking for a group to join or a cause in which to participate, they did not get what they originally thought the group had to offer. Little by little, when the group thinks a recruit is "ready" to hear it, the real beliefs and structure are revealed. Meanwhile the psychological and social pressures are in place to still the doubts and questions the person may have.

Recruitment into a cult can occur through a friend or acquaintance who has become a new member of a cult. That person shares their new experience in a way that appears to be a wonderful new truth or change in lifestyle. Or recruitment can be through an active, trained cult recruiter. The trained recruiters tend to operate on college campuses in residence halls, libraries, student activity halls, and foreign-student residencies. They look for people who are alone and may seem vulnerable or depressed. They become instant friends, using a technique that has become known as "love bombing." They invite unsuspecting students to a dinner, a party, a Bible study, or a lecture given by the group. The appeal is emotional, seldom intellectual, according to many former cult members. To the recruiter, the ends justify the means.

How Do You Know If Someone You Love Is in a Cult?

There are some signs that would indicate a cult involvement. A person may not exhibit all the signs. Some signs may be an indication of involvement in something other than a cult, so a thorough investigation should be undertaken by a family before coming to a conclusion. Some indications are:

Personality changes, such as a person who is an introvert suddenly becoming an extrovert or an easy-going person becoming aggressive. Change in language with an emphasis on certain in-group vocabulary. A person's speech may become slow and deliberate and very brief. If questioned, the person may become defensive or stop communicating. It may seem as though the cultist is spouting tape-recorded lines. If involved in a religious cult, he or she may only want to discuss religious and not "worldly" subjects. The cultist may quote endless Scriptures to answer any question you pose.

Secrecy. The person may not want to talk about the group or his or her involvement. When he or she comes home, he or she may spend most of the time in his or her room, not engaged with the family. He or she may resent questions about future plans, activities, or group involvement.

Change in reading material and interests. If the person had been involved in sports or music, this interest may drop. He or she may stop watching television, going to movies, and may not want to engage in political discussions or normal family discussions. He or she may spend much time reading the Bible or cult books, or listening to audiotapes from the group.

Change in emotions. The person may withdraw emotionally from the family. There may be a physical change in expressing his or her emotions — no more hugs. In some groups, it may be just the opposite change: a normally non-physically expressive person suddenly hugs everyone.

Change in sexual attitudes. This may involve both sexual activities and attitudes toward females' roles.

Change in life goals. The group's goals become more important than the goals the individual had before becoming involved. This may include career changes, or leaving a career to work for the group, dropping out of college or dropping enough courses that would still enable him or her to stay on campus in order to recruit for the group.

Changes in eating and sleeping patterns.

Changes in dating habits or in marriage plans. A cultist will usually break a relationship with a non-cult member if unsuccessful at an attempt to recruit him/her.

Changes in appearance, cleanliness, wardrobe.

Attempts to recruit others into the group: family, friends, strangers on the street.

Changes in financial matters. Large amounts of money are sometimes donated to the group, dissolving savings accounts, selling material goods, asking parents for inheritances or loans; not paying bills, never seeming to have enough money.

When visiting home, there can be an inordinate amount of phone calls from other members of the group. Often, the person will not come home alone, but will bring another member along.

The person may look at his/her past life as more negative than it was. Some Bible-based group members may "confess" their past sins to parents. Some large-group awareness training group members or therapy group members may be confrontational with family about past family relationships.

Change in bonds with others. People the cult member was close to before joining are not important any longer. It is as though he or she has found a new family.

Sense of elitism, of being better than others outside the group. If friends and family will join the group, they, too, will become better. If not, there is a change of attitude toward non-members.

Changes in scholastic performance. There may be a drop in scholastic average, failed courses, courses dropped, and extracurricular activities dropped.

Signs of distress. The person may sleep inordinate amounts of time while visiting home (to make up for the little time he or she sleeps while with the group); signs of depression; loss of weight; frequent illnesses; times when he or she seems "tranced out"; an inability to hold logical conversations; emotionless facial expressions; stories of seeing visions, of "God speaking to me," hearing voices, or reexperiencing or recalling past lives.

What Do We Do?

The first task is to find out whether your loved one is really involved in a destructive cult. You will need to learn the name of the group and/or its leader. Then you should contact the Cult Awareness Network, (312) 267-7777, or American Family Foundation, (212) 249-7693, to request a packet of information about the group, if available.

Your next task is to educate yourself concerning destructive cults, mind control and the specific group in question.

What NOT to Say or Do

Don't say, "You're in a cult; you're brainwashed."

Don't say "You can't make any decisions for yourself."

Don't argue with the cultist about the cult's beliefs.

Don't criticize the group or the leaders.

Don't be confrontational.

Don't give them large sums of money or relinquish trusts or bank accounts to cult members.

Don't turn over titles/deeds to cult members.

Don't give them the books and material you've gathered about the group.

What TO Do

It is important, especially if considering an intervention, that the family keep open the lines of communication with the loved one. If the family is negative toward the group, the cultist becomes defensive and often feels personally attacked. Often, this results in even further alienation of the cultist from family and friends. It is best that parents and other family members maintain a neutral position toward the group involvement.

Other suggested activities that can be important for relating to cultists are:

What Else to Do

Maintain an interest in their activities.

Reaffirm your approval of their positive actions and motives, their good intentions, but do not approve of the group.

Attend group activities or church with them, but don't go to retreats or long seminars.

Negotiate with them: "I'll attend (church or Bible study or whatever) with you. Will you give me equal time in the future?"

Take your time, educate all those who will be involved in the intervention, talk to other parents who have gone through this process, talk to former members.

What Is Exit Counseling?

Family intervention specialists knowledgeable about cults and mind control have inherited the label "exit counselors" from the network of individuals and organizations providing information on cults. The term "exit counselor" originally came into favor in order to distinguish voluntary interventions with cultists from "deprogramming," which was associated with physical restraint of cultists (e.g., refusing to let the cultist leave the family's home until he or she had listened to a deprogrammer). "Exit counseling," however, does not adequately describe most voluntary interventions today. "Counseling" often connotes a systematic attempt to help clients change their behavior. Most "exit counselors," on the other hand, focus on sharing information rather than changing behavior, although clients may change their behavior as a result of the information they receive.

I believe that the terms *cult information specialist* or *cult information consultant* better describe what most "exit counselors" do. But since the term exit counseling is so widespread, I will use it in this chapter, even though I would prefer to use other terminology.

Exit counseling is a family intervention process in which the family of a cult member, along with the cult member, participates in educational sessions. The family has as much responsibility to be educated about the issues of mind control and cult involvement as does the exit counseling team.

The approach taken here is one way to implement an intervention; it is *not* the only way. The important issue is the thoughtful and thorough preparation of the family that is necessary to undertake an intervention. Families should work closely with the exit counselor(s) in order to determine the best approach for their situation. The goal of an intervention is to help a loved one evaluate his or her involvement in a cultic group.

How to Find and Evaluate Exit Counselors

Often parents are referred to an exit counselor by a former member of their loved one's cult or by a family who has had a family intervention. Referrals to exit counselors can come through such organizations as the American Family Foundation (AFF) and the Cult Awareness Network (CAN), as well as the cult clinics and rehabilitation facilities listed at the end of this chapter.

Families should take their time in making a selection. They should interview exit counselors. During the interview process, there are several factors to keep in mind. These can be evaluated by asking about and discussing the following:

How will my family member relate to this person?

Ask for the exit counselors' experience in interventions with the particular cult in question.

Do the exit counselors seem knowledgeable about mind control and cults in general; do they present this information clearly?

Ask for fee structures and other expenses that may be involved.

Ask for references of families for whom they have worked.

Ask for references of people in CAN or AFF and/or mental health professionals. Are they in good standing with these organizations?

Ask for approximate percentages of the people they have worked with who have ultimately left a cult.

Are they willing to spend the time needed to adequately prepare the family for the intervention?

Information Gathering by Exit Counselors

During the initial contact with the inquiring parents or family, the exit counselors need to gather the following preliminary information: name(s) of inquirers and relationship to cultist; name, age, and sex of cultist; name and location of cult; length of time the cultist has been involved; and extent of involvement (for example, does he/she have a leadership position?).

The family is sent an extensive intake form to fill out and return.

A summary of the exit counselors' fees and expenses is sent at this time.

Information from the family regarding the cultist's personal history, as well as the family background, is crucial to help exit counselors understand the cultist, assess the procedure to be followed, and weigh the probable success of the intervention. Also it will help to determine particular areas of concern the exit counselors need to identify, such as control issues between parents and cultist, possible hidden agendas of the parents or family, and special mental health issues.

A mental health professional should be consulted if certain areas of concern become obvious. These areas include, but are not limited to: serious defects in interpersonal skills, drug or alcohol abuse by the family or the cultist, prior emotional or mental breakdowns, dysfunctional family situations, physical problems (pregnancy, diabetes, any illness affected by emotional stress), prior eating disorders, self-destructive behavior, or suicidal tendencies.

If there are concerns about the client's emotional ability to deal with an intervention, the family needs to consult a mental health professional who is knowledgeable about cult issues. In these cases, the family needs to get an opinion regarding the timing of an intervention and should ask the mental health professional to be available during the intervention. In a dysfunctional family situation, the family should be referred to a professional for pre-intervention counseling.

Preparing the Family for an Intervention

Family members must educate themselves on the issues of mind control, cults in general, and the specific cult their family member has joined. The importance of this cannot be overemphasized. Families can contact the Cult Awareness Network (CAN) and American Family Foundation (AFF) for information packets and books. Local CAN affiliates are available for support. The following books are recommended so that families can be informed. Everyone who will be involved in the intervention should read this material. Those books marked with an asterisk are crucial sources.

Reading List
* *Combatting Cult Mind Control* by Steven Hassan (Rochester, Vt., Inner Traditions, 1988)
* *Cults & Consequences,* edited by Rachel Andres & James R. Lane (Los Angeles, Jewish Federation Council of Greater L.A., 1988)
* *Cults: What Parents Should Know* by Joan Carol Ross and Michael Langone (Bonita Springs, Fla., American Family Foundation, 1988)
Discipling Dilemma by Flavil Yeakley (in case of a Bible-based cult)
* *Exit Counseling: A Family Intervention* by Carol Giambalvo (Bonita Springs, Fla., American Family Foundation, 1992)
Prison or Paradise by Marcia and Jim Rudin (Minneapolis, Minn., Augsburg Fortress, 1980)
Unholy Devotion: Why Cults Lure Christians by Harold L. Bussell (Grand Rapids, Mich., Zondervan, 1983)

Through CAN or FOCUS (Former Cult Members' Support Network), the family may be referred to former members of the group in question.

If so, the family should ask former members about their experience in the group, why they left, if they were exit-counseled, and, if so, what did their family say that caused them to be willing to listen and talk to the exit counselors.

Also through CAN or FOCUS, the family may ask for referrals to parents of former members, especially parents who prepared themselves well for an intervention. This will help calm the parents.

It is best to have a meeting with the exit counselor(s) before the intervention. If this is not possible, phone consultations can take place.

Timing
Find a time when it would be natural for the cultist to visit home: family celebrations, holidays, birthdays, semester breaks, perhaps a family vacation.

Team Composition
Generally, a team consists of two exit counselors. Sometimes a team of three is helpful, for example, in the case of multiple cultists

or a cultist who is in a position of leadership. If the cultist is in a Bible-based cult, one of the team needs to have a knowledge of Scripture and be sensitive to the ethical issues involved. One of the team should be a former member of the cult in question. It is preferable that at least one of the team be the same gender as the cultist.

The lead exit counselor should have the final say on the composition of the team.

Length of Intervention

Usually an intervention lasts three to five days, sometimes longer. The length depends entirely upon the cultist's willingness to deal with issues and his or her ability to relate to and integrate the information.

The Family Team

Personal confidentiality and sensitivity in planning the intervention is important. The family should tell no one other than those who need to know.

To ascertain the main players on the family team, consider the following:

Who is important to the cultist and to the intervention?
Who was closest to the cultist before the cult involvement?
Who had or still has the most influence on the cultist?
Which non-family members may have influence, such as teachers, clergy, family friends?

Only those who are particularly significant *to the cultist* should be called upon for the intervention.

Sometimes it is necessary to do a pre-intervention intervention with a family member who is unwilling to participate in the intervention or who does not understand the issues.

Family members should exercise caution not to reveal to the cultist how well-informed they are about the group. Doing so may result in the cult's taking measures to counteract the family's influence. For example, the cult may order the cult member not to visit his or her family.

51

The exit counselors should advise the family on the extent of involvement of specific family members and/or friends in the family part of the intervention (that is, when the family tries to convince the cultist to speak with the exit counselors). The more loving, open, and honest the relationship is with a parent or family member, the more that person should be involved.

If any relationship between the cultist and another family member is problematic, it may be best for the other person to be less involved. He or she can show support simply by being present. Occasionally it is preferable that the person not be there at all. A similar assessment should be made of all siblings, other family members and friends.

Family Meeting With the Intervention Team

This meeting occurs the day or evening before the actual intervention. It takes place in the town where the intervention is to happen, usually somewhere nearby, such as in the motel or home where the exit counseling team is spending the night. It is important that steps previously outlined have been taken to educate all family members taking part in the intervention.

All team members and family participants should be included in this pre-intervention session.

The purpose of this session is to reassure the family (especially if they have not met the team in person) and to address any anxieties and calm the family. It serves as an opportunity to provide the exit counselors with any additional pertinent information. It helps to ensure that family members know how to talk to the cultist the following day in hopes that the cultist will be willing to work with the exit counselors.

Each family member should be given an opportunity to express his or her feelings about the intervention and to ask about areas of concern or his or her role in the intervention. It is the last chance to clear up any confusions or hesitations before meeting with the cultist.

At this meeting, each family member is also asked for his or her expectation of how the cultist may respond to the intervention.

Bear in mind that the exit counselors and the family are attempting to present reality to a person who is out of touch with reality — due to a complex combination of emotional, psychological, and social manipulation. These manipulations are part of cultic group dynamics, performed without the cultist's knowledge.

Remember, do not argue with the cultist. It will only trigger his or her cult mind-set. It is better to remain nonconfrontational, nonjudgmental, and supportive. Let your warmth and concern shine through. The best point of view to take is to acknowledge that the intervention is about helping the *whole family* — and the cultist is an INTEGRAL part of that whole.

What to Expect During the Intervention

Some things the family may see happening during the intervention are:

> Vacillation: It may appear that some progress is being made, then following a nap or after a night's sleep, it seems that the cultist is back to the first step again.
> Anger: It is focused at the family or at the situation. Anger is usually expressed in body language, but sometimes it is expressed verbally or physically.

Stages of Intervention (These don't always follow a progression; the person may vacillate.)

> Denial
> Resistance
> Interest
> Participation

Post-Cult Counseling

A growing body of research indicates that the cult's environmental pressures and psychological manipulations cause people to experience considerable psychological distress when they leave cultic groups. Therefore, it is advisable that former cultists seriously think about getting professional psychological assistance during their recovery period.

Some ex-cultists may require only a few hours of consultation to help clarify their needs and identify a strategy for coping with the problems they are likely to encounter. Others may require psychotherapy. Some may need a period of "rehabilitation" at a live-in facility. The American Family Foundation can provide a list of mental health professionals with some knowledge of cults.

Because the demands of day-to-day living can consume so much time, few ex-cultists pay as much attention as they should to their post-cult psychological needs. Therefore, even for those whose problems are not severe, a strategic "retreat" from the pressures of practical life can greatly facilitate a smooth transition.

Rehab/Reentry Facilities

Not every ex-cultist *needs* to go to a reentry facility. Those who are able to, however, seem to recover from their cult experience at a faster rate and with less difficulty than those who do not. At present, there are two rehab/reentry facilities available in the United States.

Rehab facilities offer an opportunity to take time away from the pressures of immediate changes in the life of an exiting cult member — changes in school, job, and living arrangements. Here ex-cultists are given time to relax, to continue to educate themselves about undue influence and mind control, and to further integrate the information they received during the intervention.

Also, the ex-cultist may have issues about the intervention, his or her family, or pre-cult matters that were unresolved before cult involvement. These issues are likely to surface at this time. Rehab facilities are an excellent place to sort through these concerns with professional help and begin to resolve them.

Having been involved in a cult and under the influence of mind control is a serious situation. The family may need to evaluate the ex-cultist's job or school schedule. In some cases, the family may want to consider whether the ex-cultist would be better off leaving school for a semester. This may be necessary, particularly if she or he had been deeply involved in the group.

Even though interventions give the ex-cultist tools for recovery, leaving a cult is a traumatic event in a person's life. Its seriousness should not be minimized. The ex-cultist will be going through an intense identity crisis as well as a period of grief. For these reasons, attending a rehab/reentry facility is highly recommended, if it is at all feasible.

Families can contact facilities directly to evaluate their services. See the Resources section at the end of this chapter for the names and locations of the rehab facilities.

Future Plans

Former cultists who seek professional psychological assistance or attend a rehab/reentry facility will devote considerable time to thinking about future plans. Those who don't seek help must also address this issue at some point. Families should try not to pressure the ex-cultist.

Below are listed some important concerns that family and friends can help the ex-cultist identify and think about.

(1) Is he or she living with other group members? How can the family help the ex-cultist move out, retrieve belongings, and deal with the other members?

(2) Is he or she employed by the cult or are there other members of the cult at the workplace? Will the ex-cultist need some financial support before she or he becomes reemployed or financially independent?

(3) Has the former cultist chosen the school he or she is attending because the group wanted recruitment done on that particular campus? He or she may want to transfer schools. There may be a loss of tuition or school time.

(4) Is there a need for long-term counseling or therapy with mental health professionals?

(5) Are there FOCUS contacts or a support group in the area? Provide the ex-cultist with a list of such contacts.

(6) Does the ex-cultist have family support? This is extremely important: the cultist needs to have something to come out *to*.

The Intervention: The Author's Philosophy

The author's family interventions are based on an educational model. The cultist has been a victim of a sophisticated set of manipulations. Once she or he becomes aware of these manipulations, basic integrity usually will not allow the cultist to remain a part of a system that victimizes others — no matter how lofty the goals. An intervention, for the most part, is a discourse on ethics, values, and integrity.

The material is to be presented in a manner that respects the cultist's dignity. In particular, it is important to be sensitive to the emotional trauma the client may undergo while confronting these issues. Material is to be put forth at a pace that allows the cultist to assimilate the information and, simultaneously, deal with its emotional impact.

The goal is for the client to reevaluate his or her commitment to the group. Although parents and exit counselors may hope that he or she chooses to leave, leaving is not the goal. Informed choice is the goal.

It is important that if the cultist leaves the group, he or she does so with dignity and self-respect intact. There are some positive aspects to a person's cult involvement. Encourage the cultist to be patient, to sort out the positives from the negatives, and to integrate the positives into present and future life.

Once a person understands mind control techniques, that person has the basic tools with which to sort out these issues and deal with them. This process takes time. But there is much less time involved and much less stress on the individual if she or he has had the opportunity for exit counseling and rehabilitation. It is imperative that the family understand this whole process so they can be supportive to the ex-cultist.

The Intervention Begins: Introductions

At this point, it is assumed that the family has been successful at getting the cultist to engage with the exit counselors. Now, the exit counseling team should be introduced to the cultist. Once the cultist agrees to speak with the exit counselors, he or she then becomes their "client," that is, the person whose welfare is the paramount concern of the exit counselors.

All the members of the exit counseling team should let the client know their names, where they are from, and their experience with the group in question.

During the initial getting-acquainted session, it should be made clear to the client that the purpose is not to take the individual away from his or her beliefs or faith in God (or, in the case of a New Age group, from his or her transformation) — no one can do that. Tell the client that there are many good things he or she has learned about himself or herself, such as how to relate to others. Point out there have been some good effects on his or her life while a part of the group. Go on to say that there are many truths found in this group, and probably it is the people and the "truth" found in the group that attracted the client to the group.

These facts need to be stated in the beginning because much of the information to be gone over in the ensuing sessions may seem negative.

It should also be stated at this time that the purpose of the process is to explore this information together, not to argue or debate. The goal is to provide information that will enable the client to make a fully informed choice — the exit counselors are on *the client's* side. The information will speak for itself and will be well documented.

In an exit counseling situation, the word *doctrine* refers to the beliefs and practices of the group. While the particular beliefs of a group are not at issue in an intervention, they must be addressed because the practices and techniques that are employed get twisted around the beliefs. The beliefs or doctrine are usually what "justify" the use of techniques of emotional and social manipulation.

The client's positive motivations (wanting to do what God wants, wanting to change the world for the better) and good intentions are acknowledged and respected. The client's integrity is most important. Also the client's sincerity is valued as is the sincerity of those in the group. Sincerity and good motives are not being called into question.

The issue that does get addressed is the process by which a person's sincere desires may be channeled into something quite different, one step at a time, without the awareness of the individual. Examples are given that point to sincerity of members of other cults, illustrating how those people are manipulated. Methods of manipulation — social, emotional, and psychological — are discussed at length and in detail so the client can begin to recognize what may apply to his or her experience.

Areas Covered During the Intervention

The areas outlined below need to be covered during the intervention. Depending on the group in question, there may be other pertinent information to go over while certain topics may not be discussed as thoroughly.

The order of topics covered varies according to the client's desires or expressed interest.

The models of mind control are discussed, with a brief description of whose models they are and who the experts are: Dr. Margaret T. Singer and Dr. Robert Jay Lifton.

Dr. Margaret T. Singer's Model of Mind Control Conditions

Dr. Singer points out that there are six conditions for mind control:

1. Gaining control over a person's time, especially his or her *thinking* time.

2. Creating a sense of powerlessness in the recruit, while providing models that demonstrate the new behavior management (leadership) wants to produce.

3. Manipulating rewards, punishments, and experiences in order to suppress the former social behavior of the recruits. Use of altered states of consciousness to manipulate experience.

4. Manipulating rewards, punishments and experiences in order to elicit the behavior that management (leadership) wants.

5. Creating a tightly controlled system; those who dissent will be made to feel as though there is something inherently wrong with them to be questioning.

6. Keeping recruits unaware and uninformed. Management (leadership) cannot carry out a thought reform program with a person's full capacity and informed consent.

Dr. Robert Jay Lifton's Eight Psychological Themes for Thought Reform

These should be discussed at length, citing examples of the way in which the group in question uses the criteria.

1. Milieu Control
2. Mystical Manipulation
3. Demand for Purity
4. Confession
5. Sacred Science

6. Loading the Language
7. Doctrine Over Person
8. Dispensing of Existence

Other subjects covered during an intervention:

The history of the group and the leader(s)
Issues of deception and how this group uses it
Cognitive dissonance
Behavior modification/control
Information control
Phobia indoctrination
Thought-stopping techniques
Trances/altered states of consciousness; vulnerability to suggestion
Hypnosis — what is hypnosis (in depth)?
Videos: Educational videotapes are used during an intervention. The family should be encouraged to watch the videos so that all the participants are educated. A VHS VCR will be needed for this purpose. A remote control is necessary so that the videotape can be paused for discussion. The use of videos depends upon the type of group. If the client processes information more easily through videos and discussion, this medium can be relied upon more heavily.

For more detailed information regarding the intervention process, refer to: *Exit Counseling: A Family Intervention* by Carol Giambalvo, American Family Foundation, 1992.

Things to Remember

An intervention usually lasts from three to five days, depending on the client's ability to process the information. It is important to direct questions to the client regularly to make sure she or he understands the information.

Remember, the client needs time to assimilate the information, reestablish relationships with the family, and allow his or her "former identity" to resurface. Along with this, he or she must deal with all the related emotions.

No one can really set a schedule for how this process will transpire. Each client is different.

When the Client Decides to Leave the Cult

If the client leaves the group, the following areas may be important to address, depending on the needs of the client.

How to help friends still in the cult.

Whether or not to talk to the cult leadership.

How to move out of the group house.

How to handle feelings of embarrassment.

How to deal with temporary loss of the power of concentration, a common post-cult problem.

What to say to friends not in the group and how to rebuild relationships outside the group.

What is the value of counseling and rehabilitation facilities? (These should be strongly encouraged.)

What are the role and value of FOCUS support groups, individual contacts for support, and conferences on cult recovery issues.

How to recognize and deal with residuals and floating. What is it and how long does it lasts? How to help oneself deal with it, including identifying "triggers."

What to do about spirituality. (If the client will be going to a rehab/reentry facility, this issue should be addressed there rather than with exit counselors.)

When the client raises issues and concerns such as those described above or asks exit counselors for advice, it is important for the exit counselors *not to advise the client; rather they should merely explore options with the client.*

Exit counselors should always keep in mind the extreme vulnerability of those who have just left cult groups and mind-control environments. It takes some time to relearn how to make decisions for oneself, especially when a person has been dependent on a group or leaders. Foster independent decision-making from the very beginning. Explore this important matter with the parents and family as well.

Under no circumstances should an exit counselor influence a client in any particular direction regarding his or her religious practice or faith or any other beliefs. In all these areas, it is best only to *explore options* with the client. One option, however, is for the client to talk to clergy about specific religious issues. The client need not be left "hanging" with regard to religion. But, in my view, the exit counselor should not proselytize or evangelize the client.

When the client leaves the group, the parents should be on guard against creating a watchful atmosphere, known as the fishbowl effect. Parents need to resist their natural instincts to pull the ex-cultist back under their wings. Instead, they need to give their loved one his or her wings. Parents should be there for the ex-cultist when needed, and they should not be afraid of every phone call from a cult member.

Both parents and client should be told about two helpful resources:
(1) *Influence*, by Dr. Robert Cialdini, a book available through the Cult Awareness Network.
(2) *Recovery from Cults*, edited by Dr. Michael Langone, a comprehensive book that provides guidelines for ex-cultists, families, and professionals (to become available in 1993).

The things former cultists need most from their families are:

> Unconditional Love
> Support
> Time
> Space

The things a former cult member needs least from the family are:

"I told you so!"
"Just put this behind you and get on with your life."
"Whatever made you join this group anyway?"
"We spent a lot of effort and money to get you out of this group."

It is important for families and ex-cultists alike to remember that when a person gets involved with a cult group, they have made the best decision possible *given the limited information they had available at the time*. It took a lot of courage to deal with further information. Leaving a cult following an intervention is a courageous, ethical, and moral decision that is indicative of the strength and integrity of the individual. That is something of which to be proud, not embarrassed.

Post-Intervention: Rehab/Reentry

If the client goes to a rehab facility, it may be necessary for a member of the intervention team to accompany him or her. This serves two purposes: (1) it will ease the transition, and (2) the team member can inform the facility staff of any issues the exit counselors feel the client needs to address. Also the exit counselor can let the staff know if the client is experiencing any episodes of floating.

Ongoing Therapy or Counseling

Some clients may have issues that were present before joining the cult and these may resurface after leaving the group. Or they may have problems that arose during cult involvement which were not treated properly. For example, a client might have been experiencing addictive behavior, anxiety, or depression before the cult involvement. A client might have been dysfunctional due to illness, divorce, death in the family, or addictive behavior of a parent. Often such issues can be exacerbated in a cultic environment.

Clients with difficulties should be encouraged to engage in ongoing therapy following the intervention and/or the time spent at a rehab facility. When possible, refer them to appropriate resources.

At all times, exit counselors must keep in mind that they are not mental health professionals. When in doubt in any situation, they should refer the client and/or family to mental health professionals. Having access to mental health professionals with a knowledge of cults and mind control issues is, of course, the best situation.

Resources: Informational Services

American Family Foundation (AFF), P.O. Box 2265, Bonita Springs, FL 33959 (212) 249-7693

Cult Awareness Network (CAN), 2421 W. Pratt Blvd., Suite 1173, Chicago, IL 60645 (312) 267-7777

FOCUS (Former Cult Members' Support Network) c/o CAN, 2421 W. Pratt Blvd., Suite 1173, Chicago, IL 60645 (312) 267-7777

International Cult Education Program (ICEP), P.O. Box 1232, Gracie Station, New York, NY 10028 (212) 439-1550

Spiritual Counterfeit Project, P.O. Box 4308, Berkeley, CA 94704
(415) 540-5767 [Mon., Wed., Fri.] or (415) 540-0300

Pre-Intervention and Post-Intervention Counseling Services
   Cult Hot Line and Clinic, Jewish Board of Family and Children's
Services, 120 W. 57th St., New York, NY 10019 (212) 632-4640
   Cult Clinic, Jewish Family Service, 6505 Wilshire Blvd., 6th
Floor, Los Angeles, CA 90048 (213) 852-1234

Rehab Facilities
   Wellspring Retreat & Resource Center, Albany, OH (614)
698-6277; Dr. Paul Martin, Barbara Martin

Catholic Resources
   Father Kent Burtner, St. Dominic's Church, 2390 Bush St., San
Francisco, CA 94115-3186 (415) 567-7824
   Father Walter Debold, Seton Hall University, South Orange, NJ
07079
   Father Lawrence Gesy, Our Lady of Victory Church, 4414
Wilkens Ave., Baltimore, MD 21229 (410) 242-0180
   Father James LeBar, 2 Harvey St., Hyde Park, NY 12538 (914)
471-2537
   Carol Giambalvo, P.O. Box 2180, Flagler Beach, FL 32136-2180
(904) 439-7541
   Doris Quelet, 7 Birchbrook Ct., Baltimore, MD 21236 (4 01)
529-0640

4.

The Fundamentals of Fundamentalism

Father Lawrence J. Gesy and Michael Summers

PART I — OVERVIEW OF FUNDAMENTALISM

"**H**AVE you been saved?" Most of us are asked this question at least weekly by a friend or an acquaintance who would be termed a Fundamentalist. This question can be asked in the business place, the supermarket, the library, and of course, at your front door, by zealous proselytizers of Fundamentalist religious groups.

One Sunday morning during my homily at Mass, I asked my parishioners how many had been asked that question. Most of the congregation raised their hands vigorously. I followed that by asking them whether this question had been addressed to them by someone belonging to a Fundamentalist church. Many members of the congregation responded that the question had come from such a source, even from a family member who had left the Catholic Church to join a Fundamentalist church or Bible study and prayer group.

Who Are These Fundamentalists?

Persons or groups committed to the fundamentals of Christianity are not simply by that fact part of a destructive religious movement. It is important to make this clear at the very beginning of this chapter.

We are dealing with the *ism* of fundamentals. I will critique the way some persons who believe in the fundamental teachings of Christianity misuse, misunderstand, and misappropriate these fundamentals. Fundamentalism is a rapidly growing movement which is captivating many members of mainstream churches. Often the invitation to join a Fundamentalist church or fellowship includes some form of psychological coercion, accompanied by an attack on the teachings and customs of mainstream churches, especially Roman Catholicism.

We are not dealing with the stereotypical "Bible thumper," for Fundamentalism has within its ranks people from all social, economic, and educational classes, although one might actually find among them those who could be classed as "Bible thumpers."

Anthony E. Gilles, in *Fundamentalism, What Every Catholic Needs to Know* (Cincinnati: St. Anthony Messenger Press, 1984) states:

> "Fundamentalism connotes a distortion — a hyperextension, one might say — of the fundamentals. Attaching -*ist* or -*ism* to *fundamental* suggests adhering to doctrines for their own sake, without seeing their purpose. This is precisely the problem with Fundamentalism: It is such an absorption and fascination with doctrine that it actually distorts doctrinal meaning and significance. Fundamentalists are so preoccupied with religious doctrine that they have made it an end in itself rather than a means to an end. They are so preoccupied with the trees that they can't see the forest."

The *Oxford English Dictionary* defines fundamentalism as ". . . a religious movement which became active among various Protestant bodies in the U.S. after the war of 1914-18, based on strict adherence to traditional orthodox tenets (e.g., the literal inerrancy of Scripture) held to be fundamental to the Christian faith; opposed to liberalism and modernism."

The *American College Dictionary* states that fundamentalism also teaches that "inerrancy of the Bible not only in the matter of faith and morals but also as literal historical record and prophecy, e.g., of creation, the virgin birth of Christ, his second advent, etc. (opposed to modernism)."

The Roots of Fundamentalism

With the exception of the earliest years of the Colony of Maryland and the entire colonial history of Pennsylvania, each of our original thirteen Colonies, which became the thirteen States, had an "established" religion.

The people of the northern Colonies generally adhered to some form of Calvinist religion. Most of the settlers of the New England Colonies had immigrated there to find freedom to practice their religion, in addition to finding more land on which to spread themselves and their families. It is interesting to note, however, that the Puritans of the Massachusetts Bay Colony were so rigidly attached to their own beliefs that they could condemn a Quaker woman to death and could not tolerate Roger Williams expressing his somewhat different beliefs. By exiling him from Massachusetts, the Puritans made it possible for Williams to found the Colony of Rhode Island.

In the northern Colonies, the settlers founded the Colleges of Harvard in Massachusetts, Brown in Rhode Island, Yale in Connecticut, and Princeton in New Jersey to educate men for the ministry in their respective churches.

Pennsylvania alone welcomed settlers of almost any faith, with the result that immigrants from every northern and central European country brought their several different faiths to that colony. Since there was such a variety of denominations in Pennsylvania, each church group had to provide its own ministers if their congregations required an educated ministry. German Lutherans swarming into Pennsylvania in the late 1600s and early 1700s were largely without ministers for more than thirty years. This condition resulted at least in part because the Lutheran Church in northern Europe was the "established" or state church of each nation or duchy in which that religion was functioning, and the state officials saw no reason to send ministers (salaries paid by the German state) to serve people who had left to reside in and pay taxes to an English Colony.

Most of the southern colonies were officially Anglican, i.e., Church of England, or what we now call the Episcopal Church. Since it was the "established" church, by law every child born in those colonies had to be registered and baptized in the Anglican Church, and marriages also had to take place in and be registered in the Anglican Church. It was the Church of the colonial governors and other royal officials. Anglican clergy were supplied to the southern Colonies from England and supported by taxes. The result of this situation was that the Church of England was the greatest religious casualty of the American Revolution. Because many of the clergy had the privileges of royal officials as well as support from taxes, called "tithes," they had been Tories. Together with other royalists, many emigrated to Canada or returned to England during or immediately after the American Revolution. Since there was no bishop of the Anglican Church in the U.S. to ordain clergy between 1783 and 1820, the diminished, now Episcopal, congregations had to muddle through somehow.

Those colonists who had only been registered members of the Church of England by force of colonial law hastily formed congregations reflecting the beliefs which they had formerly held privately.

In the mid-1700s, people from the New England colonies and new immigrants to the middle and southern colonies began to cross the Blue Ridge to explore and to settle in the open lands beyond the Alleghenies. As the new American frontier opened to the western movement of settlers, educated and ordained clergy from Europe were not available in sufficient numbers to accompany the pioneers. Consequently self-appointed leaders began to fill the void of ordained clergy.

Most of the colonists believed that each Christian is guided by the Holy Spirit to interpret the Bible for himself, what is called "private interpretation of Scripture," a generally accepted Protestant belief. Additionally, most of the pioneers came from Calvinist congregations in the Eastern Colonies or from Calvinist congregations in Europe who accepted the principle that the governing of a church resided in the congregation as a whole. Many believed that "the Church invisible" was distinct from and had little need for a visible administrative structure, ritual, or hierarchy. This led to every little community in the new territories sprouting a church, with the members of the congregation determining for themselves whatever organization and teaching they believed necessary.

Since few of the leaders of these new congregations had any formal ministerial education, they could pass on only their own ideas about what the Bible taught. Later, as the territories became states and the population grew, Bible colleges or seminaries were established, not all of which had ties to what are now called "mainstream" churches.

In *Voices of American Fundamentalism* (Philadelphia: Westminster Press, 1976), Dr. C. Allyn Russell, professor of religion at Boston University, presents the view that the rise of Protestant Liberalism was "a major catalyst . . . which brought Fundamentalism into existence. . ." (op. cit. p. 15). Religious liberalism, which had strong roots in European Protestant thinking in the middle of the nineteenth century, did not become influential in American religious life until after the Civil War. It attempted to adjust to new thinking in science, particularly the theories of Darwin, and new advances in the study of ancient languages, especially as they pertain to the understanding of Scripture, while still retaining the core of religious truth. Liberals stressed mankind's progress in morality as a counterpart to or even a component of human evolution. Liberals generally viewed the Bible as a human record of a people's religious history rather than as the inspired word of God. Generally, liberals eschewed the supernatural and the miraculous, emphasizing reason, but also emphasizing what came to be called "the Social Gospel." Thus, Fundamentalism developed as a response to what was perceived by many as a threat to basic Christian beliefs.

> "As the fundamentalists saw it, all persons were faced with a crucial decision. They must choose either the fundamentalist interpretation of Christianity or that of Protestant Liberalism. In their judgment, there was no middle ground" (Russell, op. cit. p. 17).

Fundamentalism developed through the latter years of the nineteenth century by way of Bible conferences, religious literature, associations, and particularly through the voices of prominent preachers.

The strongly conservative movement which ultimately came to be called Fundamentalism began with a series of annual summer assemblies, meeting at Niagara-on-the-Lake, Ontario. Their literature expressed not only a very conservative Calvinist position, but led ultimately to the production of *The Fundamentals: A Testimony to the Truth*, a series of twelve booklets on current theological issues, published and distributed by two wealthy laymen from Los Angeles, Lyman and Milton Stewart, from 1910 to 1915. These publications were sent to every pastor, seminary and Bible school, Sunday school superintendent, and YMCA and YWCA secretary in the English-speaking world.

Despite theological differences, the authors of *The Fundamentals* managed to stand on belief in the Bible's literal inerrancy, yet also succeeded temporarily in avoiding increasing the developing contention between the Seminary-based denominational Christians and the Bible institute Christians who saw liberalism as a threat to dearly held basic Christian beliefs.

The Fundamentalists accepted (and accept) the "five fundamentals" adopted by the General Assembly of the Presbyterian Church in the U.S.A. in 1910, and reaffirmed in 1916 and in 1923: ". . . the inerrancy of the Scriptures in the original documents, the deity of Jesus including his virgin birth, and the substitutionary atonement, physical resurrection, and the miracle-working power of Christ" (C. Allyn Russell, op. cit. p. 16).

In addition to the Catholic Church, mainstream Christian churches, at least in their official teachings, then and now would concur with those same beliefs. The Fundamentalists, however, then and now generally accept the following additional basic principles or beliefs: ". . . belief in the natural depravity of man [contrary to Catholic teaching, Ed. Note], justification by faith alone (which Roman Catholics did not [accept]); the personal, bodily return of Christ and, normally a literal heaven and a literal hell" (ibid. p. 16).

After World War I, the spokesmen of the Fundamentalist persuasion reached the height of their influence. Most of the prominent Fundamentalist preachers began their ministry in the Baptist and the Presbyterian churches in which the Liberal/Modernist-Fundamentalist controversy was raging. Some Fundamentalists remained within their denominations while others left to start congregations of their own. The high point of their influence was reached in the 1920s. But Sidney E. Ahlstrom states, in *A Religious History of the American People* (New Haven: Yale University Press, 1972, p. 914):

"The Fundamentalist controversy neither began nor ended in the twenties, but that decade did witness the climactic confrontation of American evangelical Protestantism and modern thought."

Protestant liberalism may have been "a major catalyst" bringing Fundamentalism into existence, but it has its roots deep in the history of those Protestant churches which were started among the pioneers who crossed the Blue Ridge and then the Appalachians with only their Bibles as their religious and moral guide.

While the Christian Church, started by Barton Stone, a former Presbyterian minister, in Kentucky in the early 1800s, and the Disciples (some congregations later called Disciples of Christ), started by Thomas and Alexander Campbell, also formerly Presbyterian, in western Pennsylvania, strictly speaking, cannot be identified with Fundamentalism, their rejection of creeds, their option of the right of every Christian to interpret Scripture for himself/herself, and their position that the General Assembly exercises no authority beyond moral persuasion, all of these factors lay the ground for the twofold developments of the later nineteenth century: social activism, taking the form of the antislavery movement prior to the Civil War and the "Negro Schools" staffed by mostly northern volunteer teachers in the years immediately following the war, then on the other hand, the Revivalist movement with emphasis on personal Christian experience, which led to the summer conferences and eventually to Fundamentalism on the part of some. All of this is a specifically American religious phenomenon.

Just as Fundamentalism was beginning to develop in American religious life, the Ku Klux Klan was gaining strength in the South. Both Fundamentalism and the Klan peaked in influence on American society at about the same time, in the 1920s. Both are attempts to control elements in thought and in social/cultural conditions which seem to be difficult for us to understand or hard to manage in our lives.

The Fundamentalist phenomenon seemed to fade from prominence after the Scopes Trial in 1925 in Dayton, Tennessee. The trial arose out of an act of the Tennessee legislature which forbade the teaching of evolution in the public schools in the state. The jury favored William Jennings Bryan, who had the backing of almost every Fundamentalist preacher in the country, but the flamboyant oratory on both sides did not enhance the image of Fundamentalism in the minds of the public.

A characteristic of Fundamentalism which has evoked comment and discussion within Fundamentalist ranks, as well as among its observers, is a criticism of society focusing on personal sins without a compensating interest in and activity for social reform (one might add, with the exception of the strong Fundamentalist drive for Prohibition, resulting in the Eighteenth Amendment, adopted during World War I and repealed in 1933).

Regarding the Fundamentalists' criticism of society, Russell remarks:

> "What irritated people, however, was not so much the correctness or incorrectness of the fundamentalists in these areas as it was their dogmatic, absolutist, haughty insistence that they and they alone were right. They made no allowance for other views and they saw no gradation in the evils they condemned. In dealing with dancing, for instance, they made no distinction between folk dancing and nightclub sensuousness" (op.cit. pp. 214-215).

Since the 1950s, Fundamentalism has not only revived as a force in the religious life of the United States (and Canada) but has grown rapidly and among persons who would not seem to be predisposed to accept either its beliefs or its attitudes.

Who Are the Fundamentalists?

A question commonly asked about any religious movement is: Who are the people involved? A Fundamentalist can be simply anyone. Fundamentalism encompasses all classes of people — the rich, the poor, the young, the middle-aged, the elderly, the uneducated, the educated, people of all races and of all religious denominations. Anyone can become involved in Fundamentalism. How? Usually a person is drawn in by the invitation of a Fundamentalist, since Fundamentalists are unceasing in their zeal to bring others to be "saved" as they have been.

Some Types of Fundamentalists

The most visible and easily recognizable Fundamentalists are those who strike at the teachings and even at the members of mainstream churches with distorted information, through broadcasts and publications. Their antagonism and bigotry is evident. Dialogue with them is impossible. The best thing we can do is to love them and to pray for them. Examples of this type of Fundamentalism can be found in the Jack Chick comic books and his other publications. Jack Chick attempts to prove that Catholicism is not a Christian religion, that the Catholic Church is the "Whore of Babylon," that the Pope is the Anti-Christ, and all members of the Catholic Church are going to hell. Bob Jones University in Greenville, South Carolina, is another example of this sort of Fundamentalism, one of whose graduates is the Reverend Ian Paisley, known for his ranting leadership of the most militant anti-Catholic groups in Ulster.

Most leaders of this type of Fundamentalist movement have had little if any formal seminary training in Scripture, in theology, or in Church history. Their preparation for leadership has been in home Bible study circles. Such groups can use scriptural texts without being aware that they are taking them out of context to support their personal dispositions or beliefs. While we may credit them and the members of the group with good will, nevertheless, that is what we call "Scripture twisting." This personal and biased use of Scripture fuels continuing bigotry and strengthens the control of the leaders over the members of such groups, enabling them to continue teaching that salvation is to be found only in their groups.

The so-called "snake handling" congregations in the Appalachian mountain areas of western Virginia, West Virginia, Kentucky, Tennessee, and the Carolinas are an example of Fundamentalist "Scripture twisting" pushed to the extreme. Admittedly they are not typical of the Fundamentalists whom most of us meet almost daily, but it may be helpful to look at their position from the point of view of Jesus' temptation in the Desert of Judea (Lk. 4:1-13).

The third temptation is ostensibly spiritual. What could be a quicker way for Jesus to prove His spiritual leadership and to gain followers than to throw Himself down from the pinnacle of the Temple, safely because of the protection of the angels? It appeared that He was being asked to trust God, not to renounce or to change any of His teachings, nor to compromise with evil.

But notice Jesus' reply: "You shall not put the Lord your God to the test" (Mt. 4:7; Lk. 4:12).

What was wrong? Christian faith trusts in God, but with humble hope. And Christian faith learns from the *whole* of the Bible, noticing how God leads us to grow slowly, by faithful effort. *Demanding* that God do what seems best to us is misguided faith, an attempt to manipulate God.

A second type are the TV evangelists and media personalities, with their followers. Religious TV programs can be a source of real spiritual good for the housebound elderly or for persons with handicaps. For others, however, TV evangelism might be called "Couch Christianity" or "Fast Food Religion." Some TV evangelists appeal to the emotional problems, pain, needs of their viewers, promising an "instant fix" based on "the more you pray/pay the more God loves you." For these evangelists the degree of bias and antagonism shown against mainstream churches varies from that of Jimmy Swaggart to the relatively harmless tears of Tammy Fay Bakker.

The informed moderates are a third type. Most of them are also TV evangelists and media personalities, but they are generally concerned to promote the Gospel rather than a personal bias, sincerely good Christians trying to do good for others. Although their doctrines may differ little from those of the other Fundamentalists, they often prefer to be called Evangelicals. Because they are not antagonistic toward mainstream Christianity, honest dialogue is possible. Jerry Falwell, with his Liberty University in Lynchburg, Virginia; Pat Robertson, and Robert Schuller are good examples of this type of Fundamentalist, as is also Charles Stanley of Atlanta, Georgia, with his television ministry.

In a very real sense, certain evangelicals can be called Fundamentalists. The word, "Evangelical," can be found in the names of several Protestant denominations, but persons who would describe themselves as evangelical belong to many Protestant denominations. They adhere to the teachings and authority of Scripture, especially the New Testament, rather than the authority of a church itself, or of reason. They stress the importance of a personal experience of guilt for sin and of reconciliation with God through Jesus Christ. Evangelicals are very open to dialogue. A good example would be Billy Graham, who has visited the Pope, and who refers persons who come forward at his rallies to accept Jesus to ministers and priests of their own churches.

What Draws People to Fundamentalism?

Many persons living in the Southern States, often called "the Bible Belt," and in some parts of the Midwest, are raised by their families in Fundamentalism, joining Fundamentalist churches in their youth. Later in this chapter you will read an account of some of the experiences of a young man who grew to adulthood in a Fundamentalist family and who has converted to Catholicism.

As we have seen, those who have not been raised in Fundamentalism are sometimes drawn to Fundamentalist groups because they are disheartened by what they see as a compromise with the spirit of the world in some of the mainstream churches; they are disillusioned by the compromises and by what they perceive as dishonesty in government. They are disheartened and frustrated by the evils which seem to be tolerated by modern society. The Fundamentalists whom they meet are evidently totally committed to their beliefs, which seem clear and uncompromising. Fundamentalists focus on an apocalyptic view of the end of the world and on Divine Judgment to solve the world's present ills.

The Position of Fundamentalists on the Bible

The Bible, and in some Fundamentalist circles only the King James Version, is the source of all truth and contains the answers to all of life's problems and questions. God's word is absolute and unchangeable. It can be read and interpreted by anyone who desires to be saved. Since every Fundamentalist interprets the Bible as he or she sees it and presents that interpretation as absolutely true for all, this denies the need for and the legitimacy of authoritative interpretation, the Holy Spirit's role in the traditional interpretation of Scripture. Any scholarly study of Scripture is condemned as distortion leading to modernism and secularism.

In 1943, Pope Pius XII encouraged Biblical scholars to seek out what the human authors of Scripture meant and the purpose for which they wrote, to study the culture of the people who lived in biblical times in order to better understand the literature of the Bible.

The Catholic Church teaches that the Bible, Sacred Scripture, is divinely inspired, by the Holy Spirit moving the human authors to compose the various books of the Bible to convey truth, but in their own words, that is, using such images and words as would be understandable to the people of their time. The writers, therefore, conveyed the truth as they saw it, which may not be what the people of our time see as historic or scientific truth, yet the message is what God wanted conveyed. A good example of truth being conveyed by something which is scientifically untrue is the word "sunrise," which we sometimes use to express the earliest time of the day. We all know what is meant, although we know now that the sun does not "rise," but that the earth moves around the sun.

The *Dogmatic Constitution on Divine Revelation* of Vatican Council II, #11, states:

> "To compose the sacred books, God chose certain men who, all the while he employed them in this task, made full use of their power and faculties, so that, though he acted in them and by them, it was as true authors that they consigned to writing whatever he wanted written, and more."

Fundamentalists tend to see the human authors of Scripture as mere pen holders devoid of personality.

PART II — THE VIEWS OF A FORMER FUNDAMENTALIST

[Michael Summers was born into a Fundamentalist family. He is a convert to Catholicism, studying at a Catholic college. His writing about the Fundamentalist movement gives us a view through the window of his experiences and from his present perspective as a Catholic.]

As I begin to write about "Fundamentalism As I Know It," which might be a most accurate title for my part of this chapter, I wish to make very clear that I do not have the proverbial "axe to grind." The Fundamentalists whom I know and have known are, with rare exceptions, kind and loving people who are sincerely and resolutely dedicated to what they believe is true Christianity. Their ardor stands as an example to every Christian. What the Fundamentalist believes, he believes with his whole being.

Nevertheless, there are many problems inherent to Fundamentalism which can and do cause much suffering and animosity, both within and without the household of Fundamentalism. I hope that any light which I can shed on this situation will prevent persons who are not now Fundamentalists from becoming prey to Fundamentalism's deceptive simplicity, and perhaps ultimately move some Fundamentalists to take an objective look at their own faith. If I achieve nothing more than that some Fundamentalist reaches a better understanding of the Catholic Church, recognizing that Catholicism is not as Pastor X has portrayed it, then I will have accomplished a great work.

* * * * *

Bible Christians
> "Jesus loves me,
> This I know,
> For the Bible
> Tells me so. . . ."

This verse, from perhaps the most beloved children's hymn in Protestant circles, most closely approximates a creed in Fundamentalism. Those words contain the foundation of all theology for the Bible Christian. No true Christian would deny the truth of that little song, since all Christians believe that Jesus does love us and that the Bible truly states that fact. The ultimate truth for the Fundamentalist, however, can be found in the chorus of that song:

> "Yes, Jesus loves me;
> Yes, Jesus loves me;
> Yes, Jesus loves me;
> The Bible tells me so."

That which distinguishes all Fundamentalists from other Christians is absolute reliance on the Bible for all religious truth. It is the Bible, and no other source, which tells the Fundamentalists not only that Jesus loves them, but that He exists at all.

Three Scripture passages form the basis for the Fundamentalist proclamation that the Bible proclaims itself as the sole source of revelation: "Your Word is a lamp to my feet and a light to my path" (Ps. 119:105). "Everything in Scripture has been divinely inspired and has its uses; to instruct us, to expose our errors, to correct our faults, to educate in holy living" (2 Tim. 3:17). "So much has been written down, that you may learn to believe Jesus is the Christ, the Son of God, and so believing find life through his name" (Jn. 20:31) [All quotations from NRSV].

Clearly these passages are not explicit declarations of the Bible's unique position as sole judge and supreme authority of the Church. Psalm 119:105 states that God's word is *a* lamp to guide us, not *the* lamp. Likewise, 2 Timothy 3:17 merely states that all Scripture is inspired and that it has several uses, but nowhere in this quotation is it asserted that Scripture alone can fulfill these purposes. John 20:31 does not claim that one can only come to believe in Christ and gain eternal life by means of the Bible — John's purpose for writing is indeed to tell us about Christ, but John himself does not state that this is the only source of information about His life.

In fact, the Bible states that it is not the complete storehouse of Revelation. John states in his Gospel, Ch. 20:30, that "Now Jesus did many other signs in the presence of his disciples, which are not written in this book." Additionally, St. Paul writes in Romans 16:17 the following: "I urge you, brothers and sisters, to keep an eye on those who cause dissensions and offenses, in opposition to the teaching that you have learned." He states explicitly in 2 Thessalonians 2:15 that the believers are to "stand fast, and hold the traditions which you have learned, *whether by our word or by our epistle*" [emphasis mine]. The previous Bible quotation, for whatever reason or intention, is normally glossed over by Fundamentalists; nevertheless, it is necessary for these individuals to look at what Scripture actually says about itself.

That the Bible is self-interpreting is a logical consequence which follows, for if the Bible is the sole authority in Christian matters, then human exposition of the Scriptures is impermissible. But the Bible clearly rejects that position. Second Peter 1:20-21 states:

"First of all you must understand this, that no prophecy of Scripture is a matter of one's own interpretation, because no prophecy ever came by human will, but men and women moved by the Holy Spirit spoke from God."

If Scripture is not a matter for personal interpretation, then there must be some external source or agent that guarantees the authenticity of Scriptural interpretation and exegesis.

Further in 2 Peter 3:15-17 (NRSV):

"So also our beloved brother Paul wrote to you according to the wisdom given him, speaking of this as he does in all his letters. There are some things in them hard to understand, which the ignorant and unstable twist to their own destruction, as they do the other scriptures."

This indicates that it is indeed possible to twist and distort the meaning of Scripture, even if the person or persons in question are completely sincere in their approach. St. Peter in no way attributes malice to those who erroneously interpret the Scriptures.

William Reichert, a former Fundamentalist, states:

"Authority, in all our daily experiences, means a person or institution empowered to enforce a rule. . . . A book by its nature can only be *authoritative*, not an authority.

"If I were to proclaim a heresy, it would not be the Bible that would contradict me. The Bible would be mute until a Christian chose a particular text or texts from Scripture to refute what I say. It is the Christian interpreter who claims authority — his own or that of his tradition — to determine that what I teach is a heresy" (William Reichert, "I Will Be Where Peter Is," *This Rock*, San Diego, Calif., January 1990, p. 9).

The First Century Church

It is true that all Protestant churches state that they rely only on the Scriptures for guidance, for each of the mainstream Protestant churches follow traditional biblical interpretations and church discipline that they derive to a greater or lesser degree from Martin Luther, John Calvin, John Knox, John and Charles Wesley, or Henry

VIII. But while the churches which profess to stem from the Reformation also profess their foundation on Scripture, they express their beliefs in creeds, confessions, and turn with varying degrees of respect to the writings of their revered leaders. In addition, great liturgical traditions influence the worship of both the Episcopalian (Anglican) and Lutheran churches, while the worship services of those churches based on Calvinism are more plain because they are not so influenced.

The Fundamentalists, however, who have heard of the Reformation, of Luther, Calvin, Knox, Henry VIII, the Wesleys, etc., hardly ever give the Reformation or the reformist leaders any thought, for they believe with great fervor that as Fundamentalists *they are the Apostolic Church*, and that all other churches, including the Church of Rome, came from Fundamentalism, better known as the First Century Church. A Fundamentalist will, without hesitation, state that all other denominations have rejected the simplicity of the Gospel for "religion," which they do not mean in the ordinary sense of that word, i.e., belief system, but in the sense of a set of man-made traditions or customs.

Since the "Bible-believing" church receives all information regarding church organization from the few passages found in the New Testament, each individual Fundamentalist church or congregation is entirely independent from others, not only in organization but also in matters of doctrine or teaching.

A typical Fundamentalist church consists of a pastor, the elders or deacons, and the congregation. The pastor holds no greater authority in the church, nor do the elders or deacons, than do the members of the congregation, for whatever authority they possess is received directly from the congregation by election, by majority vote, and they can be removed the same way. Although this appears very democratic and fair, this unstructured structure can and often does lead to chaos.

Do you wonder why there seem to be so many small, apparently unaffiliated churches throughout this country?

Essentially, each member of a Fundamentalist church is a church unto himself or herself. Fundamentalism is not so much a church or denomination as a confederation of believers who agree on only one thing: the Bible is all-powerful. Each individual is the sole judge of what is orthodox and what is heresy. The pastor may be referred to for guidance, but ultimately it is up to the individual to decide what is the true interpretation of any Scripture passage.

The pastor does little more than preach sermons and run the operations of the church. As a preacher, he is expected to be very dynamic, sometimes presenting in his sermons his own new personal revelations about a particular Scripture passage, what he perceives to have been an illumination by the Holy Spirit, and the congregation can be caught up in a surge of emotion. But any member of the congregation is free at any time to agree with or disagree with any of his statements. This is why Fundamentalists carry their Bibles to church: one must have the Word at hand to determine whether the preacher's words "square" with the Word. It is sometimes frustrating to sit in such a congregation, watching the members flipping through their Bibles to find a verse to which the preacher has referred while he continues his sermon. The congregation which does this is not inattentive, but is seeking to verify the point the preacher is making.

I have lived through many incidents in which the pastor disagreed with the scriptural interpretations of one or more members of the church. Usually the matter is brought to a vote. The pastor can be removed by the vote, or he may become dogmatic and strongly suggest that those who disagree with his views find another house of worship. Either way, the local church ordinarily goes into schism.

It is rare, therefore, for Fundamentalists to remain in one local church for a lifetime. A church is useful for attending on Sundays in order to hear preaching and to sing and pray with others of similar, but by no means identical, beliefs. Membership, over and above attendance, is a mere formality that one goes through in order to vote for the pastor and the elders. It is not at all uncommon for a person to attend a church for a year, to leave for a year or more, and then to return to the first church because the second proved less satisfactory.

When Fundamentalists pride themselves on being the "First Century Church," a title frequently used in their sermons and Scripture studies, it indicates that the local church is patterning itself on those few tests descriptive of the early Church which can be found primarily in the Book of Acts. This often has amusing results, such as two Fundamentalist churches adjoining one another, yet in serious disagreement. In my home town there were two

Fundamentalist Baptist churches. In one it was taught that women who wore pants/slacks/shorts were doomed to hell-fire. The other church opted for a more liberal opinion. The pastors of both congregations condemned each other and forbade their respective flocks to associate with the members of the other congregation. My family and I attended neither of these churches, yet we experienced the effects of the conflict. An aunt informed me that she was praying for my mother, who was sinning because she wore pants AND wore shorts. Two of my younger cousins, whose parents were non-believers, were removed from Sunday School at that church because they had come in dress slacks.

What Is Meant by "Salvation"?

One of my earliest recollections was hearing my parents speak about salvation. Hardly a day passed that the topic was not mentioned. I can recall them conversing with relatives about whether or not a certain person was "saved," how wonderful it was to be "saved," and then how they were "saved." Sunday School and church services also stressed how important it was to be "saved." At a very early age I discovered that my parents' primary goal was for me to be "saved." By teaching me to memorize Bible verses and telling me how much Jesus loved me, they were preparing me for the day that I would "accept the altar call."

At last, at the age of six I too made the altar call and was led in the Sinner's Prayer. My parents were elated. The whole family celebrated at Sunday dinner at my grandmother's house. Unfortunately, I was not elated, for I had heard so many stories about people who had been "saved," about how they felt completely changed, totally new inside, the moment which they call being "born again." I felt none of those wonderful emotions.

In fact, I had known how to be "saved" from Sunday School and had asked my mother whether it was necessary to be "saved" at a church service. She had replied that I could be saved anywhere. So in the privacy of my bedroom I had asked Jesus to come into my heart, asked forgiveness of my sins, stated that I believed in Him, everything that I had been told was necessary for salvation. When I had felt no different, nothing special, I concluded that it was necessary to respond to the altar call at church.

After Sunday dinner at my grandmother's house, however, I was puzzled, for my aunt (the one who disapproved of women wearing pants) asked me what Sinner's Prayer was used, stating that she would give me a better one, the one used in her church. She later asked me whether the pastor had read Scripture to me at the altar rail. That too was necessary for salvation. Apparently in her eyes I had not been saved properly. At that moment I knew that something was not right, although I was unable to articulate the problem.

"Have *you* been saved?"

This question can be annoying to Catholics, who know that while we still draw breath there is no absolute way of knowing, and that if we make it to Heaven we will surely know that we are saved. Until then, we are redeemed; that is, Jesus has suffered, died for us on the Cross, has risen, and now pleads for us in Heaven, but only by our choosing to love and serve God until our death, making use of the free will He has given us, can we accept that gift of redemption from Him, so that at death we know that we have "chosen Christ" and are "saved," or have chosen badly.

For the Fundamentalist, absolute assurance of salvation is permanent. No matter what one does, not matter how horrendous the sin, "God will not pluck you from His hand." Illustrating this point, my aunt, who firmly believes that Catholics are headed for hell, on hearing that I had converted to Catholicism, remarked, "Oh well, he was saved, so he's all right."

Even though all Fundamentalists agree that "God will not pluck you from His hand," a minority believe that you are free to "jump from the hand of God," although this does not logically follow from the doctrine of absolute assurance. How can one have absolute assurance of one's election to eternal happiness, yet believe that he or she can at any time commit so grievous a sin that one would thereby separate himself or herself from God? When I asked that very question of an ardent Fundamentalist, I received the reply that you can still know if you are saved even though you could freely lose it.

What About Baptism?

Although every Fundamentalist would agree that one should be baptized, baptism is not seen as an important factor in salvation. To the Fundamentalist, baptism is nothing more then "the outward sign of an inward experience" (a statement found in most Fundamentalist literature), and one can remain a good Christian without it, but baptism is required for church membership and the right to vote. Ordinarily, after being saved, the person is baptized by immersion. If that person is a convert from a church which does not baptize by immersion, the person must be rebaptized. A puzzling feature about the place of baptism in Fundamentalism is why even the small churches go to great expense for baptisteries for immersion which are like small swimming pools, yet the congregations seem to attach little importance to baptism itself.

Fundamentalist Evangelization

Every Fundamentalist, a.k.a. Bible-Believing Christian, is expected to do his or her part in "soul winning," since there are perhaps millions of lost souls who think they are Christians but who have not made the altar call. Someone must witness to them. Nearly every person in a local church attends Sunday School, church, and Bible study every week, for this is how one learns the tactics of "soul winning." Sometimes the pastor gives special classes on this subject, at which the participants memorize specific Scripture texts for the purposes of answering questions which a prospective convert might have.

Since the act of being "saved" is so central to Fundamentalism, every Sunday sermon includes an emotional appeal for all sinners to come up to the altar and be saved. The passage or passages from the Bible which begin every sermon may deal with any topic, but the conclusion of every sermon is the same: repent, accept Jesus and be saved, or go to hell. Always there is more pleading, sometimes with the pastor addressing an individual whom he judges to be in dire need of salvation.

Sometimes the pastor gives examples of his personal experiences of "soul winning." I remember examples heard at one Sunday service. The pastor recounted two hospital visits. One person on his deathbed repented. The pastor saw a bright light on the face of the person as he exclaimed that he saw Jesus and a band of angels coming for him. Then he died. When the pastor visited another terminally ill man that same day, the second person was hostile to

God and His representative. The pastor begged and pleaded with this man, but to no avail. The pastor then related that the man saw the gates of hell open for him and died in agonizing terror.

In addition to the altar call at Sunday worship, Fundamentalist Evangelization includes visitation. It is in this that what has been learned in "soul winning" seminars is put into practice. Many Fundamentalists comply with the Gospel injunction to "go in pairs" while carrying their Bibles and handfuls of Scripture tracts. They may spend a day or an evening going from house to house or visiting a specific family that has been recommended for conversion by a fellow church member.

The approach is as direct and as emotional as the altar call: "Don't you wish you had an assurance of eternal life?" Many Scripture verses are piled on Scripture verses to prove that the individual or individuals visited are sinners and that all they need do is to invite Jesus into their hearts. If the persons visited accept the pleadings and do say the "Sinner's Prayer" their salvation will be noted and reported to the pastor, who will likely visit the newly-converted almost immediately, not only to give spiritual guidance but also to gain new members for his congregation. The local church keeps detailed records of souls won during the week and usually publishes them in the church bulletin.

If the prospective converts fail to respond to the visitors' pleading, thereby announcing their condemned state, their names are occasionally published in the church's bulletin, listed as those needing salvation, and needing prayer that they too might "see the light."

Tracts are not only distributed at Visitations, but are routinely left in public rest rooms, dressing booths at clothing stores, and are also handed to purchasers with change by store owners and cashiers. The tract contains some verses of Scripture, a step-by-step description of the salvation process, including the Sinner's Prayer, a statement congratulating the person's decision to accept Christ, a blank for the date and time one was saved, and usually the name and address of the local church with encouragement to contact the pastor.

The last form taken by Fundamentalist evangelization is aimed at children, vacation Bible school. Most people do not see this as controversial; after all, most mainstream churches sponsor such programs. The problem lies in *how* the Fundamentalists indoctrinate and convert the children.

My parents always sent me to vacation Bible schools sponsored by the local Fundamentalist churches. While we learned songs, played games, and did craft projects throughout the week, we were also instructed in the principles of Fundamentalism and were told frightening stories about the "Tribulation," the period of turmoil and horror during the "Last Days" following the "Rapture" of the "saved." We were told what would happen to us and to our parents if we were not "saved."

When I was eight years old I attended a vacation Bible school at my aunt's church. A ventriloquist and puppet master was on the schedule. After he had entertained us by performing various biblical stories using his puppets, he announced a program to be presented at the end of the week, entitled "The Devil's Banquet." Because of the nature of the presentation, only those eight years old or older would be permitted to attend. I attended this final presentation. A large table was covered with such objects as cigarettes, beer and liquor, rock music albums; the lights in the church sanctuary were dimmed; and there was background music similar to horror movie soundtracks. The puppeteer spoke to us of the dangers of becoming involved with these objects, then opened his Bible to tell us about the coming Tribulation and what would happen to those little children who would be "unsaved." At the end of his presentation, he held up to view a human skull, telling us that those who were not saved (including our parents) would end like this.

Since I was already saved, I did not respond to the altar call which followed the presentation, but many of my companions did, going up to the altar crying. In fact, I had nightmares for several weeks after this final performance. After I told my parents about this event, they did not send me again to vacation Bible school at my aunt's church. Of course, not all, not even most, of the Fundamentalist vacation Bible schools would go to such extremes to obtain the salvation of the children, but all aim to bring the children to the altar to be "saved."

After the Altar Call

One noticeable effect of the altar call is that the person responding will either become the typical energetic Fundamentalist or, surprisingly, never darken the door of the church again. There are, admittedly, a number of very large Fundamentalist/Evangelical congregations in existence. Taking into consideration the published "salvation statistics" (some churches even set a yearly goal), these churches should be substantially larger. I use this to reveal a tendency in Fundamentalism: When you're saved, you're saved, and nothing else matters. Of course, there are Fundamentalists who say that if the one responding to the altar call does not thereafter become a church-going member, then he or she was not really saved. Generally, however, those who do not continue to attend church are not considered any less saved than the rest. The Fundamentalist position is that the church or congregation has done its job by bringing the person to the altar and God will probably do whatever else is needed later.

I am acquainted with many persons in my age group who, having responded to the altar call, have since then taken part in nothing related to church. Yet when such persons are asked whether or not they have been saved, each can recite the day, the hour, and the location of his salvation experience, affirming his stance with God, usually arguing that God can be worshiped anywhere and that he chooses to do so without attending a church.

This ceasing to attend church is not rare among those who are Fundamentalist/Evangelicals, nor is it limited to those who have made a relatively recent profession of faith in Christ. Being "born again" translates into an emotion or a feeling of being regenerated. The person has been told that he or she is completely changed after having been "saved."

Many Fundamentalists, if not all, believe that every person who is saved will be graced with a "Damascus Road" experience, a reference to Saul's (later Paul) being struck down. Most people who respond to the altar call do experience some kind of catharsis. After all, the pastor's pleadings could be expected to impress a sin-tired individual, and then the sermon is brought to a soul-stirring conclusion with the altar call. The mere fact that a person is moved to walk forward to the altar in the sight of many strangers, often moved to shedding tears for sin, finally confessing one's sins before the congregation (this is a prerequisite for salvation in some churches), realizing that one's name is now written in the "Lamb's Book of Life" would be overwhelming.

The "saved" or "born again" person expects to sin no more from this moment, or at least to sin less. Among some Fundamentalists there is a belief called Sanctification, meaning that eventually one will reach perfection, literally being sinless, in one's "walk with Christ."

PART III — CONCLUSION

As you have been reading this chapter, have you wondered whether any Fundamentalists have at one time or another critiqued their own movement? Jerry Falwell, in *The Fundamentalist Phenomenon* (New York, Doubleday, 1981), lists the following weaknesses of Fundamentalism:

1. Its small capacity for self-criticism.
2. Its overemphasis on exterior spirituality.
3. Its resistance to change of any kind.
4. Its neglect of major issues and overemphasis on minor issues (beards, women's slacks, etc.)
5. Its tendency to add to the Gospel (e.g. the evils of evolution).
6. Its overemphasis on dynamic leadership.
7. Its excessive worry about labels, to insure its purity from the world.
8. Its absolutism — everything is black or white.
9. Its authoritarianism in both church and family.
10. Its exclusivism.

The Do's and Don'ts

I have always heard that one does not argue religion or politics. This is especially true of Fundamentalism. What might appear to be a simple disagreement over interpretation of a Scripture passage actually goes much deeper than the question of what we or they mean by "literal interpretation of Scripture." Moreover, any Fundamentalist knows more Scripture than most mainstream clergy.

Recall what we noted at the beginning of this chapter, the difference between the fundamentals and Fundamental*ism*. The latter indicates an attitude described by Robert T. Handy, dean of graduate studies and professor of Church History, Union Theological Seminary, New York:

"The main difference between them [the Fundamentalists and the conservatives] was probably more a matter of mood and spirit than basic theological divergence. Both subscribed to orthodox Protestant theological tenets, but the fundamentalists were more aggressive, more intransigent, more certain that they had the whole truth and their opponents had none. They not only militantly asserted the plenary inspiration of Scripture, but insisted that they had correctly apprehended its meaning and their opponents not at all" ("Fundamentalism and Modernism in Perspective," *Religion in Life*, Vol. XXIV, 1955, p. 390).

So, love the Fundamentalists with the compassion of Christ, because they sincerely believe that they are doing what is right before the Lord. Love the person, but do not condone or embrace their erroneous beliefs.

Ultimately Fundamentalism is a challenge to all mainstream churches, a challenge to reach out to the members of our congregations with carefully planned and fervent worship and more interest in and care for our members. It is difficult in large congregations to reproduce the one-on-one personal attention extended by the small Fundamentalist communities.

Additionally, the Fundamentalists challenge us to extend and deepen our study of Scripture. People today want a deep personal relationship with Jesus, and want this rooted in Sacred Scripture. If we fail to provide our people with good Scripture study programs, they may seek elsewhere for them, but more importantly, we are failing Christ in His Word and in His Mystical Body.

A final thought: study is not enough. Study of Scripture needs to be prayerful, for ourselves to grow in knowledge, understanding, and wisdom, and most of all, love for God's Word; and for others to grow likewise.

I am sure you have heard the term "Fundamentalist" used with reference to some Muslim groups, and after reading to this point in this chapter you may find that use of the word confusing, because Muslims do not hold any of the "five fundamental" Christian beliefs. Even more confusing, after reading about the almost universal anti-Catholic stance of American Fundamentalists, you may recall having heard some Catholics criticize other Catholics as "fundamentalist."

To understand this use of the term, recall what Anthony Gilles wrote, that "Fundamentalists are so preoccupied with religious doctrine that they have made it an end in itself rather than a means to an end" (Gilles, op. cit.). And recall Professor Russell's remarks, that "What irritated people . . . was not so much the correctness or incorrectness of the fundamentalists . . . as it was their dogmatic, absolutist, haughty insistence that they and they alone were right. . ." (Russell, op. cit., p. 214).

Finally, refer back to the statements of Professor Randy, who indicates that Fundamentalism is primarily an attitude.

The "fundamentalist" puts "the letter of the law" before the spirit (see 2 Cor. 3:6 and Rom. 2:29). This fundamentalist attitude can be found in some members of any religion, or of any political party, or even of any club or organization.

Error has no rights. That is a philosophical principle which is easy to accept on the practical level. We do not willingly accept short change for a purchase, which is simply expressing in practice that two plus two cannot equal four and five at the same time. Sanity requires that we bring our minds into conformity with reality. Only Napoleon was right in thinking of himself as Napoleon.

Once we accept something as true in religion or politics, however, we tend to make it "ours": "our club," "our team," "our school," "our company," "our country," "our church." And since we like to think we would never accept or adopt anything "second best," it is very easy to begin to feel superior because "our Church" teaches this or that. "Hooray for our side!"

Unfortunately, this partisanship, truth as something "belonging" to us, limits truth, diminishes it to something we can "own," begins to warp it toward error. It is a first step toward Fundamentalism.

By critiquing Fundamentalism, however, we are not advocating "indifferentism," which accepts any or all religions as equally good, that what beliefs we hold are unimportant "just so we believe in something," because "all religions can take us to God." This belief is expressed in a tolerant attitude toward all religions, but a serious commitment to none.

Between the two extremes of indifferentism and fundamentalism is the truth, which, in this case, is definitely not a compromise.

If we once accept that God is, then we immediately see the need to learn who or what God is, and whether or what God has revealed about Himself — what we can know about God. Sanity requires that of us and for this pursuit we need freedom.

One of the shorter documents of the Second Vatican Council is *Dignitatis Humanae*, ("Of human dignity") or *The Declaration on Religious Liberty* (promulgated Dec. 7, 1965). At first glance the document appears to deal with freedom of religion in a political context, but its importance to all of us is the clear statement of those basic principles on which we base our claim to seek freely the truth about God and to practice the religious truths which we believe.

> "The Vatican Council declares that the human person has a right to religious freedom. . . . that all men should be immune from coercion on the part of individuals, social groups and every human power, so that, within due limits, nobody is forced to act against his convictions in religious matters in private or in public, alone or in associations with others. The Council further declares that the right to religious freedom is based on the very dignity of the human person as known through the revealed word of God and by reason itself. . ." (DH #2, Flannery transl., p. 800).

What do both fundamentalism and indifferentism have in common? Both are responses to or reactions to what persons perceive as truth. It is at that meeting point that we can begin to discover what our attitude should be: ". . . all men, because they are persons, that is, beings endowed with reason and free will and therefore bearing personal responsibility, are both impelled by their nature and bound by a moral obligation to seek the truth, especially religious truth. They are also bound to adhere to the truth once they come to know it and direct their whole lives in accordance with the demands of truth. But men cannot satisfy this obligation in a way that is in keeping with their own nature unless they enjoy both psychological freedom and immunity from external coercion. Therefore the right to religious freedom has its foundation not in the subjective attitude of the individual but in his very nature. . ." (ibid., p. 801).

When Jesus was brought before Pilate, who asked whether he was king of the Jews, which would make him guilty of stirring up rebellion against the Roman rulers of Palestine, Jesus answered:

> "My kingdom does not belong to this world. If my kingdom were of this world, my subjects would be fighting to save me from being handed over to the Jews. . . . The reason I was born, the reason why I came into the world, is to testify to the truth. Anyone committed to the truth hears my voice." (Jn. 18:36, 37, NAB)

Let us use Pilate's question to Jesus as a question to ourselves: "What is truth?" (Jn. 18:38, NAB)

In his farewell discourse to the Apostles, Jesus had said, "I am the Way, the Truth, and the Life." (Jn. 14:6, NAB)

It is unfortunate that sometimes we speak about "fighting for the truth." Should we "fight for the truth?" And if so, how?

When Jesus was arrested in the Garden of Gethsemane, "Suddenly, one of those who accompanied Jesus put his hand to his sword, drew it, and slashed at the high priest's servant, cutting off his ear. Jesus said to him: 'Put back your sword where it belongs. Those who use the sword are sooner or later destroyed by it. Do you not suppose I can call on my Father to provide at a moment's notice more than twelve legions of angels? . .' " (Mt. 26:51-53, NAB).

Jesus, who is the fullness of God's revelation of Himself to us, is telling us that He does not need force or coercion from us to "defend" him. We are called to "defend" the truth by clearly proclaiming it, to "share" the truth with others. Whenever truth is used to manipulate anyone into acceptance of a particular point or is used as a kind of offensive weapon, a "verbal club," we are using one gift of God, the truth, to violate another gift of God, the freedom of will with which He has endowed our human nature. When God made humankind capable of seeing and accepting truth quickly, or taking longer to come to the truth, or even rejecting the truth for a while or forever, how dare any of us criticize the way we were created?

It is not enough simply to avoid force or violence in defense of the truth. We need to grow in knowledge and understanding of God, who is all Truth, and then to act toward others as He does:

> "You have heard the commandment, 'You shall love your countryman but hate your enemy.' My command to you is: love your enemies, pray for your persecutors. This will prove that you are sons of your heavenly Father, for his sun rises on the bad and the good, he rains on the just and the unjust. If you love those who love you, what merit is there in that? Do not tax collectors do as much? And if you greet your brothers only, what is so praiseworthy about that? Do not pagans do as much? In a word, you must be made perfect as your heavenly Father is perfect" (Mt. 5:43-48, NAB).

When we study those verses, it becomes evident that the perfection of God which Jesus is asking us to bring into our own lives is God's Infinite Love for all persons, and His patient waiting for us to turn to Him.

There are many other indications in Scripture that Jesus meant us to seek Him in freedom and to proclaim His teachings to our neighbors in simplicity and with great respect for their freedom: I can only suggest that readers turn to Appendix II to read the excerpts from the Vatican Council Declaration on Religious Freedom, particularly Paragraphs 11 and 14, which contain many references to the words of Jesus enjoining gentleness and respect for the freedom of others while teaching the truth.

Fundamentalism: Suggested Reading

The following books are listed not alphabetically by author, but topically, the first two providing the foundation for understanding the doctrinal stance of the men whose biographies are the subjects of Professor Russell's book and the movement which is the topic of Professor Anderson's book, which is listed last, if only because it is a sub-topic branching off from classical Fundamentalism.

Fischer, David Hackett, *Albion's Seed: Four British Folkways in America*, New York and Oxford, Oxford University Press, 1989 [Each of the four major migrations from Britain to the colonies is treated, and in each section the religious beliefs and attitudes brought from the mother country and continued in colonial times and since then are treated. Most thorough research on origins of early American attitudes toward people of different beliefs and customs, many of which perdure until the present.]

Tyler, Alice Felt, *Freedom's Ferment, Phases of American Social History to 1860*, Minneapolis, The University of Minnesota Press, 1944 [The Chapters on "Evangelical Religion," "Millennialism and Spiritualism," "The Temperance Crusade," and "Denials of Democratic Principles" provide necessary historic background for understanding Fundamentalism.]

Russell, C. Allyn, *Voices of American Fundamentalism, Seven Biographical Studies*, Philadelphia, The Westminster Press, 1976 [In-depth studies of leaders of the Fundamentalist movement in the United States.]

Anderson, Robert Mapes, *Vision of the Disinherited, The Making of American Pentecostalism*, New York and Oxford, Oxford University Press, 1979 [Anderson is professor of history and coordinator of the Division of Social Sciences at Wagner College, New York. Although many Fundamentalists and Fundamentalist congregations reject Pentecostalism per se, the doctrinal position of most Pentecostals is basically fundamentalist.]

Compendia, Guides to Specific Denominations:
Hardon, S.J., John A., *The Protestant Churches of America*, Westminster, Md., The Newman Press, 1957

Rosten, Leo, Editor, *Religions of America, Ferment and Faith in an Age of Crisis, A New Guide and Almanac*, New York, Simon and Schuster, 1975 [Part One contains chapters on the beliefs and practices of the major religions and even on the "unchurched," agnostics and "scientists." Part Two is a "collation of facts, events, opinion polls, statistics, analyses, and essays on the problems and crises confronting the churches today."]

The Catholic Response to Fundamentalism:
A Pastoral Statement for Catholics on Biblical Fundamentalism, drafted for the National Conference of Catholic Bishops by the Ad Hoc Committee on Biblical Fundamentalism chaired by

Archbishop John F. Whealon, U. S. Catholic Conference, Inc., 1987

Gilles, Anthony E., *Fundamentalism, What Every Catholic Needs to Know*, Cincinnati, Ohio, St. Anthony Messenger Press, 1984 [Excellent introduction to Fundamentalism by a Catholic who grew up in a strongly Fundamentalist part of the South.]

Gleason, S.J., Robert W., Editor, *In the Eyes of Others*, New York, The Macmillan Company, 1952 [Each of the Chapters comprising this book was written by an author chosen for special competence in the topic. While the book does not deal exclusively with Fundamentalism, some of the Fundamentalist criticisms of Catholicism are dealt with particularly well here.]

Keating, Karl, *Catholicism and Fundamentalism, The Attack on "Romanism" by "Bible Christians,"* San Francisco, Ignatius Press, 1988 [A methodical exposition of the Fundamentalists' attacks against Catholicism and an equally solid explanation of the Catholic position.]

Nevins, Albert J., M.M., *Answering a Fundamentalist*, Huntington, Ind., Our Sunday Visitor, 1990 [Explanations of Fundamentalists' beliefs and helpful suggestions for replying to their positions.]

St. Romain, Philip, *Catholic Answers to Fundamentalists' Questions*, Liguori, Mo., Liguori Publications, 1984 [Concise answers to Fundamentalists' questions, a useful short book.]

Stravinskas, Peter M. J., *The Catholic Response,* Huntington, Ind., Our Sunday Visitor, Inc., 1985 [Very good chapter on "Is the Mass Biblical?"]

None of the books listed in this section should be considered as sufficient by itself. Each contains some suggestions which supplement and strengthen the material on the same topic found in one or more of the other books. Anyone needing answers for a questioning or critical Fundamentalist would be wise to consult all of the books listed above.

5.

Shepherding/Discipleship Movement

Father Lawrence J. Gesy

"**I** CONSIDER him a charlatan — a wolf in sheep's clothing!" declared an angry father describing the leader of a Shepherding/Discipleship group to which his children belonged. His expression is typical of the comments made daily by distraught parents, spouses, or children of those involved in this movement.

The Shepherding/Discipleship Movement is composed of groups and churches that usually adhere to the cardinal doctrines of Christianity but exercise a control over their members' lives that is unethical and unorthodox. Such groups may be nondenominational, Protestant, Catholic, or both Protestant and Catholic, and almost all take a fundamentalist approach to Scripture.

Some Shepherding churches and "communities" require a covenant commitment to attain membership, thereby ensuring the members' loyalty, obedience, and cooperation toward the group and its leaders.

This movement goes by many different names and variations. The best-known, apart from the original terms "shepherding" and "discipleship," are: pastoral care, mentoring, headship and submission, and covering.

There are differences of opinion regarding the origin of the Shepherding movement. It seems to be a movement that sprang up in several groups in the United States and South America almost simultaneously in the late 1960s and early 1970s. The most prominent Shepherding leaders were Bob Mumford, Derek Prince, Don Basham, Charles Simpson, and Ern Baxter, who were affiliated with Christian Growth Ministries in Fort Lauderdale, Florida.

Some people join Shepherding groups at an emotionally low point or transitional stage in their lives. But the reader should be careful not to assume that only those with problems are targets for recruitment efforts. Most recruits are no more troubled or emotionally unstable than non-members. Statistics show that the incidence of mental illness among those recruited by cultic groups is no higher than in the population at large.

Characteristics that attract people to these groups include: a sense of belonging and of love for one another, a sense of importance in belonging to God's *special* people, the feeling of being readily understood and accepted, the discipline, idealism, and the promotion of a sexually pure lifestyle. In other words, much the same kind of idealism that draws people to Mother Teresa today, or to St. Francis of Assisi eight hundred years ago. The distinction, though, is the hidden agenda. Mother Teresa has none. But those who join the Shepherding Movement eventually find the ideals originally espoused to be secondary to the demands of obedience and conformity that underlie all else in the group.

More importantly, though, those who join are led to believe that their recruitment is part of God's plan for their lives — that He put them in the area or circumstances to be evangelized by a member of the group and that resisting those efforts would be a rejection of God.

New members are gained by "love-bombing" potential recruits. People are made to feel important, very special, and extremely welcome in order to entice them to join. Some Protestant groups include a large percentage of former Catholics, many of whom have been attracted to the movement by the enthusiasm and emotion generated in group meetings or services. Most group members are from a middle-class or upper-middle-class background and are above average in intelligence.

Shepherding/Discipleship members are taught that Christians should be gathered in small groups of "sheep" or "disciples" who have a "shepherd" over them. Shepherds have intense control over virtually all aspects of the lives of "sheep" under them. A "sheep" divulges all his personal problems to his shepherd and submits to the decisions made by his shepherd for the conduct and direction of his life. Those decisions would include where and how one is employed, where one lives, whom one marries, and all financial decisions. To question or challenge a shepherd's advice or directives is considered "rebellion." Those who cannot or will not "submit" are forced out or shamed into leaving.

Each shepherd in turn submits to the authority of a shepherd over him, pyramidically, so that as we get toward the top of the pyramid, we see a tremendous amount of power concentrated in just a small number of people.

The Shepherding Movement teaches that a shepherd provides his "sheep" with a "covering," which is a protection from sin and the demonic realm. Sheep must act in obedience to the shepherd, who takes responsibility before God for their actions. Even if one willfully and knowingly commits sin in obedience to one's shepherd, they believe that his action becomes righteous, because he has submitted to the authority of his shepherd.

Members of Shepherding groups become extremely dependent on their groups. They are taught that they will be vulnerable to Satanic attack without their group's protection. Some actually lose their ability to make decisions by allowing their shepherd to take that responsibility for them. Others maintain some ability to make decisions. Still others believe they make decisions completely on their own, while in fact they are so indoctrinated that they behave in complete conformity to the group automatically or with subtle suggestions by the leaders. They fear the "world" because of the black-and-white world view presented by the group. (The group is pure and pleasing to God — all others are tainted and under Satan's influence.)

Some Shepherding groups allow their members to maintain their ties with their denominational churches, but one's primary allegiance would be to one's shepherd and group — rather than a church. Many of the non-denominational or Protestant groups are so anti-Catholic that they present Catholics who join with a great deal of false information about Catholicism. Catholics who join one of those groups and decide later to leave usually find it difficult or impossible to return to the Church because they've been influenced by the false information and because they've been taught to disregard Catholic tradition and to take a fundamentalist approach to the Bible.

Some Catholic Shepherding groups consider the Catholic Church too liberal and believe they are destined to lead the church back to a more conservative and legitimate practice of the faith.

Leaders of all Shepherding groups are very authoritarian, although many acquired that trait from the original leaders or through the group's indoctrination processes. Many have a charismatic personality. They assume their positions of leadership without elections. Many claim a supernatural experience including a vision or revelation from God indicating that God favors them above others. Some claim to be prophets or apostles and some claim God has performed great miracles through them. Members are very impressed by these claims while under the group's influence, but often realize after separating that there was no substantiation for such claims.

Group services generate a great deal of emotion. Enthusiastic singing, vibrant music, the moving testimonies of dramatic conversions, and the cajoling of a persuasive leader can produce an exciting experience. The spiritual "high" feeling can become addictive and explains why some members endure the abuses in these groups. Such experiences can also produce almost trance-like states that can leave members vulnerable to exploitation and indoctrination.

Members can lose their ability to evaluate information critically. They can also soon learn to equate obeying the group leaders with obeying God, and disobeying their leaders with disobeying God. They might eventually "police" themselves, feeling guilty about even a thought that disagrees with the group leaders or doctrine. They can suppress their normal personalities and assume the group personality, exhibiting the group mannerisms and speaking in the group terms. Women members are often expected to acquire a "gentle and quiet spirit" which is reflected in their soft-spoken voices.

Shepherding groups use fear and guilt to hold their members. They subscribe to the theory that as long as someone is brought to Christ, it doesn't really matter how that goal is accomplished.

Members must be honest and open with one another and the group, although they are often encouraged to lie or withhold information from outsiders that might prompt criticism. Sharing their innermost thoughts, feelings, weaknesses, etc., with fellow members promotes a closeness in a remarkably short time.

New recruits are molded into the group's view of what a Christian should be, what one's goals should be, how one should behave, how one should dress, how one should relate to others inside and outside the group, and even how one should think. Single men and women recruited into such groups frequently live communally and progress through courses of instruction to foster a very "holy" but restrictive lifestyle.

Group members are taught to suppress any negative feelings and emotions about the group or lifestyle. They are discouraged from asking uncomfortable questions that might expose the manipulation or undue influence at work within the organization. They must distance themselves from relatives and friends who are not members of the group. (These people are viewed as worldly or influenced by Satan.) Members are constantly monitored and they are often corrected or "encouraged" to improve in their attitudes or behavior. Such frequent disapproval and demands for perfection can result in a lowering of self-esteem.

In most Shepherding groups, young men and women are not permitted to date until the group leadership consider them mature enough to marry. To be mature, one has had to become obedient to all the group teachings and directives, and to conform to the group's standards and restrictions. Normal sexual attraction and any romantic feelings are looked upon as "lusting" and sinful, so those feelings must be suppressed.

Many young men and women resent the restrictions on dating but don't "buck the system" for fear that permission to date will be further delayed. Young people are often discouraged from dating someone they're attracted to in favor of someone the leaders feel would make a more suitable mate. After members leave these groups, they realize that many of the marriages in the groups are influenced by or even arranged by the leaders.

Marriage is considered more utilitarian than romantic. The two parties, united in their efforts, can be more effective for God. Husbands are to be the head of the household and provide financially, while wives are to keep house, submit to their husbands, and care for the children. Group priorities take precedence over family priorities.

As head of the household, the husband has the final say on family matters and decisions. Husbands are pressured to "run a tight ship" with their wives and children in obedience to themselves and the group. Such an arrangement, however, prevents the consideration of a loving partner's advice or input. Many men become exacting and overbearing with their wives because they fear criticism from leaders above.

The role of a wife and mother becomes increasingly difficult as the family enlarges. Some groups discourage family planning even if the couple are already overburdened with more children then they can adequately care for. Both husband and wife are expected to attend all group services, teachings, and activities, often necessitating frequent use of baby-sitters. Wives are often expected to assist in food preparation, cleaning, and baby-sitting for social functions. They are required to house out-of-town guests on little notice if the group requests. Most women are worn out from the excessive demands made on their time and energy.

There is a great deal of pressure to be good parents. Children are to be well-behaved and well-mannered. Some groups advocate physical punishment for misbehavior, believing they are motivated by a higher purpose which justifies such actions. It is very easy for some overtaxed parents, under such teaching, to vent their own frustrations while spanking, resulting in child abuse.

People in Shepherding groups experience a great deal of resentment which they suppress while in the group. When they learn that their feelings were justified and normal, they relate how angry they became at the group's interference in their marriages. They particularly resented those leaders who betrayed their confidences. Women resent having been viewed as "second-class citizens" in their group and the lack of opportunities for women to use their talents and education more effectively.

Those leaving Shepherding groups often find it difficult to retain their friendships with others who have left. It is stressful to have differences of opinion with people who previously agreed with you on everything. Maintaining friendships with those still in the group is even more difficult, and often impossible.

The elitist attitude of group members results in alienation from outsiders and strains relations with family members outside the group. Having previously cut close ties to friends and families, most former members learn to rebuild close relationships but wonder how to begin. They feel embarrassed and ashamed of their previous behavior. They wonder if they should offer explanations or apologize for their actions. Some family relationships are so ruptured that they will be difficult to heal.

Shepherding groups exhibit cult-like behavior not by completely isolating their members from society, but rather by making illegitimate in the minds of their members all other sources of information and church authority. They present themselves as "God's Best" and describe other churches as lukewarm, hypocritical, or deceived. These groups spiritualize everything and have a no-lose approach with their members. Everything good that happens is because God is so pleased with their joining the group. Anything disappointing or bad that happens is due to Satan's attack and anger that they've joined.

The decision to leave a Shepherding group is difficult and stressful. Many are unhappy and chafing under the control for years before they finally get the courage to do so. Those who depart are frequently shunned by their group in order to pressure their return and to deter others from leaving.

Those victimized by these groups are usually embarrassed by their experience and might feel humiliated, exploited, and angry. Most are fearful of speaking out against their group publicly, but express concern for those they left behind and guilt if they can't bring out of the group those they recruited. Those who were in leadership positions seem to feel the most guilt because they participated in the exploitation of those under them.

Some former members find it impossible to attend any church services — sometimes for years. They yearn to worship God, but their emotional response to a church setting and preaching is too overwhelming. It is not easy to trust again when one has been hurt so badly.

Time is needed to ascertain which group teachings were valid, and which teachings were aberrant or extreme. Some experience an anger at God or the Church for not protecting them from the abuses they suffered. They frequently come to the realization that their leader has interfered with their personal relationship with God.

Ex-members often feel many ill effects from the group practices and are at a loss to know why they cannot function normally. They need help from counselors who understand their experience as they deal with their stress and reintegrate into society. Without effective help, some have nervous breakdowns and a few even resort to suicide. Many find it extremely difficult to discuss their experience years after their involvement.

Those who deprive others of their individuality and free will commit grave injustice. In order to experience the joy and freedom in Christ, we must follow the Good Shepherd rather than the self-appointed "shepherds" who have become leaders in this movement.

* * * * *

These documents promulgated by the Second Vatican Council directly apply to the Shepherding/Discipleship movements in the sense that they provide criteria for use in appraising the validity of an organization or group as to its conformity to its stated aims and the way in which the group lives out its aims. These documents are the Decree on the Apostolate of the Laity (*Apostolicam Actuositatem*, Nov. 18, 1965), the Decree on the Appropriate Renewal of the Religious Life (*Perfectae Caritatis*, Oct. 28, 1965), and the Declaration on Religious Freedom (*Dignitatis Humanae*, Dec. 8, 1965). In addition to those, the foundation for all associations of laity is to be found in the Dogmatic Constitution on the Church (*Lumen Gentium*, November 21, 1964):

> "By divine institution holy Church is ordered and governed with a wonderful diversity. 'For just as in one body we have many members, yet all the members have not the same function, so we the many, are one body in Christ, but severally members one of another' (Rom. 12:4-5).
> "There is, therefore, one chosen People of God: 'one Lord, one faith, one baptism' (Eph. 4:5); there is a common dignity of members deriving from their rebirth in Christ, a common grace as sons, a common vocation to perfection, one salvation, one hope and undivided charity. . . .
> "In the Church not everyone marches along the same path, yet all are called to sanctity and have obtained an equal privilege of faith through

the justice of God (cf. 2 Pt. 1:1). Although by Christ's will some are established as teachers, dispensers of the mysteries and pastors for the others, there remains, nevertheless, a true equality between all with regard to the dignity and to the activity which is common to all the faithful in the building up of the Body of Christ" (*Lumen Gentium*, #32).

In fervently seeking Christian perfection or closer union with Christ, it is possible for some zealous persons to overlook or to dismiss these paragraphs as too pedestrian, but they are the foundation on which the Declaration on Religious Liberty is built, and they are the foundation for many canons in the New Code of Canon Law which pertain precisely not only to associations of the laity but also to religious.

In the Declaration on Religious Liberty we read:

"It is in accordance with their dignity that all men, because they are persons, that is, beings endowed with reason and free will and therefore bearing personal responsibility, are both impelled by their nature and bound by a moral obligation to seek the truth, especially religious truth" (*Dignitatis Humanae*, #2).

The Declaration continues:

"Therefore the right to religious freedom has its foundation not in the subjective attitude of the individual but in his very nature" (ibid.).

A problem exists among some contemporary groups or organizations in that the very structures within the Church which were designed to protect that freedom of each and every individual are perhaps unintentionally bypassed.

Some persons, seeking a more perfect society and finding the structures of our contemporary society too slow in bringing about reforms, form groups to achieve that goal more quickly, at least within the group. But since human beings do not change overnight, the only way to achieve such a goal quickly is by some kind of psychological coercion or dominance. Other persons seeking the same perfection may, without sufficiently estimating the long-range cost of relinquishing some or much personal liberty, submit to that coercion. But both kinds of people fail to recognize that ". . .the right to this immunity [from external coercion] continues to exist even in those who do not live up to their obligation of seeking the truth and adhering to it" (ibid., #3).

Leaders of groups or communities which appear to practice psychological coercion sometimes say that their groups are only living according to this or that old monastic rule. While this may be literally true and the rules themselves may be approved, not all *interpretations* of old monastic rules were approved by the Church. Some, such as the interpretations of the Jansenists, were specifically condemned for not respecting the "freedom of the children of God" (for which we could substitute "the people of God").

In the New Code of Canon Law, Canon 329 is pertinent to this matter: "Moderators of associations of the laity are to see to it that the members of the association are duly formed for the exercise of the apostolate which is proper to the laity." It seems like a confusion of roles if a group or association states that its members live according to old monastic rules or practices while the group seeks to attract lay persons and is established as a lay association. If any group, functioning in a diocese even though not established by a diocese, claims to be following an old monastic rule, that group should be known to the local bishop, be legally approved as a monastic community, and then be obliged to conform to the regulations of the Church for religious institutes, because any such group would be obliged to be known to the bishop and legally approved as a monastic community.

Historically, not all superiors of religious communities have always respected the personal freedom of those who joined their convents or monasteries, but it is significant that those persons who have been declared saints by the Catholic Church have shown marked respect for the freedom of others, not coercing but patiently waiting until those over whom they had authority might respond to God's call.

For this reason, anyone thinking of joining some new group should ask himself or herself what kind of relationship do the members have with the person or persons in charge? What is the relationship of this group with the organized Church? If the leader says that the discipline within the group is like that of monasticism, then is this group an order or community recognized by the Church? What is its relationship with the local bishop? And finally, do you want to be a monk or a nun, or do you want simply to be a good lay person? If that is what you want, then why do you want to join a monastic community? Clear information at the start can prevent disappointment later.

6.

The New Age Movement

Father Lawrence J. Gesy

THERE is a story about Shirley MacLaine, the "goddess" and promoter of the New Age Movement. Shirley is standing on the Malibu beach, yelling as loudly as she can, "I'm God! I'm God! I'm God!" Her voice echoes over the roar of the waves. God, omnipresent, hears this almost inaudible voice echoing through the universe. God motions to St. Peter, "Hey, Peter, come here. Listen! Listen! She thinks she is God!" They both laugh hysterically at this speck on the Malibu beach.

Shirley MacLaine has the reputation as one of the primary proponents, evangelizers, gurus, and goddesses of the New Age movement. She promotes her "religion" and its beliefs to curious God-hungry listeners by workshops, speaking engagements, and television interviews. The story of her "enlightenment and conversion" to New Age is written in her book *Out on a Limb*. Former members who have experienced the dangers of New Age firmly believe Shirley is *really* "out on a limb."

We associate all religions with a founder and a symbol. The general public associates Shirley MacLaine, with a crystal in her hand, as one of the "gurus" of the New Age. Just as the symbol of the cross of Jesus Christ is associated with Christianity, so has the crystal become the talisman of New Age. In New Age, remember, all that glitters is not gold; it may be crystal!

The story above, as humorous and preposterous as it may seem, is my introduction to the New Age. This story about Shirley MacLaine is reflective of the whole mentality of New Age. New Age is a wrong belief about who God is and who we are in relationship to Him. We are creatures created in His image and likeness. New Age is the belief that mere humans can become God. It is the worship of the creature rather than the Creator. Just as previous civilizations have fallen into false worship, so, too, New Age is a repeat of the same error. Romans 1:25 states: "They exchanged the truth of God for a lie and revered the creature rather than the creator, who is blessed for ever" (NAB).

Recently I had an appointment with Dr. Richard Balcer, my eye doctor. Richard and I recapture the past events of our lives during my appointments. I jubilantly informed him of this book, and as I gave Richard the titles of the chapters, he stopped me and asked, "What is New Age?" My response was, "Shirley MacLaine and crystals." These four words instantly were confirmed by, "Oh! that's New Age." What do *you* think New Age is?

What Is New Age?

Keep in mind that there is nothing "new" about New Age. It has been around for centuries. The "new" in New Age refers to the belief that the "old" mainstream denominational beliefs have failed. According to the New Age philosophy, the earth has been under the astrological sign of Pisces the fish for two thousand years.

This Christian symbol undervalued the power and the knowledge of the occult world. According to its followers, a "new age" is necessary. It is the age of Aquarius that cries for humanism, brotherhood, occult truths, and occult practices. It appears that the 1960s musical *Hair* has become a reality!

Trying to get a hold on this enigmatic creature is like trying to grab a slippery eel. No one has ever totally confined New Age into a tight container. My definitions of New Age is the following:

New Age is a belief system of self-divinity, self-generated truths, and self-generated destiny that blends Western occultism, Hinduism, Buddhism, and Christianity into the spiritual, political, social, and economical aspects of society.

Russell Chandler, a religion writer for the *Los Angeles Times*, describes New Age in his book *Understanding the New Age*, pp. 7-18, as a "kaleidoscope of beliefs, fads, and rituals."

> "New Age is a hybrid mix of spiritual, social, and political forces, and it encompasses sociology, theology, the physical sciences, medicine, anthropology, history, the human potential movement, sports, and science fiction.
>
> "New Age is not a sect or cult, per se. There is no organization to join, no creed one must confess. Identifying individuals as 'full-blown' New Agers is baffling. Some subscribe to certain portions of New Age, some to others; some dissociate themselves from the movement altogether, though they embrace core aspects of its thinking.
>
> "The New Age influence touches virtually every area of life, and thousands of New Age activists seek to transform society through New Age precepts. Millions have adopted the movement's view of reality, though they may simply think of it as a pragmatic, humanistic philosophy of life.
>
> "Although 'new' in style and vocabulary, the movement is in many ways as old as the Eastern religions of Hinduism, Buddhism, Western occultism, and the mystical oracles of ancient Greece and Egypt. New Age has simply recast the theory of reincarnation into the language of Western humanistic psychology, science, and technology. . . .
>
> "Rather, the insidious danger of the New Age is its view of the nature of reality, which admits to no absolutes. History provides evidence that relative standards of morality breed chaos — ultimately — the downfall of society."

Time magazine's December 7, 1987, cover story "New Age Harmonies," by Otto Friedrich (p. 64), summed up the movement by saying:

> "All in all, the New Age does express a cloudy sort of religion, claiming vague connections with both Christianity and the major faiths of the East . . . plus an occasional dab of pantheism and sorcery . . . the underlying faith is a lack of faith in the orthodoxies of rationalism, high technology, spiritual law and order. Somehow, the New Agers believe,

there must be some secret and mysterious shortcut or alternative path to happiness and health. And nobody ever really dies."

Modern Roots of New Age

Walter Martin in *The Kingdom of the Cults* (Minneapolis, Bethany House Publishers, 1985) states that the foundation of the New Age movement can be found in the Theosophical Society, which was begun in New York City in 1875 by Madam Helena Petrovna Blavatsky (1831-91). Helena Petrovna was born in Ekaterinoslav, Russia, in 1831. After her separation from her husband, General Blavatsky, Helena embarked on the study of mystical religion by traveling to Tibet, India, Egypt, Texas, Louisiana, Cuba, Canada, and eventually to New York City, where the Theosophical Society began in 1875.

The Theosophical Society claims to be a universal world religion of a distinct nature all its own. Yet its belief is traced directly to a source in the Orient, particularly to India and the Vedas or Hindu Scriptures. The writings of Buddha and the early Christian Gnostics also heavily influence the doctrine of the Theosophical Society. Its religious belief is anti-Christian, rejecting a personal God, the resurrection of the body, and the Old and New Testaments.

> "Theosophists, then, are great admirers of the Gnostics, and this is not at all surprising, since they have adopted much of the terminology and vocabulary of ancient Gnosticism, which looked with disdain upon the material properties of both the world and man, depersonalized God, and created various planes of spiritual progression culminating in universal salvation and reconciliation though reincarnation and the wheel concept of progression borrowed unblushingly from Buddhism" (op. cit., p. 247).

The wheel concept of Buddhism is an endless cycle of reincarnation with no progress. It is like a mouse running within a wheel from which he cannot escape. There is no God of salvation Who gave mankind redemption and eternal life through Jesus Christ.

> "According to the literature of the Theosophical cult as represented chiefly by Madam Blavatsky, Mrs. Besant, I.C. Cooper, A.P Sinnet,

L.W. Rogers and C.W. Leadbeater, there is a great fraternity of 'Mahatmas' or 'Masters,' who are highly evolved examples of advanced reincarnations whose dwelling place is somewhere in the far reaches of remote Tibet. These divine beings possessed Madam Blavatsky and utilized her services to reach the generations now living upon the earth with the restored truths of the great religions of the world, which have been perverted by mankind. In this highly imaginative picture, the Theosophists add seven planes of progression previously noted, through which the souls of men must progress on the way to the Theosophists' 'heaven' or Devachan. . . .

"The Theosophical Society maintains that it has three primary objectives which are: (1) to form a nucleus of the brotherhood of humanity, without distinction of race, creed, sex, caste, or color; (2) to encourage the study of comparative religion, philosophy, and sciences; (3) to investigate the unexplained laws of nature and the powers latent in man" (op. cit pp. 250-51).

Nina Easton in the *Los Angeles Times Magazine* (September 1987, p. 10) states:

"Blavatsky might well be called 'a godmother of the New Age Movement' because, in the words of Blavatsky's biographer, Marion Meade, she 'paved the way for contemporary Transcendental Meditation, Zen, Hare Krishnas; yoga, and vegetarianism; karma and reincarnation; swamis, yogis, and gurus.' "

It must be noted that while some of the elements mentioned are older than Blavatsky, she paved the way for acceptance of these practices in Europe and the United States. Blavatsky's successors were Annie Besant (1847-1933), Guy Ballard (1878-1939), Alice Bailey (1880-1949) and Benjamin Creme, a student of Bailey and a contemporary English occultist, who heralded the immanent coming of the Christ Maitreya widely advertised in popular publications including *The New York Times* and *Reader's Digest*.

These individuals continued the vision of the Theosophical Society with inspired channeled prophecies of ascended masters. Bailey coined the term "New Age," which recurs throughout her writings. The widely accepted expression settled in when the "New

Age" was associated with the "Age of Aquarius," the title song in the 1960s musical *Hair* (Russell, op cit., p. 47).

Someone who might be called the godfather of the New Age is Joseph Campbell. It is Martin Gardner who gives this title to Joseph Campbell in his review of the book *A Fire in the Mind* by Stephen and Joseph Robin Larsen (Doubleday). This review was published in *The Washington Post* Book World, November 24, 1991, pp. 8-9.

Joseph Campbell, who died on October 31, 1987, was the best known popular writer on mythology in the English-speaking world, whose work has had a profound influence on millions.

Yet, according to Gardner, Campbell's favorite definition of mythology was "other people's religion," and his favorite definition of religion was "misunderstood mythology." Gardner continues, "He saw the great myths as Jungian archetypes, welling up from humanity's collective unconscious — lies on the outside, truth inside." Campbell made no value judgment (which of one or more statements corresponds to objective truth) of the superiority of one religion's myth over that of another.

Joseph Campbell embraced Hinduism, associated closely with theosophists, especially Jiddu Krishnamurti, and New Agers. The Larsens quoted in their book, according to Gardner, that Campbell in a journal entry stated, "Krishna is a better teacher than Christ." He was a popular lecturer at Esalen, the pioneer New Age growth center of the paranormal scene. Today his scholarship and his belief system are being seriously questioned.

Another very popular practice in modern circles is that of the enneagram, which has it roots in the occultist George Gurdjieff (1877-1947). I refer you to the book *Catholics and the New Age* by Father Mitch Pacwa, S.J. (Ann Arbor, Mich., Servant Publications, 1992). Father Pacwa has an excellent evaluation of the enneagram from his personal experience as a seminarian and currently as a professor of Sacred Scripture at Loyola University in Chicago. He also has an excellent evaluation of Jung and Matthew Fox. Please read it, it is excellent!

Who Are the New Agers?

The common question "How can I identify a New Ager?" can be answered very simply. New Agers are found in every thread of the fabric of today's society. These individuals are seeking peace and harmony in a nonpolluted and toxin-free environment. They want political and economical networking among nations, no more war, and a future for their children. Their intentions are noble, but the means to the end of attaining these goals can be destructive to the spiritual, emotional, and physical well-being of the individual as well as to our planet.

The fabric that makes the garment of New Age is intricately woven from all walks of life. New Age people appear as normal everyday people. They include the policeman directing traffic on a busy intersection, the doctor and the nurse at the bedside of the sick patient, and yes, even the sick patient! They are the tellers at the bank, the mother and the father with the child in the park, the judge at your trial for a speeding ticket, the school principal with your teenager, and even the clergyman preaching from the pulpit! Astonished? Yes, New Age beliefs and practice have permeated every aspect of our society.

I hear stories daily from concerned individuals about peculiar beliefs and practices that are taking place with family members and friends. "My son doesn't go to church anymore but talks about being God. He chants and wears a crystal around his neck." Peering over the top of my glasses, I respond "Yep, he's involved in it." "Involved in what?" the mother asks. I respond assuredly, "New Age." What the mother has described is a change in the behavior and beliefs of her son. These warning signs can be enough to alert our attention to a potential problem. In addition, the warning signs may be the new beliefs, the actions, and even the vocabulary or "buzz words" of the person involved in New Age.

Daily we unknowingly use "buzz words" that are associated with the New Age vocabulary. "Oh! No, not me — that's impossible." Every movement has its own vocabulary or "buzz words." New Age is no different. Unfortunately many of the buzz words are associated with traditional dictionary meaning. Such words as "healing, enlightenment, channel, and meditation" are examples. Our understanding of the meaning of the word is not the same as the New Age meaning. The word "channel," in Christian terminology, is associated with being instruments of God. The New Age meaning of "channel" is to be the medium for entities. It is easy to become innocently involved in the New Age movement without any awareness that we are being deceived! Do you recognize any of these words? The traditional meaning quickly comes to mind. The New Age context of these "buzz words" is quite different.

New Age Terms or Buzz Words

Altered consciousness	Occultism
Astral Projection	Ouija Board
Astrology	Past Life Regression
Auras	Reincarnation
Channeling	Séance
Cosmic Consciousness	Sensitivity Training
Crystal	Spiritism/Spiritualism
Divinization	Subliminal Tapes
Enlightenment	Tarot Cards
Fortune Telling	Trance
Global Village	Transcendent
Gurus	Transcendental Meditation
Harmonic Convergence	Wholistic/Holistic Healing
Karma	Witchcraft
New Vision	Visualization
Nirvana	Yoga

Pope John Paul II, during his ten-day pastoral visit to the United States, spoke in September 1987 at St. Mary's Cathedral in San Francisco to three thousand delegates representing thousands of the United States' Roman Catholic lay people. One of the highlights of his message referred to the growing problem of secularism in America:

"Every age poses new challenges and new temptations for the people of God on their pilgrimage, and our own is no exception. We face a growing secularism that tries to exclude God and religious truths from human affairs. We face an insidious relativism that undermines the absolute truth of Christ and the truths of faith, and tempts believers to think of them as merely one set of beliefs or opinions of others. We face an alluring hedonism that offers a whole series of pleasures that will never satisfy the human heart. All these attitudes can influence our sense of good and evil at the very moment when social and scientific progress requires ethical guidance. Once alienated from Christian faith and practice by these and other deceptions, people often commit themselves to passing fads, or to bizarre beliefs that are shallow and fanatical" (Text by Vatican via U.S. Catholic Conference).

The message of Pope John Paul II with the greatest impact is his concern that individuals are abandoning the truths of Christianity and are following a belief system that the Pope says is "shallow, bizarre, and fanatical." The book of Hebrews warns the early Church to be careful about following beliefs that are new and passing fads. Second Timothy 4:3 clearly states: "For the time will come when people will not tolerate sound doctrine but, following their own desires and insatiable curiosity, will accumulate teachers and will stop listening to the truth and will be diverted to myths" (NAB).

I have expressed that New Age is a belief system of self-divinity, self-generated truths, and self-generated destiny. Russell Chandler describes it as insidious because there are no absolutes. Otto Friedrich echoes the same concern by describing New Age's underlying faith as a lack of faith in orthodoxies.

The Yardstick of Comparison

Do you remember the analogy of the yardstick that I used in the first chapter? I used the analogy of the yardstick as a way to "measure" or "compare" the belief system of a contemporary destructive religious movement to orthodoxy in government as well as in the church. Just as a yardstick is acknowledged as a universal measurement, so too can we who work in the diagnostic evaluation of these movements have ways to measure the belief system or "theology" of any movement. In other words, how does New Age "compare or measure up" to traditional faith.

As a Roman Catholic priest, my first and primary concern is the damage that the New Age Movement can do to the faith of an individual. New Age, because it is a distortion of the truth, can destroy an individual's faith by causing confusion and doubts. Remember, I said that all destructive religious movements begin with the wrong understanding of God. Let us measure and compare the belief of orthodox denominational faith with the wrong beliefs of New Age Movement.

New Age and Self-Divinity

New Age is the worship of the creature rather than the Creator. New Age is about serving self. Self-divinity is the claim that I am God. The belief in self-divinity is the sin of our first parents Adam and Eve. Genesis 3:5 states: "God knows well that the moment you eat of it your eyes will be opened and you will be like gods [like God] who know what is good and what is bad" (NAB).

As Satan deceived Adam and Eve to eat of the tree of the knowledge of good and evil, so he deceives us in the same way today. Satan is a liar and a destroyer of dreams. He wants us to believe that we can become God if we serve him. New Age is the means to accomplish the end result of separating us from God. Philippians 2:10-11 states: "At the name of Jesus every knee should bend, of those in heaven and on earth and under the earth, and every tongue confess that Jesus Christ is Lord, to the glory of God the Father" (NAB).

New Age and Self-Generated Truths

Absolutes are truths that are pure, perfect, and unadulterated. Absolutes are traditional "spiritual disciplines" that submit to a body of teachings even when it conflicts with immediate interests or gratifications. In the New Age there are no concrete absolutes.

Absolutes are substituted with a potpourri of relativism, which means the criteria of truth varies with the individual, time, and circumstances. In other words, New Agers believe what they want to believe.

When we substitute truths that are variable and temporary, or faddish, for what is steady and constant, then we shall die like a plant uprooted from the soil. The stability of a nation is based on the observance of truths that maintain democracy and avoid anarchy and chaos.

Our nation and its constitution were founded on a commitment to create a good society. New Age is blending in and swallowing the traditional orthodoxies of our society and church. Since New Age lacks any absolute standards, it is impossible to determine the outcome of the future, whether it will be good or evil.

New Age and the Occult

A large portion of the New Age's self-generated truths come from the occult. The New Ager is led to seek knowledge that is forbidden outside the course of God's influence. The word *occult* means seeking knowledge that is beyond the veil of ordinary knowledge, hidden from view, the mysterious, not disclosed, secret, revealed only to those who are initiated. The source of this knowledge is the spirit world.

The first commandment clearly states, "I am the LORD your God; you shall have no other gods before me." Just as Moses gave this command which he received from God to the Israelites, we follow this commandment and serve God, who shines on the just and the unjust. Deuteronomy 18:10-13 forbids dabbling in the occult: "Let there not be found among you anyone who immolates his son or daughter in the fire, nor a fortune teller, soothsayer, charmer, diviner, or caster of spells, nor one who consults ghosts and spirits or seeks oracles from the dead. Anyone who does such things is an abomination to the LORD, and because of such abominations the LORD, your God, is driving these nations out of your way. You, however, must be altogether sincere toward the LORD, your God" (NAB).

There is no God to sin against in the New Age. "I am God, therefore I am now the creator of truths." Neither is there good nor evil as is understood in mainstream religions. For the New Ager, evil is an illusion, the wages of Hindu karma. Evil is denied, guilt removed, right and wrong erased, self-conscious responsibility dismissed; the ability to create one's own universe with new laws becomes unlimited. Evil no longer exists because all finite experience of it is negated.

Werner Erhard, the founder of "est" (Erhard Seminar Training), the Forum or Lifespring as it is now called, preached to his devotees that they could end world hunger by "creating the end of world hunger by 1997" in their consciousness. But world hunger still exists! It is impossible to think world hunger out of existence. We must work for the end of world hunger. Werner Erhard used valid concepts and valid words, but twisted them to suit his purpose. When he said we had to make the end of hunger, "an idea whose time had come," a reality — he was right. But the way to make an idea a reality is through action, not through some esoteric thought or philosophical belief about hunger. This explains New Age concepts very well. Use the "right" words, get behind a *good* idea, but there is no realistic follow-through.

Most of the buzz words of the New Age (see above) are related to the occult. Most people will ask me, "Why don't New Agers see the dangers of the occult?" Since the New Ager is removed from absolutes by self-generated truths, the truths about God and Satan are not an issue. "God" is seen as an impersonal creative force of the universe. Satan is seen not as a creative force but as the lack of creative force, a void.

The occult practicers enable the mind to tap into an occult world to create one's own "space" or destiny. Channeling is a good example. We have seen channelers on television. Channeling is inviting a spirit or entity to enter the channeler's mind, take control of his or her voice, and speak through the channeler.

In a trance, the channeler will contact an "ascended master" who is a "wise man" who has reached his "nirvana" and is no longer being reincarnated. This is mediumship, which is condemned in the following passages of Scripture: Leviticus 20:27, Deuteronomy 18:9-14, 2 Corinthians 11:14, Acts 16:16-1.

The use of a crystal is another example. The crystal becomes the conductor or channel of energy that brings healing into the body of the person. According to New Agers, the source of power to heal is not God, it is the occult. The truth is that God is not channeled through crystals or mediums. He personally shows His healing power in the Church through the sacraments, especially the Eucharist and the Anointing of the Sick. It is by the laying on of hands and prayer that the sick are healed. In addition, God uses the medical and the psychiatric sciences to bring healing.

New Age and the Source of Its Power

There are two sources of our power in our faith life. One is God; the other is Satan. Self-centered power is also possible. Traditionally,

God's power is good and Satan's is evil. I ask three questions in order to discern the source of *power* of any religious movement:

1. Whom is the person serving? God? Self? Satan?
2. Where does the person's power come from? God? Satan?
3. What fruits are produced? (The fruits of God are joy, and peace. The fruits of Satan are despair, fear, doubt, and confusion.)

For the Christian, the power is God the Father, Jesus Christ, and the Holy Spirit. For the New Ager the power is Satan and his dominion. Take time to discern the spirits. Discernment of spirits means that we ask God's guidance as "to distinguish one spirit from another" (1 Cor. 12:10), and "to distinguish truth from falsehood" (1 Jn. 4:6). New Agers will be afire with their experience, believing that they have found a personal relationship with God when actually they are being deceived by Satan to believe that they are God. In time the fruits of this encounter with the New Age movement will be confusion, despair, lack of hope, doubts, fear, and sometimes suicide. This is a vital point. It may take years. It may never happen while one is involved. In the movie *Angel of Light*, mentioned in the upcoming pages, the negative effects begin when one pulls away from this movement.

New Age and Self-Generated Destiny of Hinduism, Buddhism

Job's question (14:14) "If a man dies, shall he live again?" has intrigued mankind since creation.

Some interpret this question as implying that there is nothing beyond the grave.

Another interpretation of Job's question is that it implies reincarnation, the belief that there is an endless recycling of the life of the person after each death. Reincarnation and karma are major beliefs of New Age. These beliefs are rooted in the Hindu and Buddhist religions of the East. Hindus believe that when people die their souls pass into new bodies. This reincarnation of the soul into a new life form is part of an endless cycle — birth, life, death, new birth, etc. But souls can also regress into lower life forms in the course of the cycle or reincarnation, as a result of "bad karma."

Karma is the "cosmic law" of cause and effect, like a ledger of good and bad deeds that determine into which cycle an individual will be reborn. India show us the fruits of this belief. The belief in this endless cycle breeds a hopelessness which creates a nation full of poverty and hunger.

Buddhists deny the existence of the soul, aiming for a state of nirvana that will cause the cycle of birth-life-death to come to an end.

True to its nature, New Age espouses the major tenets of Hinduism and Buddhism with the exception of the downward regression of the soul because of negative karma. New Agers embrace the concept of reincarnation because it frees them from personal responsibility before God and the possibility of guilt which will follow failure to act responsibly toward God (sin). Sin is replaced by karma, which they believe allows them to make up for past errors and wrongs by doing life over again and again, working toward for nirvana.

This is quite different from the traditional Christian belief in a just God who holds us responsible for our actions resulting from our free choice. The world as it is, with its pain and suffering, is the results of wrong choices made by many persons in the past and in the present. The New Ager believes that the world, with its present pain and suffering, is the result of wrong choices made in past lives. The New Ager is thus responsible for creating his own universe and his own (hopefully?) future salvation. He is solely dependent on himself for his divinity and his self-attained redemption.

Finally, the Christian believes in the journey of the soul to God for judgment, followed by eternal life, in which resurrection is the answer to Job's question.

Hebrews 9:27 clearly rules out reincarnation: "Just as it is appointed that human beings die once, and after this the judgment. . ." (NAB).

From the beginning of the world, human beings have desired to make choices without considering the will of God, but also have not wanted to die. But Genesis 3:4-5 shows us the source of that kind of thinking, Satan speaks to Eve: "You certainly will not die! No, God knows well that the moment you eat of it [the fruit] your eyes will be opened and you will be gods [or like God] who know what is good and what is bad" (NAB).

New Age and Christian Belief

How does the New Age belief compare with Christianity? Using our yardstick, let us measure. New Age's belief system is summed this way:

1. Monism — All is one.
2. Pantheism — All is God.
3. Gnosticism — Elitist truths and knowledge by which one attains salvation that come from within the mind or soul.
4. Syncretism — All religions are one.

All Is One/All Is God

New Age belief encompasses a oneness in all things — that all things are interrelated and interdependent, that there is no difference between the essence of God, a human person, or a rock. Good and evil are the same. The potter and the clay, creator and creature, are the same for a New Ager. Thus it is understandable why New Agers can claim that "I am God." This is "monism," that God and all beings are really just one. But just as potter and clay are distinct, so God is the creator and we are distinct creatures.

Pantheism, expressed as such, teaches that everything, literally, is God, that we are, in fact, gods, that God is the transcendent reality of which the material universe and people are only manifestations. This involves denying God's personality and tends to identify God with nature. Religions based on nature, particularly those which worship the Great Mother Earth (Gaia) and the Earth Goddess of Wicca (witchcraft), find many adherents in the New Age Movement.

At various times in the history of the Catholic Church, Councils and Popes have warned that monism (which includes pantheism) is inconsistent with the true Christian teaching about God.

Gnosticism

Gnosticism states that we attain salvation by the possession of a special knowledge given to a select few. The source of this knowledge was a well-kept secret among early Gnostics. The source of this knowledge is limited to those who are willing to expand their consciousness to new dimensions of beliefs and experiences. The enlightenment of these revealed truths creates an elite group of "the saved" that have the superior knowledge or truth never before revealed to mankind.

The Roman Catholic Church teaches that we are not saved by our knowledge. The fullness of truth is in the Revelation of Jesus Christ as the Way, the Truth, and the Life. Christians believe that these truths of Divine Revelation are found in Scripture (the Bible) and sacred Tradition of orthodox belief. Sacred Tradition is the way that the Church, guided by the Holy Spirit, passes on its living faith through history. Tradition includes beliefs, customs, rituals, and laws by which the People of God have lived and continue to live their faith through the centuries. God's teachings in Scripture are not always easy to accept, but they are acknowledged to be true. Anything contrary to scriptural Revelation is not of God.

For a more extensive coverage of this topic please see the next-to-last chapter of this book on Syncretism and the New Religious Movements.

All Religions Are One

New Age teaches that orthodox Christianity is a distortion of the truth of Jesus Christ, that Christian teachings are antiquated, and that Christians are motivated by fear and guilt. A new religion is needed, therefore New Age will blend select beliefs from all major religions — pagan as well as Christian — to satisfy this need.

According to New Age beliefs, Jesus Christ is a great "ascended master" who has been misrepresented by the Church. He attained His karmic perfection in India and is no longer reincarnated. His truths have been concealed by the Church for centuries but are now being unveiled to the world by "spirit guides" who are the "ascended masters" of the New Age movement. Jesus is one of the many masters who will teach the world new truths. These new truths will usher in a new age of enlightenment. These is no distinction between the nature and role of Jesus, Buddha, and Krishna.

Of course, all Christian churches reject this view. Jesus Christ is truly God, the second person of the Trinity. He is our Redeemer and won salvation for all people by His death on the cross. Christianity teaches that redemption is not self-attained, as New Age teaches. Mankind has the gift of free will, which is the ability to accept or reject that salvation which was won for us by the death of Jesus Christ on the cross.

New Age Profile

The Catholic Church teaches that all "public Revelation" ceased with the death of the last apostle. "Public Revelation" means God's truths revealed in Sacred Scripture. We are called upon to give assent of faith to these truths, and to the doctrines of the Church drawn from them, those teachings found in the pronouncements of the Popes and the Councils, as well as to the teachings of Scripture and Tradition. As for all other revelations, whether those about which the Catholic Church states there is "nothing in this contrary to the teachings of the Church" (such as the revelations to St. Margaret Mary about the Sacred Heart of Jesus or the apparitions of the Blessed Virgin to Saint Bernadette at Lourdes) or reputed apparitions or revelation, (where *no assent of faith* is required), the Church states that giving *full* assent of faith, similar to our wholehearted belief in the articles of the Creed, to such revelation, however good, is inappropriate.

Altered States of Consciousness

There have been a variety of authentic altered states of consciousness created through licensed therapists and doctors in the mental health professions. There are legitimate states of altered consciousness in both Eastern and Western traditions of religious meditation. Peace and healing can be given in these varied practices.

New Age has created a belief extracted from standard mental health practices that hypnosis can be used to "expand the mind" to new levels never before discovered by any other human being. Visualization or "guided imagery" creates past-life regression, rebirthing, travel to other places, and more. These experiences appear to be real through the special wisdom or charism of a leader who shares his or her "truth" with the new "elect." It is very dangerous to use hypnosis and to "play with" someone's mind by creating altered states.

New Age creates altered states of consciousness from relaxation techniques, deep meditation, visualization, imaging, and self-hypnotic trances. According to New Age thinking, the mind has various levels of consciousness.

The movie *Angel of Light* is a good example of this practice. *Angel of Light*, produced by Fred Carpenter and James Reid in 1985 by Mars Hills Production, is a true story. Sara, a college-age woman, is introduced to New Age by one of her college teachers, Gloria Graham.

At first Sara and her newfound friend John relish Gloria's seminars on New Age meditation. John soon realizes that Gloria's seminars are about the supernatural world of the occult and leaves the seminar training. He then confronts Sara about the danger to her faith and that Jesus Christ is the Way, the Truth, and the Light.

John warns Sara, "We can be sincere and yet be sincerely wrong." In time, Sara's "spirit guide" changes appearance from an angel of light into a ghastly and hellish figure which shows that the entire fearful experience has been an encounter with evil. This nightmare with a New Age "spirit guide" led Sara out of the movement and back to the truth. The theme is validated by 2 Corinthians 11:14, "even Satan masquerades as an angel of light." We can be sincere and be sincerely wrong.

Final Comments: Beware

I would like to give some admonitions, warnings, and recommendations in concluding this chapter. From my experience, the best advice that I could give is "Beware." Know your Scripture, know your religion. Ask questions and know that there is no such thing as answers to all of life's questions. Beware of those who assure you that they have all the answers. Beware of anyone who forces or deceives you into making decisions against your free will.

Know Your Religion

We are non-Christians, Jews, or Christians by birth, baptism, or by choice. This is our religion. Our denominational belief is our identity. Whatever religion you may have, know its belief. Think and ask questions about your religion. Know its history, its doctrine, dogmas, and tenets. Many wolves in sheep's clothing will come along wanting you to dance to another tune of faddish faith and false doctrine. Do not follow them. If you know your religion and have faith in your heart, you will have an advantage. Please consult the *Profile* Appendix III at the end of the book to compare Christian orthodox doctrine with New Age belief.

Attend Church Weekly and Practice Your Faith

Take the third commandment seriously, Remember the sabbath day and keep it holy. Laziness, work schedules, and making materialism our God can be destructive and devastating to our faith life. Jesus warned us that we cannot serve two masters, God and money. What good will it do to gain the whole world but lose our soul in the process?

Do Not Dabble in the Occult

Let your journey of faith, your quest for God, and your personal relationship with Jesus Christ be found in mainstream, regular denominational churches. Maintain orthodoxy. Curiosity about the occult is the greatest danger to your faith. I believe that as cigarettes have a warning label, "Smoking May Be Dangerous To Your Health," so too should occult material have this warning label: "Warning: This Material May Be Dangerous To Your Faith, Your Emotional Life, and Your Physical Well-being!" The basis of all destructive religious movements is deception. Beware of anyone who wants to take away your most precious gift — your free will and the ability to make choices. Please consult the *Profile* (Tools for Spiritual Evaluation of a Movement) for a better understanding of this point.

Seek the Transcendent God by a Lived Faith

We have lost the sense of the transcendent God in our society and in our churches, and many are searching for Him. The New Age movement challenges not only youth, parents, educators, teachers, and clergy but the universal society to seek again the transcendent God and to restore our dignity as God's transcendent creation. Our intrinsic dignity as God's creation is that we are like God but we are not God. God alone has the capacity, with our assent of faith, to transform us into the likeness of Him. Self-improvement is like a dog chasing its tail in an endless circle — the dog never gets anywhere. But with God's graces everything is possible. The light of Christ must shine forth in our lives, that people who are hurting, broken, confused, lost, and searching may find a beacon of hope and a fortress of solace and strength in us that leads them to God. Lead the lost to God.

Be attentive to Wisdom: "For all men were by nature foolish who were in ignorance of God, and who from the good things seen did not succeed in knowing him who is, and from studying the works did not discern the artisan; But either fire, or wind, or the swift air, or the circuit of the stars, or the mighty water, or the luminaries of heaven, the governors of the world, they considered gods. Now if out of joy in their beauty, they thought them gods, let them know how far more excellent is the Lord than these; for the original source of beauty fashioned them. Or if they were struck by their might and energy, let them from these things realize how much more powerful is he who made them. For from the greatness and the beauty of created things their original author, by analogy is seen" (Wis. 13:1-5).

Pope John Paul II concluded his message in San Francisco in September 1987 with this powerful statement: *"Christ's message must live in you and in the way you live and in the way you refuse to live."*

The New Age: Suggested Reading

General Introduction:

See the books listed in the Chapter 1 bibliography for New Religious Movements. The following are specifically about New Age:

Chandler, Russell, *Understanding the New Age*, Dallas, Word
    Publishing, 1988 [Chandler is a religion reporter for The Los
    Angeles Times, twice honored with the John Templeton Reporter
    of the Year Award. Excellent introduction for the general reader.]
Martin, Walter, Ph.D., *The New Age Cult*, Minneapolis, Minn.,
    Bethany House Publishers, 1989 [This is a short introduction,
    utilizing much of the Chapter on New Age from his book *The*
    Kingdom of the Cults, but with additional material and has a
    useful Glossary of New Age terms as well as a good bibliography.]
Miller, Elliot, *A Crash Course on the New Age Movement,*
    Describing and Evaluating a Growing Social Force, Foreword by

Walter Martin, Grand Rapids, Mich., Baker Book House, 1989 [Among the excellent appendices, the "conspiracy theory" is addressed and quite effectively answered, also the difficulties that must be faced in trying to break through the age barrier to relate effectively to teens on this issue.]

Groothuis, Douglas, *Unmasking the New Age*, Downers Grove, Ill., Intervarsity Press, 1986; *Confronting the New Age*, same publisher, 1988; *Revealing the New Age Jesus: Challenges to Orthodox Views of Christ*, same publisher, 1990 [Three books by Groothuis provide background, guides for answering New Age promotions, and explain some of the ways in which New Age mixes pagan and gnostic myths with Christianity]

Larson, Bob, *Straight Answers on the New Age*, Nashville, Tenn., Thomas Nelson Publishers, 1989 [Groups New Age practices and beliefs, shows how some of these have been introduced into such fields as business, medicine, media, sociology and even political policies; also a list of New Age public personalities.]

Rath, Ralph, *The New Age, A Christian Critique*, South Bend, Ind., Greenlawn Press, 1990 [Excellent short introduction, covers "What is it?" and "Where is it?" with Christian response, and "Evangelizing New Agers" with list of anti-cult groups and contacts.]

Of particular interest to Catholics:

England, Randy, *The Unicorn in the Sanctuary,* Manassas, Va., Trinity Communications, 1990 [Short introduction to New Age ideas and practices penetrating some Catholic groups, probably giving more credit to the "conspiracy theory" than it deserves.]

Pacwa, Mitch, S.J., *Catholics and the New Age*, Ann Arbor, Mich., Servant Publications, 1992 [The subtitle, "How Good People Are Being Drawn into Jungian Psychology, the Enneagram, and the Age of Aquarius," gives a clue to the contents, but even more important is the fact that the author, a professor of Sacred Scripture at Loyola diversity in Chicago, was drawn into and quite deeply involved in the New Age Movement. This is his account of his experiences, of how he discovered the traps and contradictions in New Age, and of his final disillusionment with it and wholehearted return to the richness of Catholic belief.]

7.

Transcendental Meditation

Maggie Moulton

Introduction

I AM a former Transcendental Meditation instructor. I was deeply involved in the TM organization for ten years. I began meditating in 1972 and soon moved to an upstate New York TM academy, where I worked full time for the TM organization while attending their school to become an instructor of the TM program. I became a qualified Science of Creative Intelligence instructor and TM checker during 1973. I continued my practice and studies over the next three years at the New York Academy. I then went to Europe for the final stage of my training (a very intensive six-month residential program), where I was personally qualified in the spring of 1976 by Maharishi Mahesh Yogi (the founder of the TM Program) as a Teacher of the Transcendental Meditation Program. I returned to my home state, where I taught the Science of Creative Intelligence and TM Program to over two hundred people. I have not been active in the TM organization for the past ten years. At this writing, I am thirty-eight years old, married, the mother of three pre-teen children, and a full-time employee of a respected computer consulting firm.

So why am I writing this? There are lots of books available on TM and other cults, and how to deal with them if your loved ones become involved or if you are invited to participate. But what I notice is that those books are written by people who have *studied* the cult in question, or they are written by *theologians* who can point out the heresy of the philosophies involved. Don't misunderstand — I have the greatest respect for sound theology and learned theologians

. . . they have probably saved my life! My point is, I rarely see a book written by someone who has been deeply involved in the organization itself. I've not seen a book written from an *experiential* standpoint, from the inside out, so to speak. I have avoided doing this very thing for years. The memories are confusing and painful to this day, and it is very difficult to reopen this area of my life. But if my story helps shed light into the way these organizations work, if my story rings true in another's spirit, if it can help one person from opening that Pandora's Box, then it is worth it.

The Seven States of Consciousness — Definition and Experience

The Transcendental Meditation Program is based on traditional Hinduism. Maharishi Mahesh Yogi, the founder of the Transcendental Meditation (TM) Program, took fundamental teachings from Hindu religion and "redefined" them to make them more palatable to Western society. The seven states of consciousness taught in the TM Program are based on teachings found in traditional Hindu literature, the Upanishad, the Bhagavad Gita, and other Vedic scriptures. The seven states of consciousness, as presented in the TM Program, are:

1. *Waking consciousness:* mind and body awake and alert.

2. *Sleeping consciousness:* mind and body in a state of rest, not awake or alert.

3. *Dreaming consciousness:* mind resting (not awake or alert); body active (dreams are activity in the brain).

4. *Transcendental consciousness* (TC): mind conscious (awake and alert): body in a deep state of rest. This state of consciousness is described as the underlying basis of states 1, 2, and 3. It is analogous to the bottom of an ocean. The surface of the ocean, with all its wave and movement, is like the active, waking mind. During the practice of the TM technique, one "dives" from the surface of the mind to the quiet, silent, unchanging depths of the mind and beyond.

I have experienced this many times. It is quiet, peaceful, and silent. There are no thoughts — not even the thought "Gee, this is so peaceful!" You are awake and alert, but nothing is going on. It is nothingness, but without an experience of emptiness *or* fullness.

There are no emotions attached, it's not lonely, it's not joyful, it's not scary, it's not exhilarating. It's just silent.

The philosophy we taught as TM teachers was that this silence was the basis of all our activity in life. Dive into the silent transcendent state, come out into daily life. Again, we used an analogy — of hand-dying cloth. Dip the white cloth in the saffron dye, set it out in the sun to fade. Dip again, fade again. Dip and fade until that point that the sun can no longer cause the dye to fade away. The dyed cloth is then considered colorfast. We used simple analogies, then backed them up with plenty of complicated scientific charts. We were instructed to present this as a scientific technique, make it very clear this was not a religion and that it did not require adherents to give up their present religion.

5. *Cosmic consciousness* (CC): this is the "colorfast" state alluded to in the previous analogy. It is described by TM teachers as "silent witnessing." The logic, as in the cloth-dying analogy above, is that if you dive into TC and back into activity enough times, you will begin to draw the inner silence back into everyday life with you. CC is when you maintain one hundred percent of the silence along with one hundred percent of the activity.

I would say I have had this experience for a brief time (two to three weeks), but I have been unable to maintain it. This state of consciousness is maintained not only while you are awake, but while you are asleep and dreaming also! I first had this experience while on an intensive teacher training course, where we did "rounding," or greatly extended periods of meditation interspersed with rotating sets of yoga postures, called *asanas*. My experience began as I drifted into sleep one night. I was very aware of my body falling deeper and deeper toward sleep. My mind was still active with thoughts, but my limbs were, well, asleep. My breathing was naturally very slow and rhythmic, and I couldn't move my body. I was thinking, "Wow! This is great! This must be witnessing sleep!" But then my mind drifted toward sleep. Thoughts became dimmer, less focused, quieter. I was awake, aware, alert, but silent. I'd had this feeling while meditating — transcendence. Next, my mind "clicked" off — it was asleep. Yet there I was. A unique experience, and hard to put into words. Bet a psychologist would have a field day with this stuff! The analogy I came up with to describe it to my teachers was that there was a little guy in my head that I described as "me." He walked through my body "switching off" the various parts (feet, legs, arms, fingers, nose, etc.). Then he switched off my mind, and I thought, "This is it! I've got this figured out! 'I' is the little guy that controls the switches! I'm not my body, or my mind, or my thoughts! What a great revelation!" But then the little guy yawned, crawled into bed in my mind, and promptly went to sleep . . . and "I" was still there! I was the silent, unchanging, bright night light that burned in the corner of the room — no thoughts, no more, "Isn't this great?" Just silent, unchanging awareness — until morning, when the little guy got up and resumed his responsibilities of turning all the equipment back on. And somehow, since I had become so intensely aware of the background night light, I was aware of it burning brightly all day as I went to classes, ate, studied, and so on. It was the first time I had directly experienced that "I," indeed, am not my body, my thoughts, my mind or my feelings. I am spirit or soul (in TM, referred to as "Being"). This experience continued for a couple of weeks, through waking, dreaming, sleeping, and meditating. Then it just kind of slowly faded away and became a memory of the experience instead of the experience itself.

While I have not recaptured it fully, I have maintained a residual effect that I find rather amusing. I can manipulate my dreams to this day, as if a part of me is watching a movie on a screen and I'm the director. If I don't like how a dream is going, I just change it while it is going on. My point in sharing all of this? The experiences from these techniques are very real, very powerful, very enticing! But at what cost? It becomes clearer as we continue. . . .

6. *God consciousness* (GC): Maharishi really starts to address the sixth and seventh states of consciousness when a meditator is more deeply committed to the practice (during Science of Creative Intelligence courses and Residence courses, where meditators have committed time, energy, and hundreds of additional dollars). We also studied these states extensively on our teacher training courses. I have probably watched hundreds of hours of videotape of Maharishi on the subject.

In GC, we were taught that an individual is separate from all activity, acting but not acting — the silent witness to creation unfolding. GC is described as a state where one so appreciates the beauty of the creation that there comes an eternal longing to know the creator. One then "sees" the creator in all aspects of the creation. "The finest levels of creation are tickled by the melting heart" (Maharishi's analogy). Those aspects of creation become enlivened and therefore available to the person in that state. Sounds very spiritual and beautiful, doesn't it? But something begins to break down here. We aren't talking a longing to know The Creator. We're talking knowing the finest levels of creation. We're talking that all of creation *is* an aspect *of* the creator. GC is said to be a state where you "see" the creator in all aspects of creation. Maharishi's analogy was that the sap runs through the stem, leaves, and petals of a flower, but we are unaware of it when we look at the beautiful flower. GC would be analogous to physically seeing the invisible sap as being the essence of the flower, while we look at the stem, leaves, and petals of the flower. We are getting into the realm of an impersonal god: creation *is* god, *we* are all aspects of god.

Experientially, I will say I have seen golden light, an "aura" if you will, occasionally during the years I meditated. Interestingly enough, *not* when I was experiencing the silence during activity that I mentioned earlier. Usually I saw the light while watching or performing the initiation rite for TM, the "*Puja*." I still occasionally see a light around certain people. I don't know what it means. Mostly it is yellow-gold in color, transparent, and surrounds their head and hands. I see it most often these days during the Consecration at Mass, around the priest's head and hands, and falling like a blanket over the altar. I don't see it at all Masses, nor with all priests. I also see it, at times, during Charismatic prayer meetings when the group begins praying in "tongues." Take it for what it's worth — I stopped trying to figure it out years ago! Is it a true spiritual experience? Is it fantasy? Is it damaged optic nerves? Is it the delusions of a demented woman? Who knows? All I can do is share it the way I perceive it. Leave it to others to dissect and decipher.

7. *Unity consciousness* (UC): This is *classic* Hindu philosophy. On my teacher training course, Maharishi describes it as "that point where the devotee surrenders fully to the object of devotion. Where the Master must be present to give the final bit of knowledge needed to tear the veil of ignorance, and that knowledge is: 'All This Is

That.' The devotee becomes one with the devoted, all boundaries are dissolved." This is Hinduism in its purest form.

The TM Organization Comes Full Circle

I find it interesting that when Maharishi *first* introduced the TM Program back in the '60s, he called his organization the "Spiritual Regeneration Movement." I have seen old videotape of Maharishi where he referred to the fifth state of consciousness (now called cosmic consciousness) as Christ Consciousness! He talked about Jesus being a man who had attained that level of enlightenment, transforming him into "The Christ." He also said to us, "Be careful what you say! If the wall is yellow and everyone calls it white, be careful if you call it yellow, they may crucify you!" (I believe that tape has been removed from standard circulation.) He later changed the direction of the movement from spiritual to scientific, renaming the organization the TM Program and the Science of Creative Intelligence. In this way, he could present the technique as secular and introduce it to businesses, schools, monasteries, basically anywhere in Western society. I understand that Maharishi is becoming more bold in the last few years. He seems to be dropping the scientific terminology that he used in the '70s and '80s in favor of more spiritual terminology today. I guess the New Age movement has made this spiritual terminology more acceptable to the general public. The organization has come full circle, back to spiritual terms.

My point? The TM organization was into New Age long before it became popularized by Shirley MacLaine and others. I laugh when I see these supposedly "new" New Age books, or listen to the proponents of New Age talk about channeling, spirit guides, or spirit writing. Tried and true TM-ers, and many other Eastern semi-religious organizations, routinely practiced and promoted these beliefs in the early 1970s (and the traditions date back five thousand years or more). We delved into all this through the spiritual "underground." Let me explain. There were always at least two levels of knowledge going on at TM academies and teacher training courses — the words we were taught to say, and the "real" stuff that we sat around talking about after hours. I have to acknowledge that most of the "spiritual" stuff was *not* presented as standard course material, and was even openly discouraged. We were told that these were merely signs of "unstressing," and to pay them no mind. But I guarantee, these experiences were as much a part of our training as anything else we learned. The "impulses of creative intelligence" that we taught new TM-ers about were called "*devas*," or gods, in the TM underground. We met in one another's rooms at night to exchange information on psychic healers, karma, reincarnation, samsara, nirvana, soma, astrology, the names of our spirit guides, or the latest gems and crystals to wear for what effect. We routinely "contacted" spirits while we lived at the New York Academy, sometimes intentionally, sometimes not. Many of us wrote to psychic "healers" who claimed to traverse great distances on the astral plane to exorcise earthbound spirits that had attached to our auras during times of crisis in our lives. The air was alive and vibrating with psychic energies at that place. I know that this may seem fantastic or even ridiculous to many who have never delved into these types of experiences, but it is important that I make the following point: Even today, far removed from that way of thinking, I believe those experiences were real. I know part of the mystique was our *desire* to believe, our willingness to believe. But we also practiced age-old, powerful techniques that opened doors best left unopened. Our desires fueled the experience, literally inviting this "other world" into our own.

Contacting Spirits — Who's in Control?

I hesitate to share intimate stories of personal experiences. Now, years later, they seem so foreign to my life, almost ludicrous. However, I am willing to be thought a fool if it sheds light onto the thinking and actions that lead to this lifestyle. So I will share some of my stories. . . .

My first encounter with a "being," or spirit, was my very first night at the New York Academy. This event seems important to me because it was so *innocent* on my part. I was actually very surprised as it unfolded. I arrived at the Academy with a dear friend late that evening. Classes and dinner were over; the halls were dark and quiet. We checked in at the front desk and were assigned rooms. (The TM organization had purchased several old hotels in the Catskill mountains and renovated them as campuses. "Boys" were assigned one section of living quarters, "girls" another. I went to my room, tired yet happy, showered, and got ready for bed. I opened the curtains because it was a beautiful moonlit night with a fresh-fallen snow covering the golf course outside my window (no longer used for golf, of course). I fell into bed and promptly went to sleep. Some hours later I awakened, aware of motion in the room. I turned over in bed, and from the moonlight shining in the room I saw what appeared to be two people wrestling. They were between four and five feet tall, similar in body type to us (head size, arms, legs, torso). There was no sense or indication of male-or-femaleness about them. They were somewhat translucent (like the consistency or color of a jellyfish, if that makes any sense). They didn't have discernable features or hair, or lack of hair for that matter. They were more like shadows, or soft lights. I wasn't frightened, but fascinated and curious. I thought it was a dream, except it didn't "feel" like a dream — I was awake. They seemed oblivious to my presence. I watched this wrestling match for several minutes. One of the spirits was dark, like a shadow — no light emanated from it, in fact, it seemed to be a very flat darkness. The other was a soft iridescent white — it seemed to almost glow from within. There was no *feeling* of "good" or "evil" from either spirit, but in my mind I assumed the dark represented evil and the light represented good (such preconceptions we live with!). Suddenly the spirit of light was literally absorbed by the dark spirit — just whoosh!, gone. Immediately the dark spirit turned to face me, now very much aware of my presence; and, whoosh! — entered my body as if fitting a glove onto a hand. I *felt* it. What still amazes me to this day was my reaction. I thought, "That wasn't the way it was supposed to end. The good one was supposed to win . . ." and I turned over and went back to sleep! I never mentioned this experience to anyone until almost ten years later, when praying with a group of friends. I don't know what that was all about. I don't know if I assumed one of the spirits was evil and the other good, or if they were, in fact, fighting for possession of my soul that night. Was it a dream? Was it real? All I know is, it was a unique and unexpected start to quite an interesting time in my life!

Another time I was awakened by the sound of wind in my room. I turned in my bed and noticed the curtains in the room moving as if blown by a strong breeze, but the windows were closed. There was a tall, brilliant spirit at the foot of my bed. He (there was a feeling he was male) was perhaps seven feet tall, and he appeared as a deep, golden light, a brilliant fire, almost too bright to look at. I was frightened and wanted to turn away. That's when I noticed "I" was sitting up, but my body was still lying down sound asleep. Again, I had not asked for this experience, I was just observing it unfold. The spirit "spoke" to me — at least I felt I understood him, although I heard no verbal sounds. I remember to this day what he said as if it were yesterday. He said, "Do not be afraid. This is your color." I still have no idea what that means. He repeated the exact message several times, and I knew he meant the deep golden color he appeared as was the "color" he was referring to in the message. This spirit had a sense of benevolence or goodness about him (although I do not know what, in fact, he really was). I did not know then that evil spirits can appear as angels, nor that angels usually prefaced their appearances with "Do not be afraid." I was really very naïve. All I knew was that this was too strange for me and I wanted the experience to end! He sensed my fear, I felt sadness from him that he had caused me fear, and he dissolved away until I couldn't see him anymore. I thought, "This is just a strange dream. If I turn over and close my eyes, everything will go away." I turned and "fitted" myself into the sleeping body on the bed, closed my eyes, and drifted back to sleep.

These spirits are contacted in many ways. Some people consciously invite them in during rituals, séances, and the like. Others open themselves to the spirit world through abusing their bodies with drugs. Still others practice techniques and meditation that open gateways to the spiritual realm. What I have learned is that the experience usually proceeds with a life of its own. We may think we know "good" spirits, or "bad" spirits, but that realm has laws all its own that you had better not try to fit into the ideas we have of how it should be. Once you open the door, you have very little control over the outcome. Its like getting on a carnival ride — you choose to climb in the seat, then you ride out the ride.

As an aside, I have noticed that even though I no longer practice these techniques, I seem to have an openness to the spirit realm. My children are also very sensitive — perhaps "intuitive" would be a word others would use to describe them. I wonder if one opens a gateway, are they more vulnerable to this type of experience than perhaps someone who never dabbled in the occult? It seems to be true with many people. It certainly seems to be the case in my own experience.

More Recent Developments
in the TM Organization

When I left the New York Academy in 1976, they were just introducing a practice called "Siddha" techniques. That is, *enlivening* (as opposed to just experiencing) the "impulses of creative intelligence" and bringing their influence into everyday activity. Maharishi's teachers are now stating in public lectures that through the practice of the TM-Siddhi Program you can attain perfect health, and that the influence of the Siddhas (people practicing the TM-Siddhi Program) is creating Heaven on Earth. (No, I'm not kidding — these are their words!) I am still on the TM organization mailing list. I regularly receive literature advertising events to gather thousands of "Yogic Flyers" to their campus in Fairfield, Iowa (an *accredited* college — Maharishi International University!) to produce "global changes" in the "enlivened field of reality." Yes — flyers! Without planes, props, or wires. Actually, more of a cosmic "hopping" at this point, but still very unnerving to see. And I have seen it with my own eyes. I saw them drain the indoor pool at the New York Academy and line it with old mattresses. I saw them sit in a lotus position (legs tightly crossed), eyes closed. I saw their bodies being jerked up and thrown forward — some just tiny little bounces along the pool bottom, others thrown forward maybe ten feet, and up three feet in the air. Much further than could be faked. And the sounds they made! Whooping and hollering, like souls possessed. Something is definitely happening there . . . but again, my fundamental question. *At what cost?* Have my friends who continued in this program ever stopped to ask themselves who or what is at the *foundation* of these experiences? I find it profoundly upsetting and frightening. *At what cost?* At what cost to feel the power of overcoming gravity? Didn't Satan promise our Lord dominion over all the world and its powers if only He would bow down and worship at Satan's feet?

I want to make the point that I believe these experiences to be real. The technique *does* produce the results they claim to produce . . . it *was* and *is* powerful! In fact, it feels *wonderful*!! The problem I had was in hiding the true origins of the program, of getting people involved without revealing the whole story to them first. I believe it is all individuals' right to choose whatever path they choose. They are responsible for their choices. They will pay the price or reap the benefits of their choices. But I believe it is wrong to disguise a technique in scientific terms when it clearly has religious origins.

From Mediator to Teacher —
The Steps Along the Way

When you first learn the TM technique, you are taught the actual technique in about a half hour on the first day. You then practice it for twenty minutes morning and evening, while attending three consecutive days (two hours each) of informational classes. On the third night of class, CC is held up as the ultimate goal of practicing the TM Technique. No time limit is set for an individual to reach this state, but you are definitely left with the impression that it's quite attainable. The teacher will not directly answer the question "Are you in CC yet?" They will usually divert it with a joke, or say, "We're all on the path, some further along than others." Teachers are highly trained in every word used, every inflection in their voices, every answer for every imaginable question, how they look, how they act, what they eat, how they live, and how they present themselves. During the initial three-day follow-up to learning the TM technique, teachers kind of gloss over the higher states of consciousness (GC and UC). They are mentioned in passing, as is the siddhi program, but a lot of detail is not given out at this time in order to "avoid confusion." (Or perhaps in order to avoid questions they don't want to deal with, or to avoid raising doubts about the underlying philosophy of the TM Program?) They walk a very fine, well-defined line at each level of teaching.

After someone has been practicing the technique for a while, there are advanced lectures (voluntary classes offered to those who have completed the basic TM program) and residence courses (weekend retreats where additional meditation and siddhi techniques are practiced, and yoga asanas, or stretching postures, are taught). Here's where the Hindu philosophy begins to get more ingrained. The participants have been practicing the TM technique for a while, and are obviously experiencing benefits if they are willing to spend their time and money on further courses. On these courses, cosmic Self versus individual self begins to be introduced. Cosmic consciousness is now expressed as the "I" (Eternal Self or "Being"), the silent witness to the "i" (individual self). The "i" performs the daily activity of life. The "I" is the perfected, universal Self (or higher self, or personal godhead — lots of New Age names have been given to this state of consciousness).

The next logical step is to become a teacher. After attending several residence courses, interest is naturally peaked to find out the "Big Secrets." There is an invisible line drawn between "The Teacher" and "The Student." As a TM practitioner, I knew how to meditate, but I didn't know the secrets — like how the mantras were chosen and what the initiation ceremony meant. Even when I began to feel uncomfortable with the material being presented on teacher training courses, I continued to work very hard at becoming a TM teacher. By this point I had paid a lot of money, and had dedicated a lot of energy to discovering the tantalizing "secrets" of being "The Teacher." Yet those secrets were not even revealed until the last week of teacher training. Daily we were being told that not all the students would be made teachers, that only those fully devoted should continue, that this was a great calling. The pressure was tremendous. We were required to rote-memorize pages upon pages of Sanskrit. We drilled day and night. We were tested and retested. I probably memorized word-for-word at least a hundred pages of information (most of which I can still recite to this day). We were in an isolated environment, away from family and friends — no TV, no radios, no newspapers — fully focused on memorizing the vast amounts of material being presented to us. It was imbedded very deeply in our minds because of the extended meditations we were doing, and because of the intensive environment in which it was presented.

The Big Secrets

Here it is, folks! The secrets I sold ten years of my life for. I write these down to take the mysticism out of them and to show the underlying religious tones. As Maharishi's teachers, even we were not privy to the depths of the knowledge. We were used by Maharishi to get the technique out on a mass scale. We were trained by rote memorization, without full disclosure of the meaning and depth of the information. How are the mantras chosen? How many are there? It seemed so mysterious, with the initiation ceremony and all. Maybe some greater power chose a mantra just for me and whispered it in my teacher's ear during that ceremonial trance! Nothing so magical. When I became a teacher, there were fewer than twenty mantras. The teachers memorized them by rote. The mantras were assigned to individuals based on their age at the time of initiation. If you were between, for example, eighteen and twenty-four, you got a particular mantra; twenty-five to thirty-two, another mantra. Yet the secrecy surrounding this is so steeped in mysticism! Even one teacher to another doesn't know what particular mantras Maharishi imparted to each during those private minutes when he conferred the title of teacher on you! And *no one* talks about it!! In later years, I understand new teachers were required to sign disclaimers stating they would not reveal any of this information under penalty of legal action. By the way, even this particular technique of choosing mantras is also steeped in Hindu tradition. Traditional Hinduism states there are "stages" of life based on age, such as the student (*Brahmacharya*), the householder, and so on. Each mantra is selected to magnify the stage of life that the meditator is in. Time and space limit my sharing all the knowledge I have gained of traditional Hindu practices and ceremonies, but I guarantee, TM is steeped in them at every level.

We taught that the mantras were merely sounds, used only on the level of sound, not meaning. That may very well be true, but they *had* meaning, whether it was used or not. The more recent TM-Siddhi program delves into ancient techniques in the Upanishads (Vedic scripture) that state: inherent in a sound is its form; in other words, whether you knew the meaning or not, you were invoking the form associated with your mantra each time you meditated. The mantras, at least the ones I was given to teach with, *were* the names of Hindu gods. We were not told this even when we were made teachers. I found it out years later while reading classic Hindu literature — and there was my mantra, along with the others I memorized to give to the people I taught. My mantra literally translated was: "To the goddess of wealth, I bow down." Chilling revelation. . . .

The ceremony that a new meditator is asked to witness is a classic Hindu "ceremony of thanksgiving" called a "Puja." It invokes names of the masters in the long line of Maharishi's tradition, including Brahman, the Hindu god of creation, Vishnu, the god of maintenance, and Shiva, the god of destruction, and ending with Maharishi's master, Sri Brahmananda Saraswati of Jotir Math (also known as Guru Dev, a very highly respected Hindu spiritual Master during his lifetime in India). The TM teacher recreates this classic ceremony by singing the Puja in Sanskrit while performing various acts of devotion, and centering the mind and heart on certain thoughts and feelings. During the ceremony, a new white handkerchief, fresh fruit, and fresh flowers (all brought by the new initiate) are placed by the TM teacher on an altar. The altar consists of, among other things, a brass offering tray set at the feet of a large picture of Maharishi's teacher, Guru Dev. Other items are offered up while the teacher is singing, "To the divine master, *I bow down*," each time substituting another divine title as the teacher places a new item on the altar. Yet we taught this was *not* a religious ceremony!

Prior to the initiation, we explain that the Puja is a "ceremony of preparation" that teachers perform to prepare them to impart the technique, and that the initiate is not asked to participate, merely witness. (Yet the initiate provides three of the items offered up on the altar, in my mind making them an unknowing participant.) At the end of the ceremony, the teacher *literally* bows down before the altar prior to imparting the mantra to the new initiate. We were taught to look toward the initiate as we started to kneel, with our eyes cast downward, and our hand making a slight lowering gesture. Notice, we did not *ask* the initiate to bow down, but the intent was clear! In my experience, eight out of ten initiates *did* bow down before the altar. There was always an underlying sense of saying one thing and meaning another in this organization. And the participants were kind of drawn in, little by little, until they were so deep it was hard to extricate themselves.

Involvement by Intent or Innocence:
Still Involvement!

Remember that problem in basic geometry about two lines on a plane, moving toward infinity with a one-degree difference in direction? They appear to be parallel, but over time they begin diverging, until eventually they are so dramatically different they are totally irreconcilable? (I'm not a mathematician, but can you get the picture?) My point is, it seems you can be drawn into this type of organization innocently. You may have valid, beautiful intentions. But you choose the path, and it immediately begins diverging from the "straight and narrow" ever so slightly. So slightly that you aren't even aware of it. It's not until you're fairly far down the road that you can see that you're heading in a completely different direction than you thought you were when you started. Trust me, I speak from experience. So do thousands of others.

Here is my concern: How many people are drawn totally innocently into this practice, or other organizations, for that matter? TM happens to be my area of expertise — but this phenomenon happens *everywhere*, from Fundamentalism to mysticism to New Age to Satanism and beyond. *Not* that I am comparing extreme fundamental Christianity to Satanism! My point is simply that there are cults in *all* areas of life . . . and it is hard to know at first contact about some of them. I believe some are intrinsically evil, intent on destruction. I believe some are sincerely seeking good. But it is the *results* and the *foundation* that ultimately come into question. By their fruits they are known . . . and fruits may not come forth for years and years! What is a beautifully flowering tree may, in the long run, produce deadly fruit. How many people, like me, were seeking some spiritual truth, some spiritual experience, and were innocently attracted to the potential offered by these organizations? How many started a program, and found powerful, exciting, satisfying experiences? It may take *years* to begin to question the foundations of these organizations, if you *ever* reach that point! And by then you are so deeply entrenched, it is difficult to walk away, even if you want to.

I spent ten years of my life deeply involved in the TM organization. I have been fully out of it for ten years. For me personally, I believe that by the grace of God, I walked away. *But at what cost?* To this day, I struggle to stay away. I *miss* the experience, the power, the camaraderie, the community. It truly is an addiction. I want it *every day*. I wake up and consciously *choose* not to practice those techniques — one day at a time. It is just as powerful an urge as a smoker's urge to smoke, an alcoholic's urge to drink, a cocaine addict's urge to use. It is excruciatingly painful, a hunger in my soul. It is *always* there. That's why it has been so painful to bring this all up again, to write this down. I have to look at it all over again, and it hurts.

I have no firm spiritual foundation. I *choose* my Catholic faith — by sheer *choice* and grace I practice my faith. I have been prayed with and over, I have received a renewed baptism in my faith through the charismatic renewal. I have been very active in my parish, and my faith is very important to me. Yet still, I don't have a deep, solid, unchanging belief. I don't have peace, I don't have joy. I walk purely by faith, not by the knowledge that I am doing the right thing, nor by a deep sense of joy or satisfaction. I fail often, and have to pick up the pieces and begin again. It is painful, and it is the price I pay for filling my heart and mind with too many diametrically opposed beliefs. It's as if it "blew out" the belief circuitry in my brain. I envy those who have a simple faith and joy in their beliefs.

Baby and Bathwater . . .

Remember the old saying, don't throw the baby out with the bathwater? The intent of most of these groups is *not* to corrupt and destroy human souls. I know many good, loving, honest, wonderful people who are practicing and teaching these things. They truly believe, in the depths of their souls, that they are on the right path for them. And honestly, who am I to question them? I am no learned scholar, nor judge, nor priest. But I *do* know each of us is responsible for our choices. I used to believe with all my heart that what I was teaching was true. Now I believe with the same fervor that it is illusion. I guarantee individuals still involved in TM will use my very words to invalidate what I have said. They will call it "unstressing," as I have done to others who have spoken out when I was an active teacher. I guess what I *have* learned through these past ten years is some humility. The bottom line is, my experience has led to confusion and sometimes despair, and sometimes I don't know what is true and what isn't. I can only act as I must and stand accountable for my actions.

What would be my response if I were asked, "Why couldn't someone practice the *techniques* of these traditions to enhance their strong Christian experience and enrich their prayer life, without embracing the parts that conflict with their beliefs?" The ultimate confusion, despair, and loss of faith it can bring about is enough reason to stay away. You can't *really* separate the techniques from the beliefs, even if you think you can. The very foundation of these organizations is in direct conflict with the basic tenets of our Christian faith. Those who are trying to balance both worlds are doing a dangerous juggling act that can backfire at any time.

More than that, I would answer that *there is no need to look outside our own Catholic faith to find the fullness of all traditions.* My experience in the last ten years has been that all the fullness I longed for in the other practices exists right here in my own tradition. I'm a Catholic . . . for me, the Catholic faith is rich and full of Christian mystics. If my searching spirit had been directed some twenty years ago to the writings of Teresa of Ávila, or St. John of the Cross, St. Augustine, St. Francis of Assisi, the writings of the *Philokalia* (*The Way of the Pilgrim*), and how many countless others, even to the Litany of the Saints, the Office of the Hours, or the Holy Rosary, where might I be today? I might have heard a different call . . . there may have been no need to seek out TM, or est, or Buddhism, or Scientology. (Then again, perhaps I was supposed to walk that path so I could write this paper . . . I have given up figuring out the why and wherefore!) Yet still, doesn't some of the responsibility for others turning to foreign traditions fall on us, the Body of Christ? Where have we failed, that seeking hearts feel the need to look elsewhere to be fulfilled? Where have we failed, that our children don't appreciate the fullness of their own faith, or the deepest mysteries of life, or listening for the touch of God Almighty on their hearts? *Interior Castle* by Teresa of Ávila has the dearest description of Christian mystical meditation I have ever read. Over and over I thumb through her descriptions and say, "Yes, I *know* what she's talking about!" I don't say it arrogantly, but with great awe, that God would allow me even a glimpse of that great beauty. The Litany of the Saints is our *own* ceremony of thanksgiving. I now often pray the litany when the urge to return to TM becomes strong. And I meditate, using one of the many Hebrew names of God as my meditation vehicle.

God-Given Grace vs. Self-Improvement

Beneath all the "right" and "wrong"; beneath all the spiritual mysticism; beneath all the controversy, there are some fundamental differences between New Age, Hinduism, Buddhism, and Christianity. From a theological standpoint, I'm sure there are volumes of information supporting one position or the other. From an experiential standpoint, I *cannot* hold both to be truth. The basic struggle I dealt with when I left the TM way of life was to choose one path or the other. I'd like to offer two observations based on my personal experience of two very different paths:

1. In TM (and in many other religions as well) we are considered perfected souls who must, through our own hard work and lifetimes of experience, remove the impediments (or "stress," as we taught in TM) to realizing our own perfection. The basic ground of understanding is that, through meditating, we could reach perfect enlightenment, here, on this planet, this plane of existence. I bought that belief for many years. The TM mentality simply ignored any experience that didn't fit the mold — we wrote it off as "unstressing." We always focused on the perfection, the enlightenment. I even "felt" enlightened, or at least well on the path, while I lived in the enclosed "womb" of the TM organization. There were never any stimuli to bring out my own brokenness, so I didn't know it existed!

The "real" world is a very different place from the enclosed environment of the TM Academy, the college in Fairfield, Iowa (MIU), and the teacher training courses. I guess that's part of a cult mentality — denial of reality, creating your own reality, separation from everyday life. When you're in the middle of that cult environment, it seems so natural and real, so true. But when you meet the real world head on, with jobs, earning a living, paying bills, raising kids, washing dishes, and all the rest, that fantasy land of "Perfected Spiritual Being" seems pretty far away.

2. The truth is, I am far, far from being a perfected soul. I have a *lot* of broken places (just ask my husband and kids!). In being able to

embrace my imperfection, my sinfulness, and in being able to embrace God's love for me in spite of my brokenness, I have found I am at last able to address my shortcomings and begin to heal. It is a slow and painful process. There are no quick fixes — just a lot of hard work and continuing the battle each day.

The fundamental difference between the perfection philosophy and sinner philosophy *can't* be ignored. They are *not* reconcilable, *as much as I would like them to be*. It's a lot nicer to think of myself as an enlightened soul on the path to realization than as a broken soul born into this world stained with sin, in need of a Savior. Sometimes the harder path proves to be the one worth climbing. . . . Remember, there is a world of difference between grace transformation and self-realization.

In Conclusion

I'd like to leave you with this thought: There *is* a spiritual realm. It is full of powerful experiences and powerful beings. One of the main dangers I see in the New Age movement is that those who lead others into this realm may not be equipped to deal with what they find there — angels, demons, spiritual battles. What begins as an innocent weekend retreat to rediscover your "inner self" may leave you shaken and open to evil influences — or it may take *years* before it becomes clear it is a negative influence! Think long and hard before you choose to dabble in the New Age, for it *is* your choice. And your choices may have far-reaching effects that you cannot possibly imagine. I will close with one more story to make my point:

A year after I left the TM organization, my mother died of breast cancer. I had two children under the age of three at that time, and was an active member of a prayer group at my church. Within several months of my mother's death, I found a lump in my breast and had to have it surgically removed and biopsied. Anyone who has been through this experience knows that in the time between the diagnosis and the biopsy results, you have to deal with the fear and reality of possible cancer and even death. I was deep in prayer, and asked God how He could take me when my children were so young. I feared for their future, I felt betrayed, I felt scared. After several hours in deep prayer, I began to feel a sense of peace. I felt God's love leading me through each step, showing me that should I have to deal with this, my children would be fine, they would be well cared for and loved. Indeed, He showed me in a new way that they were not *my* children but His. Each fear was somehow revealed and then released, until I said simply, "Lord, let Thy will be done! If you want me to walk the path of cancer, so be it. I trust in your plan for my life and the lives of my children!" It was a profound moment. It was surrender. In prayer I "heard" the words, "I have given you life, now go and raise My children the way they should be raised." I had been sitting with my eyes closed in prayer during this time. I fell off into sleep for a while.

After some time I sort of stirred, and I became aware of "whispering" over my left shoulder — "You dumb @($&%*. You really believe all this garbage? You're going to die, you @($&%*. And you're going to suffer. See how far your faith gets you then!" I *clearly* realized that the "inner voice" many of us hear judging our actions and beliefs in our head was pure evil — and it *wasn't* me. I quickly turned and "looked" over my left shoulder and "saw" (all this happened in an inner trance-like state, not physically) this awful, slobbering, rage-filled, hateful, stinking, massive, animal/man-like, frightening, evil being. He became even *more* enraged when he realized I had "seen" him, that I knew the "whispering" in my ear was him. He pointed at me and *bellowed* in a thundering, deep voice, "If I can't get you through your body, I'll get you through your children!" I shouted, "Begone, in the name of Jesus Christ! You have no place here!" He literally shrieked and was ripped from the room in a whirl of wind. I was shaken. I still feel the hair on the back of my neck stand up when I tell this story.

The tumor was benign. But the irony is, when you open the gates, the impact can be so much more than you can imagine. My children have had a hard life. They have had to grow up much sooner than they should have. They have dealt with abandonment, poverty, welfare, violence, illness, and confusion. I have had to struggle desperately to be true to the command to raise them as I know they should be raised. We're making it, by the grace of God and the extraordinary effort of the whole family. But was it necessary? If I had not opened those doors, not spent years inviting those influences into my life, would this family have walked this path? Would I have made the choices I made? I will live with those questions the rest of my life.

My advice, based on my life experience, is this: Keep your eyes open and be cautious. What may seem to be a wonderful experience may turn quite frightening further down the road. The people leading you into these experiences may not have much more experience than yourself, and that can be dangerous. Your actions are far-reaching, and *you are responsible for your choices*. Channeling and contacting spirits *does* exist, there *are* ways to touch the spiritual realm. Back to the ocean analogy I used to describe the experience of meditating: we're all bobbing around the surface of the ocean, hoping to dive to some deeper level of life. There are "ships" that can carry us to the beautiful silent depths. It's our choice whether or not to board one of the vessels. The only question I ask you to answer is this — who is piloting the vessel you choose to board? Our Savior Jesus Christ, through the grace of God and the power of the Holy Spirit? Or Shiva, the Hindu god of destruction? Or a New Age teacher who has given command of the vessel to some unknown entity? Or your self, who has never traveled these waters before? Who captains your vessel? It's your choice. . .

Please see Appendix IV at the end of this book for the 1984 Pastoral statement of His Eminence Jaime Cardinal Sin, Archbishop of Manila, on *The Basic Conflict Between Maharishi and Christianity*.

an appeal to authority

meditation should be taught gratis.

8.

The Ku Klux Klan and Neo-Nazism

Jane Petrie

WHY does a book on Contemporary Destructive Religious Movements contain a Chapter on the Ku Klux Klan and Neo-Nazism? Are they not political organizations rather than religious movements?

Remembering my own earliest acquaintance with both of these groups may bring them into clearer focus for all of us.

Al Smith, popular governor of New York State, was the Democrat candidate for the presidency of the United States in 1927, running against Herbert Hoover, who had distinguished himself as head of Red Cross Relief to the European countries which had been devastated during World War I. Both were talented and experienced administrators. Hoover, a Quaker, was a kind but somewhat sober man. Al Smith, vivacious, with sparkling Irish wit, was a Catholic.

I was about seven years old, living in one of the northeastern states. Every school day began with the Salute to the Flag and the Oath of Allegiance, which included the words: ". . . one nation, indivisible, with liberty and justice for all. . ."

That Presidential Campaign of 1927 introduced me to prejudice and to the fact that some people belonged to an organization called the Ku Klux Klan.

My father was Protestant with a respected old American family name. My mother was Catholic, third generation American, with a somewhat Irish appearance. Until the presidential campaign started, we would joyfully drive out in the family car on Saturday for a picnic in a state park or at a beach, or on Sunday afternoon to visit some scenic spot or to have dinner in a newly discovered restaurant in a distant town. The great American love affair with the automobile was starting, and my parents were enjoying their new "toy."

"The campaign" changed our happy-go-lucky ways. Suddenly it became dangerous to visit certain places, "because the man is strong" in this area or that, or because someone had warned us that there was to be a "cross burning" in a certain place. Above all, we had to be sure that we would be home by dark, because Dad did not want to chance running out of gas or having to change a tire on a strange road or in a strange town. At the very least, a person who "looked Catholic" would find it difficult to buy gasoline or to get help changing a tire, might even be beaten if he met a militant member of the Klan after dark.

My parents told me that "the Klan" hated equally Catholics, Jews, and negroes (whom "they" called "niggers," a word I was taught never to use because it would show disrespect for a fellow human being).

In the early 1930s, a few years after the Hoover-Smith presidential campaign, we were traveling during summer vacation in the Berkshires. We had stopped at a "tourist home" for the night. Today it would be called a "bed and breakfast." Dad had signed the register and had paid for our lodging. When mother and I came to the entrance with our bags, the hostess/owner looked at mother and asked bluntly "Are any of you Catholic?" I can remember Dad's furious answer to this day: "I'm not, but I *am* a law-abiding American citizen paying with good American money, so what difference does our religion make?" The owner replied to the effect that Catholics were not welcome in that town. Dad took back the money for the room, scratched his name from the guest register, and we left. As we drove to a larger town, I recall him saying that he had heard that place was "Klan territory" but that he had thought it looked "clean and decent." "The Klan" soon faded from my mind because there were so many other events claiming attention.

In the late 1930s, just before Hitler and Stalin invaded Poland, starting what came to be called the Second World War, Adolf Hitler's face and ranting voice came to be well-known through newsreel films and broadcasts of his speeches. Some of us met Jews and Gentiles as well from Germany and Austria who had fled from their homelands to escape restrictions or death.

In college I met some Catholic "refugees" who had chosen to leave Germany or Austria rather than compromise their beliefs. Some told me that nurses and doctors in Germany were required to kill persons who were mentally retarded, those who were permanently crippled, patients in mental hospitals, and the senile elderly. Others mentioned that children were under extreme pressure to attend Nazi youth meetings scheduled for Sundays at the same time as church services and Sunday school. Young people who did not attend the Nazi youth meetings had no hope for advancement in school or employment.

The refugees I met from Germany and Austria were decent people, some hard-working craftsmen, some former owners of small shops, housewives and mothers, some very well educated professional persons, all puzzled and confused that the German and Austrian people among whom they had lived and whose countries and culture they considered their own could turn on them as if they had never conversed in a friendly manner in the neighborhoods where they had lived or worked.

In the year 1992, every day brought more news of violent uprisings of ethnic groups throughout the former Soviet Union; bloody fighting in what was formerly Yugoslavia between Orthodox Serbs, Muslims from Bosnia-Herzegovina, and Roman Catholic Croats; Kurds fighting against both Iraq and Turkey for the right to create (or re-create) a homeland for themselves; Ulster still a bloody battleground after more than three hundred years of fighting; Sri Lanka in ethnic turmoil, and less publicized "small" wars or revolutions in countless "new" countries of Asia, Africa, and Latin America.

Why is this? After all these thousands of years that human beings have lived upon the earth, and after the hundreds of years that some of us have been exposed to Christian teachings, what leads some people to accept belief systems or such manipulation of their emotions that they appear willingly to embark on wholesale killing sprees?

During World War II the common goal of working for victory seemed to unite people to the extent that I heard nothing of "the Klan," but the attitude of the people toward Japanese-Americans on the West Coast, and even of the rest of the nation, reminded me of the irrational fear which led to irrational anger on the part of "the Klan" when I was a child. I asked myself why few, if any, German-Americans on the East Coast were put under any kind of restriction, while Japanese-Americans, even second- and third-generation citizens, were herded into concentration camps, having to trust their homes and businesses to what they hoped were the mercies of their neighbors. Later, it was thrilling to read that the U.S. Army unit composed of Nisei (Japanese-Americans) had won so many awards for valor in the Italian campaign.

If we look at American history, we can see movements of "Nativism," which, by the way, does not refer to "Native Americans," i.e., the Amerindians, but attempts by white Americans of mostly northern European descent to restrict immigration of Catholic Irish and people of Eastern and Southern European stock, and to keep persons of those ethnic groups from equal access to jobs. In the mid-nineteenth century, a sign, symbolic of that mentality, "Hiring. No Irish Need Apply," was often seen at factory gates.

A similar attitude toward people of different race was common on the West Coast of the United States resulting in on-again-off-again exclusions and quotas for Chinese and Japanese immigrants.

It is a natural human trait that we find it easier to associate with people whose racial, national, and religious backgrounds are similar to our own. We are comfortable with people with whom we are familiar. Even the word "familiar" (it echoes "family") hints at humans clustering in "tribes." Are not family reunions, class reunions, and various "homecoming" activities of schools, churches, even towns, a normal part of the American scene?

This clustering of "like with like" can quickly become prejudice, especially when "one of our own" cannot find work while a person of another nationality or another race gets a job, perhaps by accepting a lower wage. Or simple recognition of differences in language or customs can turn into a habitual attitude of prejudice when we meet people whom we find difficult to understand. So there has always been some prejudice against "outsiders," people of different races, different language, different religious affiliation, different from "our own," whatever that might be.

What makes the Ku Klux Klan and Neo-Nazism more destructive

or dangerous than noisy Yankee or Dodger fans or Dallas Cowboy fans arguing against Redskin rooters?

How Did the Ku Klux Klan Come to Be?

When Robert E. Lee surrendered the Confederate forces in Virginia at Appomattox Court House on April 9, 1865, and General Joseph Johnston surrendered a slightly larger Confederate force at Durham Station, North Carolina, on April 18, 1865, the fight for States' Rights, which as a matter of fact included the right to own slaves, seemed to have ended. In the Emancipation Proclamation of January 1, 1863, Lincoln had freed the slaves, but the surrender of the Armies of the Confederacy marked only the barest beginning of the work of bringing that proclaimed freedom into reality.

Giving negro slaves their freedom was not a simple matter either for the blacks themselves or for their former masters. The Civil War had barely touched the Northern States, but much of the South was devastated: "slash and burn" had not only wiped out large areas of Georgia but also much of the wheat fields of the Shenandoah Valley, where General Sherman had tried that tactic before his march through Georgia. Additionally, anything metal — plows, farming equipment and tools of all kinds — had been melted down to make weapons. Houses and barns were burned. Cattle and horses had been confiscated either for food or for use by the Army, or those that had been passed over as unfit had died for lack of fodder. Confederate paper money had so little worth that the small (to save paper) bills were called "shin plasters." Enormous numbers of strong young men had been killed or wounded so as to be unfit for the hard labor needed to rebuild the shattered economy.

Factories in the Northeast needed only to turn from producing shoes and clothing for the Army to making similar items for civilian needs. Not only had the farms of the Midwest been untouched by battles, but the farmers depended not on slaves but largely on the newly developed machinery being produced in the factories located around the Great Lakes.

The demobilized and defeated Confederate troops returning to their homes, however, faced devastation and what appeared to be, for them, the loss of the labor they would ordinarily have expected to have used to rebuild.

The Emancipation Proclamation did not simply grant freedom to slaves. It gave legal expression to a principle which was already contained in both the Declaration of Independence and in the Constitution of the United States, and also gave legal expression to a basic teaching of Christianity.

The Declaration of Independence states clearly:

> "We hold these truths to be self-evident: That all men are created equal; that they are endowed by their Creator with certain unalienable rights; that among these are life, liberty, and the pursuit of happiness. . . ."

The Thirteenth Amendment to the Constitution abolished slavery. The Fourteenth Amendment granted citizenship to all persons born or naturalized in the United States and stated that

> "No State shall make or enforce any law which shall abridge the privileges or immunities of citizens of the United States, nor shall any State deprive any person of life, liberty, or property, without due process of law; nor deny to any person within its jurisdiction the equal protection of the laws. . . ."

The Fifteenth Amendment declared:

> "The right of citizens of the United States to vote shall not be denied or abridged by the United States or by any State on account of race, color, or previous condition of servitude. . . ."

These Amendments, adopted by Congress between 1865 and 1869 and all ratified by the states by 1870, simply codify the principle stated in the Declaration of Independence that ". . . all men are created equal."

Historians of the Ku Klux Klan tell us that it was organized in the law office of Judge Thomas M. Jones in Pulaski, Tennessee, about eighty miles south of Nashville, on December 24, 1865. Most if not all of the original organizers had fought for the Confederacy: Calvin E. Jones, Frank O. McCord, Richard R. Reed, John B. Kennedy, John C. Lester, and James R. Crowe.

One of the founders, Captain John B. Kennedy, chose the name

Ku Klux from the Greek word *kuklos*, which means band or circle. James Crowe is reported to be responsible for making two words out of it and changing the final letter to *x*. John Lester suggested that since all of the founding organizers were of Scottish descent, *clan* should be added, but for uniformity with the rest of the name it should be spelled with *K*.

At the second meeting of the group, a few days later, the men "dressed up" and paraded through the town on borrowed horses, also disguised. Masquerades were common forms of social entertainment in the mid-nineteenth century, so costumes were made of sheets, since the impoverished South could hardly be expected to provide more elaborate materials. The pointed headgear, covering the face except for providing holes for the eyes, reflects certain medieval penitential garb.

Very soon, the Klan members discovered that the anonymity provided by their garb, even the garb itself, provided opportunities for frightening the mostly uneducated former slaves in the area.

From the beginning, the Klan did not recruit new members. If a member overheard someone express interest, the potential applicant would be told when and where to go for further information. Applicants were almost always brought blindfolded before the group for the first time. If the applicant met with the approval of the group, he would be invested and told to repeat the Klan oath, in which the new member vowed never to reveal his membership in the Klan. If not approved, the applicant would be led outside, away from the meeting place, and dismissed.

Very soon after the Klan's founding, friends of the founders in other towns asked for advice to start chapters, and the term "regulation," meaning preserving the old order of race relationships, began to appear. Within a year there were hundreds of local chapters with the same name, same titles, same purpose, "regulation," but whose behavior ranged from crude practical jokes on the negroes to serious physical punishment and even death for any behavior contrary to what the Southern whites considered acceptable.

Klan Philosophy

To this day, the Klan disavows most of the extreme offenses, but concealed identity and secret membership lists make it impossible to say who did commit most of the crimes for which the Klan was blamed.

Just after Congress had passed the Reconstruction Act, which divided the South into five military districts in which the commanding generals had authority even over the courts, Klansmen from many parts of the South gathered at Nashville early in 1867 for an organizational meeting.

In the documents which the Klansmen accepted at that meeting, we read:

> "We recognize our relation to the United States government, the Constitutional laws thereof, and the Union of the States thereunder" (*Prescript*, drafted by General George W. Gordon).

It may seem contradictory for the Klan to swear allegiance to the Constitution and to the Union while defying federal law, but the Southern understanding is that the North had violated the spirit of the Constitution. This view is expressed in the questions addressed to candidates for membership in the Klan, in which the person is required to express commitment to "a white man's government" and to work for restoration of states' rights.

In the official charge read to the new recruit we can read:

> "Our main and fundamental objective is the maintenance of the supremacy of the white race in this Republic. History and Physiology teach us that we belong to a race which nature has endowed with an evident superiority over all other races, and that the Maker, in thus elevating us above the common standard of human creation, has intended to give us over inferior races a dominion from which no human laws can permanently derogate" (William Pierce Randel, *The Ku Klux Klan, A Century of Infamy*, Philadelphia-New York, Chilton Books, 1965, pp. 15-16).

The entire area in which the Klan had members was called the Invisible Empire, which was divided into Realms (individual states) each under a Grand Dragon, Dominions (congressional districts) each under a Grand Titan, and Provinces (counties) each under a Grand Giant. Robert E. Lee is reported to have refused to become the first Grand Wizard, the head of the Invisible Empire. General Nathan Bedford Forrest accepted that honor at Nashville but served for only two years. Many of the other original Klan officials were also former Confederate officers, even though the terms under which they had accepted amnesty at the end of the Civil War they had sworn never again to oppose the federal government, but the expected answer to the final question to prospective recruits explains this: "Do you believe in the inalienable rights of self-preservation of the people against the exercise of arbitrary and unlicensed power?"

In addition to former slaves and those negroes who dared to run for public office, especially those supported by the federal troops, those federal employees who had been sent South to implement Reconstruction, and such "carpetbaggers" as were obviously trying to profit by the Reconstruction, the Klan especially victimized northern teachers, mostly women, whose minimal salaries were paid by northern churches and who had come to the South to teach negroes who would become living disproof of the claim that negroes were an inferior race, incapable of learning.

The Roots of Racist and Ethnic Prejudice

The "first settlers" of the American Colonies came here to seek religious freedom, right? That is a statement which is true as far as it goes, but "the rest of the story" shows us the other side, the dark side of what appears so bright.

The Puritans, who settled the Massachusetts Bay Colony in 1629 and in 1636 began to settle Connecticut, were strict Calvinists like Cromwell's Covenanters, who rebelled against King Charles I in England in the 1640s, ultimately condemning Charles to death in 1648. It is interesting to note that the Puritans in England were among those called "Independents" of whom Antonia Fraser, biographer of Oliver Cromwell, says

> "Independency had originated as 'a form of decentralized Calvinism,' as one historian has described it, based on the theory that religious authority rested with the local communities, since Christ had deliberately chosen certain people to 'walk together.' Each particular local group was therefore believed to hold within it the autonomous power to decide its own religious destiny. Thus the independents would

of their very nature tolerate many different shades of opinion, as represented by variations in the different communities" (*Cromwell, the Lord Protector*, New York, Alfred A. Knopf, Inc., 1973, p.68).

It is interesting that Roger Williams was banished by some of those very Independents, the Puritans of Massachusetts, in 1635, partly because of his unwillingness to coerce others into uniformity of religious belief. (Modern Congregational Christians, who have merged with the Evangelical Reformed Church to form the United Church of Christ, hold not the slightest bit of that original rigidity.) Many "Independents," Presbyterians and Baptists from the British Isles, settled in the southern colonies with the officially established Church of England, but after its disestablishment they became the religious majority in those new states.

Note that the spirit of independence, nonconformity even to the point of rebellion and regicide, is part of the colonial heritage.

Another element in the Calvinist heritage is that of belief in a chosen people, an "elect," the "saved." Still another belief was not simply in the inerrancy of Scripture, but that the words of the Bible must be understood in the strictly literal sense.

The "habit of independence" undoubtedly contributed to the thinking of the men who led the American Revolution. That same "habit of independence" was strong in those states which seceded to form the Confederacy. Note the issue: a *union*, the United States, or a *Confederacy* of individual states.

Several additional strands of thought were woven together to create a climate of thinking which culminated in the Civil War.

Almost from the beginnings of the colonies, race was a problem. The first difficulty arose from the fact that the colonists inevitably met with at least some degree of opposition from the Native Americans as soon as the colonists wanted more land, even those colonists who attempted to "buy" land from the Indians, because, to the Indians, the land was not for sale. Not only did the Native Americans, a.k.a. Indians, appear different; they spoke a non-European language and had a totally different culture. Moreover, they were not Christians, not "saved," not of the "elect." Hence the term often used for them, "savages."

The Native Americans did not make good field hands, so quite early in colonial history the Southern planters began importing Africans to use as slaves. They were sufficiently different in appearance from the white colonists that they could be treated as chattel without a feeling of revulsion on the part of most colonists against that treatment. Moreover, anyone who interpreted the Bible in the strictly literal sense could point to Genesis 9:18-27, in which they could read that Ham, as the father of Canaan, is called "cursed" and ". . . the lowest of slaves shall he be to his brothers" (Gn. 9:25, NAB).

The Enlightenment, which viewed humanity as essentially equal, met practicality in both England and the colonies. On the practical level, many British saw the slave trade as extremely lucrative and saw the blacks as savages, even "beastly." One of our most popular hymns, "Amazing Grace," is the paean of John Newton (1725-1807), former slave trader, thanking God for his conversion. The Wesleys and Bishop Asbury preached the equality of all persons as children of God and laid the groundwork for some Southern families to move to the upper midwest away from a slave-based economy, even though many of those pioneers left close relatives behind.

The representatives of the several states who met in Philadelphia from May to September 1787 to draft the Constitution of the United States had a full spectrum of beliefs, not only about slavery but also about persons of other races and of other religions than their own. In the Virginia Convention of 1776, Thomas Jefferson joined with James Madison to frame a draft constitution which would eventually disestablish the Church of England in the colony. In that draft, the Declaration of Rights stated: ". . . all men are equally entitled to the free exercise of religion according to the dictates of conscience." This principle would be incorporated eventually into the First Article of the Bill of Rights of the Constitution of the United States.

While the Church of England was disestablished in Virginia at the very start of the Revolution, the Congregational Church remained firmly established in Massachusetts by the state constitution of 1780 and even for many years after Massachusetts ratified the Constitution of the United States. Some of the very legislative bodies of the states which ratified the Constitution of the United States retained in their own jurisdiction religious restrictions among the qualifications for public office or for civil service, which restrictions remained in effect in several of those states beyond the middle of the nineteenth century. The Massachusetts constitution, for example, declared that religion was the foundation of morality and of the state, requiring that "public funds be used to maintain the churches and that a man be a Christian before he could hold public office" (Esmond Wright, *Fabric of Freedom*, New York, Hill and Wang, 1961, p. 149).

The legal proclamation of liberty in the First Article of the Bill of Rights, while religious restrictions continued to be tolerated in practice, provided ground in which some of the ideas could grow which culminated in the Ku Klux Klan.

The Constitutional Convention in Philadelphia also provided a rationale for the racist orientation of the Ku Klux Klan. Some of the delegates were wholeheartedly anti-slavery. Others owned slaves but either freed them over the years or freed their slaves in their wills, e.g., Thomas Jefferson. Still others not only owned slaves but defended slavery as an economic necessity. Nevertheless, the debate ended with the southern states conceding that the importation of slaves would end in 1808. The account of that concession is important in American history.

Dr. James McHenry of Maryland feared to give congress the power to pass navigation acts or to collect any taxes or imposts or to regulate "commerce among the several states." The northern states restricted the congressional right to pass navigation laws by mere majority, but required a two-thirds vote of each house and decreed that the import tax on slaves would not exceed ten dollars a head. Next, however, we see the "slavery compromise" without which Alexander Hamilton said "no union could possibly have been formed." For the purpose of numbering the population of a state for mapping congressional districts and for taxes, slaves would be counted as five to each three free white inhabitants, which came to be known as the "federal ratio." From that moment, anyone could justify the principle of racial inequality by pointing to the "federal ratio." The grave injustice of that compromise was reiterated at the height of the Civil Rights Movement in this century with the publication in 1969 of Floyd McKissick's book *Three Fifths of a Man*.

So, by the time of the constitutional convention and the early nineteenth century there was a serious split in American thinking on race. This developed into the strong anti-slavery stand of many staunch Calvinists in New England, and after the Civil War led to many young men and women from the northern and midwestern states volunteering to teach in the South in spite of danger from the Klan.

In North America, however, and also in Europe a semi-scientific, even pseudo-scientific, set of opinions on race was being developed which appeared to give an intellectually respectable foundation to the notion of the superiority of the white race, especially the Anglo-Saxon and/or Germanic branch. By the 1830s many southern writers accepted as fact not only inequality of the races, but that blacks were innately inferior to whites and therefore unfit for freedom, even that negroes were a distinct species.

> "By 1850 American expansion was viewed in the United States less as a victory for the principles of free democratic republicanism than as evidence of the innate superiority of the American Anglo-Saxon branch of the Caucasian race. . . . Many think of rampant doctrines of Caucasian, Aryan, or Anglo-Saxon destiny as typical of the late years of the nineteenth century, but they flourished in the United States in the era of the Mexican War.
>
> ". . . The debates and speeches of the early nineteenth century reveal a pervasive sense of the future destiny of the United States, but they do not have the jarring note of rampant racialism that permeates the debates of mid-century. By 1850 the emphasis was on the American Anglo-Saxons as a separate, innately superior people who were destined to bring good government, commercial prosperity, and Christianity to the American continents and to the world. This was a superior race, and inferior races were doomed to subordinate status or extinction" (Reginald Horsman, *Race and Manifest Destiny, The Origins of American Racial Anglo-Saxonism*, Cambridge, Mass., Harvard University Press, 1981, pp.1-2)

Horsman recounts the English interest in Anglo-Saxon Christianity at the time of the Reformation, when early Christian institutions and practices in England were studied to provide justification for Henry VIII's break with Rome. During Queen Elizabeth's reign, Archbishop Matthew Parker sponsored

Anglo-Saxon studies. The continental Reformers of that same period were stressing the strength of their German heritage.

The philosophy of the Enlightenment period included and even emphasized the principle that all humans were of one species and capable of indefinite improvement, and that differences in achievement between races could be accounted for by environment rather than by heredity (see Rousseau and the Encyclopedists). This was the philosophy of most of the leaders of the American Revolution of 1776, but also of most of the leaders of the French Revolution of 1798. Until the middle of the nineteenth century, both the religion of Christian believers (based on the Bible) and the science of both believers and rationalists seemed to point to a single origin for the races of humankind.

In the mid-nineteenth century, the views of a Scot, Robert Knox, were widely accepted in the United States as well as in Europe, including the notion that ". . .God had given the whites, for their own preservation and purity, a strong feeling of racial antagonism. When superior and inferior races met, the only hope for the latter was serfdom or slavery" (Horsman, op. cit., p. 147). Horsman states that some authors of that period asserted vaguely that other races would simply fade away before the expansion of white America (ibid.).

Among European nations, views such as these served to support the wars of colonial expansion in Asia and in Africa during the latter half of the century.

The pseudo-science supporting white racial superiority also provided support for the Chinese Exclusion Act of 1882, in spite of the Fifteenth Amendment to the Constitution.

One of the most flagrant expressions of racial superiority and militant nationalism combined with a certain religious flavor is Rudyard Kipling's poem, "Recessional," written for Queen Victoria's Diamond Jubilee of 1897. It so perfectly exemplifies the spirit of racial superiority combined with a gracious nod to religion that it bears quoting in entirety.

> "God of our fathers, known of old —
> Lord of our far-flung battle line —
> Beneath whose awful Hand we hold
> Dominion over palm and pine —

Lord God of Hosts be with us yet,
Lest we forget — lest we forget!

"The tumult and the shouting dies;
The Captains and the Kings depart:
Still stands Thine ancient sacrifice,
An humble and a contrite heart.
Lord God of Hosts be with us yet,
Lest we forget — lest we forget!

"Far-called, our navies melt away;
On dune and headland sinks the fire:
Lo, all our pomp of yesterday
Is one with Nineveh and Tyre!
Judge of the Nations, spare us yet,
Lest we forget — lest we forget!

"If, drunk with sight of power, we loose
Wild tongues that have not Thee in awe,
Such boastings as the Gentiles use,
Or lesser breeds without the Law —
Lord God of Hosts, be with us yet,
Lest we forget — lest we forget!

"For heathen heart that puts her trust
In reeking tube and iron shard,
All valiant dust that builds on dust,
And guarding, calls not Thee to guard,
For frantic boast and foolish word —
Thy mercy on Thy People, Lord."

The British Empire was expanded greatly ("Dominion over palm
and pine . . .") during Queen Victoria's reign, through something
over three hundred "little wars" ("Lord of our far-flung battle line
. . ."), but the attitude of the British toward the colonials is expressed
only too clearly in "Lesser breeds without the Law. . . ."

Victoria and all things Victorian were much admired in the United
States during the later years of the nineteenth century. At present,

nearly a hundred years later, there is a strong revival of interest in Victoriana.

* * * * *

In the Ku Klux Klan we see the spirit of independence extended to the extreme of rebellion against what was seen as restrictive government, the belief in the superiority of one race and the inferiority of another attributed to biblical authority, and finally the support for that belief by apparently scientific findings, come together at a time when the grief which follows defeat was compounded by severe economic hardship.

The strength of the Klan in the South seemed to decline during the early part of the twentieth century, and especially during the First World War, but it revived vigorously in the early 1920s, until scandals affected its credibility with the public, especially that involving the Grand Dragon of the Indiana Klan, D.C. Stephenson, who was convicted and found guilty of second-degree murder for his part in kidnapping and killing a young woman in 1925.

The Klan revived again in the late 1930s, and in 1940 Klansmen and members of the German-American Bund joined in a great meeting at Camp Nordland in rural New Jersey (August 18, 1940) to stress what they called true Americanism.

In the spring of 1944 the Internal Revenue Service billed the Klan for $685,305 in back taxes. How they managed to arrive at that figure is not clear, but the Klan lost its tax-exempt status, and in one final Klonvokation in Atlanta on April 23, 1944, the members voted to disband.

Since the official disbanding of the Ku Klux Klan, individual Klan members formed local Klans under such titles as White Knights of the Ku Klux Klan, the Christian Knights of the Ku Klux Klan, the Confederate Knights of the Ku Klux Klan, or The Invisible Empire, Knights of the Ku Klux Klan, who are presently (1992) recruiting in the middle Atlantic states with "International Offices" at Gulf, N.C., and Shelton, Conn., but using various post office boxes in Virginia under the title The Robert E. Lee Society.

Between 1944 and the present, individual Klan members or small groups within local Klaverns continued harassment of blacks, especially those who attempted to exercise their civil rights by registering at previously all-white public colleges and universities, or who worked to increase black voter registration. In several instances this harassment, not only of blacks but of anyone who dared to help them, was carried to the extreme of murder.

The following quotation will instruct those who are unaware of the intensity of hatred which fuels the actions of some present-day Klan members. It is excerpted from *The Conversion of a Klansman*, by Thomas A. Tarrants III, with a foreword by Leighton Ford (New York, Doubleday, 1979):

> "During the previous five years I had become a hardened radical. Starting innocently in the Goldwater for President campaign [1964] at the age of sixteen, I soon became involved with members of the John Birch Society. A short time later, I moved into the National States' Rights Party, the Ku Klux Klan, and the Minutemen. For nearly a year, I had headed a small, highly secret, elite terrorist group. I was largely responsible for planning and directing the Ku Klux Klan's terrorist operations against civil rights forces, communists, liberals and Jews. I was a leader of Mississippi's dreaded White Knights of the Ku Klux Klan, the most violent right-wing organization in the United States. Among its achievements in five years were nine murders and more than three hundred other acts of violence, including bombings, burnings and beatings" (op. cit., p. 2).

> "During the previous six months, the Klan had maintained a reign of terror in the Meridian area. Since January 15, 1968, eight black churches had been fire-bombed or burned and two black homes, as well as one white home, had been fired into" (ibid. p. 3).

In this book, Tarrants tells of attempting to place a bomb at the home of a prominent Jewish businessman who had been outspoken in denouncing the Klan after the bombing of Meridian's Jewish Synagogue, and was attempting to raise funds for a reward in an attempt to identify the perpetrators. Police sharpshooters and FBI agents were watching the house on June 29, 1968. Tarrants fled through gunfire, but was captured at a roadblock after a battle with state police during which he shot a state trooper and was himself shot.

After imprisonment, he escaped once, was recaptured, and was sent to maximum security. There he was converted through reading the Scriptures.

> "One verse of Scripture was especially penetrating: 'What does it profit a man if he gain the whole world and lose his own soul? And what will a man give in exchange for his soul? . . .' For the previous five years I had been selling my soul to gain the world. Although I was motivated by dedication to my ideals, in truth I used my activities to receive recognition, acceptance, and approval from my peers . . . my activities provided me with a sense of worth. They fed my ego" (ibid. p. 102). "In my early teens I had made a profession of faith, been baptized, and had become a member of a church. But my relationship to the Lord and my behavior remained the same — even though I thought I would go to heaven when I died. I was like so many good people in churches who think that they are religious although they do not know Jesus Christ personally. This is true throughout the United States, but it is particularly prevalent in those areas where religion has been a strong part of culture, and people have an outward form of good behavior and religion" (ibid. p. 103).

After his conversion, Tarrants studied in order to share his newfound faith with other prisoners, which he has continued to do very quietly since his release.

Sometimes we can read a news story of the change of heart of a former Klansman (generally not at the time of the change, but in an obituary or in an account of the person's death), but there are many more accounts of shootouts, the FBI and state police sharpshooters against white supremacists at cabins in remote areas.

The Birth of Nazism

At the same time that pseudo-science was developing theories of white racial superiority in the United States, that same pseudo-science was at work in Europe. In addition to racial theories, it spawned new fashions in art and in music. Glorification of all things Germanic (or Nordic) became almost a fad. Richard Wagner with his Ring of the Nibelung cycle of operas comes to mind, of course. Two theoreticians of racism are important for understanding Nazism: Arthur de Gobineau, author of the essay *The Inequality of*

Human Races (1853), and Houston Stewart Chamberlain, who became Richard Wagner's son-in-law, author of *Foundation of the Nineteenth Century*, written in German and published in Munich in 1899. Chamberlain renounced his British citizenship and became a German citizen during World War I, in 1916. In *The Foundations of the Nineteenth Century*, Chamberlain extols the Germanic invasions of the Roman Empire for "saving" European civilization from Roman decadence.

Adolf Hitler met Chamberlain himself on several occasions in 1923, but a stronger influence on Hitler was Alfred Rosenberg, student of Chamberlain and author of the sequel to Chamberlain's *Foundations — Myth of the Twentieth Century* (Munich, 1930). Just as southern slave owners and later the Klan used pseudo-science to support the myth of black inferiority, so Gobineau, Chamberlain, and Rosenberg used biology to support their anti-Semitism and racism.

But how could generally well-educated Germans of the 1920s and early 1930s, people living at the same time as our parents and grandparents, accept the theories of Nazism seemingly without question?

Germany had been soundly defeated in World War I, 1918. Defeat included loss of all German colonies in Africa, mainly. Loss of the colonies and the destruction of German shipyards and ships by bombing wrought severe economic hardship. The people were dissatisfied with their new republic and were looking for something or someone to restore their self-esteem and to give them some semblance of prosperity.

I remember a German couple who owned and operated a small grocery in the neighborhood in which I grew up. In the late 1920s Mr. Ludwig (not his name) returned to Germany for a short visit to his family. Both husband and wife were decent Christian people. On his return, Mr. Ludwig told my parents, with great astonishment and sorrow, how he had awakened one night in his brother's home to discover his brother standing over him with a large knife, prepared to kill him for his traveling funds. Newsreels had shown pictures of German women dragging wheelbarrows filled with paper Deutschmarks to buy a loaf of bread. The similarity to the Southern states after the Civil War is unmistakable.

Where is the difference?

Nowhere among the Klansmen of the nineteenth or twentieth centuries do we find such a charismatic leader as Hitler. The Klan became, and was called, The Secret Empire, but it never became the legally acknowledged government of any state. Hitler came to power through an open, legal election. He maintained his position by persuading the majority, however slim that might have been at the end, to keep him there, admittedly with force not too far in the background. But he played on the German people's desire for the return of governmental power and its trappings, prosperity and international recognition, and success in the expansion of national boundaries.

In addition, Hitler used occult arts to gain his power and to keep it. He used the music of Wagner deliberately to arouse emotions which would fuel racist theories of Aryan supremacy.

It is important to remember that those who do not believe in the God of Jews and Christians have no religious or philosophical basis for dealing compassionately or even justly with other persons. It is only when we recognize God as Creator and Father and, as Christians recognize Jesus as Redeemer and Brother, that we can reach out to others as Jesus taught us to do in the Parable of the Good Samaritan. Many "naturally good" persons of other faiths are very kind to their neighbors, but their kindness comes from a sentiment or from rational ethics rather than from compelling laws given by the God to Whom we owe adoration and obedience. Sentiment and ethics can sink rapidly when one is in a leaking lifeboat with too many other people.

It is not hard for those of us who have good jobs, decent housing, good food, and ordinary pleasures to criticize the Germans who allowed Hitler to lead them into persecution of the Jews, but it is important to realize that people who are experiencing grinding hardship can easily be led into doing what they would never think of doing under different conditions. This is precisely the starting point of the Book of Job.

Most of us think of the theme of the Book of Job as the examination of how evil and misfortune permitted by God can enter the lives of good people. Job can be looked at, however, from another point of view: how people react when tested by misfortune. Do we rail at God and lash out at anyone we may think is in our way?

Some Germans stood firmly by their Christian principles, some even to the sacrifice of their lives in concentration camps. Others slipped little by little into acceptance of Nazi principles. It felt good to cheer victories.

More important was the fact that Hitler's elite troops, the SS, were inducted at occult ceremonies and trained in castles where they renounced Christianity and accepted induction into Hitler's special corps in pagan, even Satanic, rituals. Hitler admitted more than once to his close associates that he intended to replace Christianity in Germany and the territories he had conquered with his own religion, a restored, warlike paganism.

Conclusion

It seems an impertinence for any one person to attempt to summarize two movements, each of which is so destructive, not only of the victims of the respective movements, but also of those who embrace their ways of thinking, their philosophies. Both have wrought enormous damage in the world, bringing about millions of deaths, not only on the battlefield but in individual lynchings and in mass killings in concentration camps, or leveling whole villages with their inhabitants killed in the process.

It is important that we examine our thinking in this regard, because I am very sure that the majority of Germans in the early 1920s and the majority of Southerners immediately after the Civil War had no desire to hound anyone to death. But as any reader of detective stories can testify, the first killing is difficult, the next a little easier, and so on.

When, where, how does the drift into wrong action begin?

Who is my God and what is my relationship with my God?

Most of those who colonized the East Coast of what is now the United States honestly believed they were right, not only in their personal beliefs but also in the way they expressed those beliefs in their control of their fellow colonists and in their treatment of the Native Americans and the Africans whom they brought here. But their God was a God of heavy-handed justice. The passages of Scripture dealing with mercy and with love of neighbor were not taken to heart. Those who could beat former slaves until they died, those who could lynch blacks or northern Jews trying to aid blacks to gain the right to vote, failed to discern the emotions leading to pride and the desire for power, control of the weaker members of society, which led them into such destructive acts. Failure to "discern the spirits" which can lead us into acts directly against the laws of God is the first step into destruction of others, but really of ourselves.

Young people throughout the world have normal desires for success in whatever they may do in life. They (and not only young people) are easily swayed by appeals to emotions. Natural disasters and economic problems can weaken our commitment to the principles of true Christianity, and then emotions can be played on by clever leaders. The admonition of John is just as important today as it was in the first century:

> "Beloved, do not trust every spirit, but put the spirits to a test, to see if they belong to God, because many false prophets have appeared in the world. . . . We belong to God and anyone who has knowledge of God gives us a hearing, while anyone who is not of God refuses to hear us. Thus do we distinguish the spirit of truth from the spirit of deception" (1 John 4:1,6, NAB).

The Ku Klux Klan and Neo-Nazism: Suggested Reading

Readers may question the heavy emphasis on history in this bibliography. The emphasis was deliberate: to point to the *roots* of racism and religious prejudice rather than to recount current episodes which anyone can find in newspapers and in radio and television newscasts.

Blee, Kathleen M., *Women of the Klan, Racism and Gender in the 1920s*, Berkeley, Calif., University of California Press, 1991 [The author is associate professor of sociology at the University of Kentucky. Interviews with dedicated members of the Klan in the 1920s indicate women played a major role, using rumors, gossip, and boycotts to influence elections and to drive opponents out of business.]

Nelson, Jack, *Terror in the Night: The Klan's Campaign Against the Jews*, New York, Simon & Schuster, 1993. [The author is

Washington bureau chief for the *Los Angeles Times* and a close friend of former terrorist Tom Tarrants (see above and below).]

Randel, William Peirce, *The Ku Klux Klan, A Century of Infamy*, Philadelphia and New York, Chilton Books, 1965 [Probably one of the best in-depth studies of the beginnings of the Klan in general and particular activities of the Klan in representative southern States, with 29 pages of bibliographical notes, carefully compiled.]

Roper, John Herbert, *C. Vann Woodward, Southerner*, Athens, Ga. and London, The University of Georgia Press, 1987 [Professor Woodward's contributions to historical scholarship have contributed immensely to our understanding of racial prejudice in the United States, and occasionally in other parts of the world. "The Strange Career of Jim Crow," recounted in Chapter 7, may seem at first glance to be about a minor matter, long since corrected, but it shows how a half-hearted attempt to treat persons of another race justly can lead to very great injustice, not only in this country, but in South Africa, where our "separate but equal" laws were used as patterns and precedents for Apartheid.]

Silver, James W., *Mississippi, The Closed Society*, New York, Harcourt Brace, 1964 [*Mississippi, The Closed Society*, dealing with a particular time and feature of Mississippi history, happens to have been brought out on Monday, June 22, 1964, the day following the disappearance of the three civil rights workers, Chaney, Goodman, and Schwemer, near Philadelphia, Mississippi.]

Silver, James W., *Running Scared: Silver in Mississippi*, Jackson, Miss., University Press of Mississippi, 1984 [This is a biographical essay dealing with Professor Silver's life as a scholar at the University of Mississippi, which was compiled in self-defense against what he considered unjust termination of his position. It includes the three years of James Meredith's residence (1962-65), as well as accounts of incidents when Professor Silver's life appeared to have been in danger because of his position on the civil rights of blacks.]

Tarrants, Thomas A. III, *The Conversion of a Klansman, The Story of a Former Ku Klux Klan Terrorist*, Introduction by Leighton Ford, Garden City, New York, Doubleday and Company, 1979

Hitler, National Socialism [Nazism], and the Occult:
Angebert, Jean-Michel, *The Occult and the Third Reich*, transl. from
the French by Lewis A.M. Sumberg, New York, Macmillan, 1974
(French copyright, Editions Robert Laffont, S.A., 1971)
[Jean-Michel Angebert is the pseudonym of Michel Bertrand and
Jean Angelini. The original French title of this book is: *Hitler et la
tradition cathare*. This book may be hard to find in any except the
larger university libraries. . . . The ability of new paganism to
reaffirm itself militantly and contest with Christianity for men's
minds and bodies tells us that the Nazi nightmare is the most
recent but not the final act in a larger human tragedy that is still
being played out. It would be foolish to see the phenomenon as a
specifically 'German problem'; . . ." from the translator's preface,
p. xiii.]
Fredborg, Arvid, *Behind the Steel Wall, "A Swedish Journalist in
Berlin, 1941-43,"* New York, Viking Press, 1944 [See esp. p. 237:
"Hitler has tried to give the German people a new religion . . . by
keeping German youth away from the churches and giving them
something new to believe in. . . . German youth has been
inoculated with . . . nature-worship — a gospel of blood, power
and Germanism."]
Höhne (Hoehne), Heinz, *The Order of the Death's Head, "The Story
of Hitler's SS,"* transl. by Richard Barry, London, Secker and
Warburg, 1969 [See especially pp. 150ff for description of pagan
ceremonies of the SS at Wewelsburg.]
Sklar, D. (Dusty), *The Nazis and the Occult*, New York, Dorset
Press, 1989 [Originally published under the title of *Gods and
Beasts: The Nazis and the Occult*, Crowell Publishers, 1977.]
Suster, Gerald, *Hitler: The Occult Messiah*, New York, St. Martin's
Press, 1981
Tauber, Kurt P., *Beyond Eagle and Swastika, German Nationalism
Since 1945*, Middletown, Conn., Wesleyan University Press,
1967, 2 vols. [Vol.2 consists entirely of footnotes. Provides
background on Germany in 19th century, World War I, the Third
Reich, the Nuremberg Trials, the development of war veterans'
organizations, the "built-in ambiguity" of the Combat SS's
relationship with the rest of the SS, the continuation of nationalist
and National Socialist literature post-World War II. Limited,

however, in scope by listing only European organizations and personalities. Very detailed list of folklore and culture societies, many of which are fronts for neo-Nazi secret societies.]

Waite, Robert G.L., *The Psychopathic God, Adolf Hitler,* New York, Basic Books, Inc., 1977 [Note Appendix, pp. 427ff on spurious sources, incl. Reinhold Hanisch, Josef Greiner, Konrad Heiden, Brigid Dowling Hitler, sister-in-law, quoted by John Toland, and Kurt Krueger, reputed to have been Hitler's psychiatrist.]

On Puritan beliefs and attitudes as contributory to and formative of both American racism and religious bigotry and also of American abolitionism:

Billington, Ray Allen, *The Protestant Crusade, 1800-1860, A Study of the Origins of American Nativism,* originally published by The Macmillan Company, New York, 1938, reissued by Rinehart & Company, New York, 1952 [Classic study of anti-Catholicism and "nativism" prior to the Civil War.]

Cords, Nicholas, and Gerster, Patrick, *Myth and the American Experience,* 2 vols., New York, Harper Collins Publishers, Inc., 1991 [From the Preface: "The selected historical myths discussed and analyzed in this work can best be understood as a series of *false beliefs* about America's past. They are false beliefs, however, which have been accepted as true and acted upon as real. . . ."]

Cromwell, A Profile, edited by Ivan Roots, New York, Hill and Wang, 1973

Frank, Joseph, *The Levellers, A History of the Writings of Three Seventeenth-Century Social Democrats: John Lilburne, Richard Overton, William Walwyn,* New York, Russell and Russell, 1955 [The "Leveller" movement among English Protestants had a greater influence on the political and religious thought of America than its strength in English politics would lead one to expect.]

Fraser, Antonia, *Cromwell, The Lord Protector,* New York, Alfred A Knopf, 1973 [Considered a definitive study.]

Horsman, Reginald, *Race and Manifest Destiny, the Origins of American Anglo-Saxonism,* Cambridge, Mass., and London, England, Harvard University Press, 1981

Myers, Gustavus, *History of Bigotry in the United States,* New York,

Random House, 1943 [A detailed chronicle of manifestations of racial and religious intolerance compiled, fruit of seventeen years of research.]

O'Neill, James M., *Catholicism and American Freedom*, New York, Harper and Brothers, 1952 [This book primarily addresses the charges against Catholicism that it is repressive at its core and, therefore, anti-American, specifically Paul Blanshard's attacks. It contains a concise account of the history of anti-Catholicism in the United States. See Billington's for details.]

Tyler, Alice Felt, *Freedom's Ferment, Phases of American Social History to 1860*, Minneapolis, The University of Minnesota Press, 1944 [Part Three, Humanitarian Crusades, is especially important for the sections dealing with "Denials of Democratic Principles" and "Like a Firebell in the Night" and "A House Divided" dealing with the abolitionist sentiment and its opposition.]

Details about American constitutional history were drawn from many books, but in particular:

Bowen, Catherine Drinker, *Miracle at Philadelphia, The Story of the Constitutional Convention, May to September, 1787*, Boston, Little Brown and Company, 1966

Peterson, Merrill D., *Thomas Jefferson and the New Nation*, New York, Oxford University Press, 1970

9.

Infestation, Obsession, Possession

Father Lawrence J. Gesy

WHY do we include a chapter on "Infestation, Obsession, and Possession" in a book entitled *Today's Destructive Cults and Movements?*

At first glance that chapter title itself can be very upsetting. Obviously, none, not one, of those conditions is a "religious movement." Nevertheless, the chapter is included in this book, and could not properly be omitted, because some practices of destructive religious movements *can* pave the way for diabolical intervention — that is, the entry of Satan or demonic influence — in a person's life. *Notice*! I say "can." This does *not always* result from practices connected with destructive religious movements. It may not happen "often," but *it can happen*, and *it does happen* often enough that I would be failing in my priestly duty were I to omit this subject.

TV and radio news broadcasts, the daily papers, even friends and neighbors relating what they have heard "on the grapevine" remind us that almost incredible evil takes place in the world around us. A recent book, *When Bad Things Happen to Good People*, became a best seller almost overnight, not only because it is well-written, but also because the topic is one which touches everyone. It has been an issue with which some of the greatest minds in history have struggled for many centuries, probably as long as there have been human beings. It is, in fact, the central theme of the *Book of Job* in the Old Testament.

In the *Book of Job* we read that God allowed Job, a man of great faith well known for his goodness, to be tested by Satan. (In the *Book of Job*, the word "Satan," which means "adversary," is preceded by

175

the article, indicating that the word is used as a noun, but not as a *proper* noun, i.e. a name. Its meaning, however, is clarified by the preceding words of the verse:

"One day when the sons of God came to attend on Yahweh, among them came [the] Satan. . ." (Jb. 1:6).

What is especially interesting about this verse is the picture which it presents of God reigning over the universe, receiving His creatures as a king receives his subjects at a court. In many books of the Bible "sons of God" is a term used for invisible creatures with superhuman powers — that is, what we call angels, or the fallen angels we call devils or demons (reference: *The New Jerusalem Bible*, Doubleday, 1985). In the rest of the Book of Job which follows we see very clearly that Satan or "the adversary" is presented as a creature of God who, regardless of his power, is still and always only a creature, operating only by God's permission.

Job's faith remained firm in the midst of seemingly endless, crushing adversity. Without losing faith, Job raised many questions: If God is all good and all knowing, why is there so much misery, suffering, sickness, and pain in the world? Why do good things come to bad people, and, even more puzzling, why do bad things happen to good people?

We may be asked, what does the problem of good and evil have to do with a chapter on obsession and possession, beyond the fact that, if possession, as it is generally viewed, is an objective reality, it is undoubtedly a bad experience for the person concerned, as well as for the person's friends and family.

At this point we need to clarify the meaning of two words: bad and evil. "Bad" is an adjective which properly qualifies nouns referring to objects or events. Actually no object, anything created by God, can be bad, but it can be the occasion of something "bad" happening to persons, for example, a person who trips against a stone may fall, breaking a leg. The stone is not bad. The broken leg is "bad," i.e., painful, for the person. Neither the stone nor the broken leg can be called "evil." A knife is neither good nor bad. If it is used to cut meat or vegetables for persons eating a meal, it is good and is used for good. If it is used to threaten or to injure or to kill someone, the knife itself is still good, but the person using it is doing evil. "Evil," therefore, refers to morality, that is, to human acts.

An interesting event casts light on our examination of this subject. St. Thomas Aquinas was hard at work on his great compendium of theology, the *Summa Theologica*. St. Louis, King of France at that time (about 1269 or 1270), invited St. Thomas with some of his fellow Dominicans to dine with him. According to accounts of this event, St. Thomas went along but was still so absorbed in his thinking that during the meal he forgot where he was. Suddenly, he banged down his fist on the table, exclaiming: "That settles the Manichees!" Louis had such respect for St. Thomas as a Catholic thinker that he immediately sent for a secretary to take St. Thomas's dictation so that the good idea might not be lost. (This episode in the life of St. Thomas is recounted by all of his biographers, including Father Angelus Walz, O.P., *St. Thomas Aquinas*, Westminster, Md., The Newman Press, 1951, and G.K. Chesterton, *St. Thomas Aquinas — "The Dumb Ox,"* New York, Sheed and Ward, Inc., 1933).

How does this episode connect with the problem of good and evil?

St. Thomas Aquinas, in treating of questions about the existence and the nature of God, shows that most of the objections come either from problems presented by natural science, which may be the occasions of persons attempting to dispose the existence of God, or from the existence of evil in the world, which is used by persons who find it difficult to believe in an infinitely good God. Mani, the founder of the teachings which bear the name Manichaeism, was born in a region of Mesopotamia under Parthian (Persian) rule in A.D. 216. His parents were Christians, holding Christian beliefs strongly influenced by the teachings of John the Baptist. Moreover, Mesopotamia had been the home of Zoroaster. In the teachings of Mani we find both echoes of Christianity and echoes of Zoroaster's radical *dualism*, that is, that there are *two equal first principles, good and evil creators of the world* (Ormuzd and Ahriman), neither more powerful than the other.

Manichaeism, the teaching of Mani, was declared false by the Council of Nicea in 325 and by the Council of Constantinople in 381. The basis for these declarations that the teachings of Mani were heretical is found in the Epistle of St. Paul to the Colossians, 1:16:

"For in him were created all things in heaven and on earth, the visible and the invisible, whether thrones or dominions or principalities or powers; all things were created through him and for him."

True Christian teaching is that God alone is the Supreme Being, the Creator, who made all things good; that the devil, or Satan, is a creature of God, who chose to rebel against his Creator, but is, nevertheless, still only a creature who can function only by God's permission. Moreover, the Church has consistently taught that whatever evil has come into the world has come as the result of Adam, i.e., the first man, to whom God gave rulership over the world to rule it under God's Headship, abdicating that position to serve the devil. The Church also consistently teaches that Christ won the victory over Satan, over sin and death, by His passion, death, and resurrection, but each individual person can only participate in that victory over Satan by choosing to serve God. Father Corrado Balducci, called ". . . one of the world's most highly respected living demonologists," says:

> "Satan has been conquered, but his hatred and warfare against mankind still goes on. As Raponi observes: 'The victory of Jesus over his adversary is a radical victory, but it is not a total victory; it must be completed by the followers of Christ.'. . . The life of Christians is therefore a warfare against Satan. . ." (*The Devil, ". . .alive and active in our world"*, pp. 39-40).

The great problem for the Church in Europe in the twelfth and thirteenth centuries was that Manichaeism in the form of the religion of the Cathari or the Albigenses, as they were called, from the town in France which was their center, was spreading throughout the continent of Europe. St. Dominic founded the Order of Preachers, of which St. Thomas Aquinas was a member, more or less in response to the need to address that very issue.

Knowing that God is all good and all powerful, St. Thomas Aquinas was faced with the problem: If all that God made is good, what, then, is evil? It cannot be "a thing" because all *things* are good. The discovery which occasioned St. Thomas' table thumping was that *all things are good, but evil is the absence of that good which properly belongs in particular human acts.* Let's return to our example of the knife: using a knife to cut food makes distribution of portions easier, an obvious good; but a person who uses a knife to harm another takes from that other person some good to which that other person is entitled, health or even life itself.

Then, you may ask, but is not evil *some thing?* Analyze any action which appears evil to us. Whatever we call evil is a thought, words, or an action (more likely a series of actions), the result of which is a lessening of the good which should exist in a person, place, thing, or function.

Books dealing with morality generally treat only of ordinary morally good or evil actions. Everyone knows of temptations. Most temptations arise from within the person, from our tendencies to respond improperly to "the world" and to "the flesh," but some do come from "the devil." What we are concerned with here are not the everyday kind of temptations, nor those issues which are treated in ethics or in general moral theology. First Peter 5:9 states clearly that some temptations are of diabolical origin: "Be calm and vigilant, because your enemy the devil is prowling round like a roaring lion, looking for someone to eat." In the first centuries of the Christian era, with Christians who had professed their faith literally facing lions, that was surely a vivid word picture.

Evil and the Devil

It is possible to explain evil in philosophical terms, but the Church has consistently taught that the devil himself, called Satan, and the demons who are his followers, the legions of fallen angels, exist. Father Balducci says:

> ". . . From the Gospels we learn only the bare essentials: the fact that the devil exists, how he acts toward us, and how we should conduct ourselves in relation to him" (op. cit., Introduction, xviii).

Some modernists, if they accept the existence of a devil or Satan, see the devil as neither good nor evil but as a kind of cosmic force in the universe; others see the devil as a fabrication of the Church, intended to frighten people into changing their ways, so that belief in the devil is portrayed as medieval. Yet the signs of his presence are more and more evident.

According to Father Joseph Brennan, a counselor for victims of Satanic worship, writing in *The Priest* ("Satanic Worship and Possession: Truths and Myths," April 1992, p.38), there are more than nine thousand Satanic covens in the United States with more than one hundred fifty thousand members.

> "The devils still have an angelic nature because sin does not change the nature of the sinner. They are purely spiritual beings, but what a pure spirit is surpasses our understanding and imagination . . . an angel transcends every sense image; he exists in an entirely different sphere, where matter, space and time do not apply . . . those very elements that condition our human knowledge" (Balducci, op. cit., p. 15).

It is fatal and foolish to eliminate the devil from our thinking, the devil whom Jesus called the Father of Lies, since if we do so we shall end by believing the lie of the liar himself. Just as dangerous as denying the reality of the devil's existence is to blame the devil for everything which is attractive, seductive, and sinful, which thinking can be a way of removing personal responsibility for our actions. Another attitude toward the devil is often found among those who have a fundamentalist, simplistic faith, by which they sometimes feel moved or even required to cast out demons from other individuals, using the name of Jesus Christ.

It is easy to blame problems such as physical ailments or various forms of mental illness on the devil and his demons. I have met persons who were seriously frightened by a Christian with strongly fundamentalist beliefs who told them that some physical or emotional problem was caused by demon infestation when the problem really required a competent medical doctor, psychologist, counselor, or clergyman. A good example of this is epilepsy: in former times, anyone convulsing and foaming at the mouth was considered demon-possessed. Now we know that the condition of epilepsy can be treated and controlled by medication, even though it cannot be completely cured.

The Church requires that all possible medical and psychological causes of the behavior in question must be examined, and only after medical and psychological experts have declared that the behavioral symptoms cannot be explained by their sciences does the Church examine the possibility of obsession or possession. This is the way of prudence.

The Church and the Devil

Discussing the teachings of the New Testament on the devil, Monsignor Balducci writes:

> ". . . the designation most frequently used in the New Testament is the one that depicts the devil as an evildoer, for that is the whole purpose of his activity. He is the 'evil spirit,' and that name is used in Scripture, in the singular or in the plural, seventy-six times. The next name most frequently used — sixty three times — is the word 'demon,' and usually in the plural. It is a Greek word of uncertain origin, but it refers to the evil and malicious influence of the devils on the world, in contrast to the beneficent influence of the good angels. Next, the names 'Satan' and 'devil' are both found thirty-six times in the New Testament. The former name is the one preferred in the Old Testament; it comes from the Hebrew and it means adversary, persecutor, accuser, or slanderer. The word 'devil' is from the Greek verb meaning to separate or divide, since the devil tries to separate us from God. These are the four generic names most frequently used (211 times) in the New Testament to designate the fallen angels" (op. cit. p. 21).

It may be noticed that one name popularly used for the devil is not found in this list, "Lucifer." It is a popular term for the devil, but it is never used in that way in the Bible itself. The English word is derived from St. Jerome's translation of the Old Testament into Latin. In predicting the return to Jerusalem of the exiles from Babylon, Isaiah writes satirically of the death of the King of Babylon: "How did you come to fall from the heavens, Daystar ['Lucifer,' that is, 'light-bearer'], son of Dawn?" (*New Jerusalem Bible*, Is. 14:12). Daystar and Dawn were among the Canaanite divinities. In the New Testament references to Satan's "fall," e.g., Luke 10:18 and three references in Revelation 8:10, 9:1, and 12:9, quite different words are used.

Monsignor Balducci summarizes the New Testament teaching about the devil:

> *"The devil exists.* This is stated so frequently and so clearly that there cannot be the slightest doubt about the fact of the devil's existence.
> *"The devil is a personal being.* He is not an abstract concept but a real spiritual being with a personality of his own.
> *"The devil (or Satan) is not simply another word for sin.* St. John says: 'The devil is a sinner from the beginning' (I Jn. 3:8). He is therefore an entity distinct from sin, having his own proper existence and personality.
> *"Human beings are free to consent to the devil and to sin or not.* The Gospel message of redemption and salvation would make no sense at all if we were not endowed with free will. Thus, Jesus says: 'From the mind stem evil designs — murder, adulterous conduct, fornication, stealing, false witness, blasphemy' (Mt. 15:19), and St. James says: 'The tug and lure of his own passion tempt every man' (1:14).
> *"The devil, however, can exert influence on the sinner.* The sacred writers, and especially St. Paul, see sin for what it really is: a personal free choice of the individual person. Secondly, they were able to distinguish the degrees of culpability in relation to the influence that the devil can have on an individual" (Balducci, op. cit., p.40).

In the writings of the Church Fathers, the bishops and teachers who lived and preached in the first six centuries after Christ, we can see that they were faithful to the traditional teachings about the devil which they had received from the Apostles. Some contemporary cases of diabolical possession are reflected in their writings. Their primary concern, however, was the pastoral care of the people, instructing the faithful to avoid the devil's influence as a tempter to evil.

Many Councils of the Church confirmed the Church's belief in the existence of the devil: the first Council of Braga in Portugal (551-564), the Fourth Ecumenical Lateran Council (1215), the Ecumenical Council of Florence (1431-1437), the Council of Trent (1545-1563), and the Second Vatican Council (1962-1965). In the official documents of the Second Vatican Council, the devil is mentioned specifically 18 times, showing the consistency of the Church's belief about the devil from its very beginning.

Speaking to the people of our times, Pope Paul VI stated in a general audience on November 15, 1972:

> "One of the greatest needs (today) is defense from the evil which is called the Devil. . . . Do not let our answer surprise you as being over simple or even superstitious or unreal. This evil is not merely the lack of something but an effective agent, a living spiritual being, perverted and perverting, a terrible reality. It is contrary to the teaching of the Bible and the Church to refuse to recognize the existence of such a reality . . . or to explain it as a pseudoreality, a conceptual and fanciful personification of the unknown causes of our misfortunes . . . that it is not a question of one devil, but of many, is indicated in various passages in the Gospel. But the principal one is Satan, . . . the Adversary, the enemy, and with him, many, all creatures of God, but fallen . . . A whole mysterious world . . . of which we know very little. The question of the devil is a very important chapter in the Catholic doctrine which is given little attention today, though it should be studied again" (L'Osservatore Romano, English Edition, Vatican City, Nov. 13, 1972).

In his address, Pope Paul VI gave two good reasons to speak of the devil: a trend in theology to deny the existence of the devil and the widening of the evidence of Satan working in the modern world.

Pope John Paul II has also spoken many times about the devil. Some of his statements are reprinted in Appendix V at the end of this book.

* * * * *

We can read in the Gospel how Jesus is accused of casting out Beelzebul, the prince of demons, by the power of Satan (Mt. 12:22-37, Mk. 3:22-30, Lk. 11:14-23, 12:10). Jesus replies to the accusation:

> "Every kingdom divided against itself will be laid waste, and no town or house divided against itself will stand. . . . How can anyone enter a

strong man's house and steal his property, unless he first ties up the strong man? Then he can plunder his house" (Mt. 12:25, 29).

If we look at the architecture of some ancient Palestinian houses, we will see a square of rooms surrounding an inner courtyard. From the road, access to such a house is gained through a massive gate/door which leads to the central courtyard through a corridor-like passageway between two of the rooms. Except for sleeping, the household lives, works, and plays in the courtyard. (See illustration.) This design protected families from unfriendly strangers or marauders. For an enemy to gain control of the household, he had first to enter, by permission or by breaking down the massive gate/door, then to enter the corridor, and finally to enter the courtyard. Once in the courtyard, he would have access to the surrounding rooms and to their residents. The European castles of the Middle Ages with which we are more familiar from history and from fiction were simply a later development or improvement on this design.

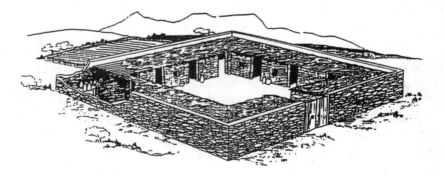

I will be using this model of a Palestinian house to explain temptation, infestation, obsession, and possession.

Temptation

Absolutely no one is exempt from temptation, and at no stage of life is anyone without temptation, although the manner and kind of temptation may change at different periods of our lives, as our interests and circumstances change. Jesus, the God-man, consented to be tempted as a step toward His final victory over Satan on the cross, to show His solidarity with us, His human brothers and sisters, and also to show us how to overcome temptations. In the Letter to the Hebrews (4:15) we read of Jesus:

> "For we do not have a high priest who is unable to sympathize with our weaknesses, but one who has similarly been tested in every way, yet without sin. . . ."

Temptations come to us in many ways, traditionally we say "from the world, from the flesh, and from the devil." Nevertheless, many, probably most, temptations come from within ourselves. Speaking of temptation, St. James (1:12-14) tells us:

> "Blessed is the man who perseveres in temptation [or 'trials' which the footnote gives as an alternate translation] for when he has been proved he will receive the crown of life that he [Christ] promised to those who love him. No one experiencing temptation should say, 'I am being tempted by God '; . . . he himself tempts no one. Rather, each person is tempted when he is lured and enticed by his own desire. . . ."

St. Paul gives additional insight into temptations or trials, after writing to the Corinthians about the overconfidence of the children of Israel whom God had brought out of Egypt with Moses. They had been released from slavery through a series of miraculous events, yet many desired some of the things which they had had in Egypt, and some grumbled about the food and water which they were receiving from God. St. Paul writes (1 Cor. 10:5-13, NAB):

> "Yet God was not pleased with most of them, for they were struck down in the desert.
> "These things happened as examples for us, so that we might not desire evil things, as they did. And do not become idolaters, as some of them did. . . . Let us not indulge in immorality as some of them did. . . Let us not test [the Lord] as some of them did. . . Do not grumble as some of them did. . . These things happened to them as an example, and they have been written down as a warning to us, . . . whoever thinks he is standing secure should take care not to fall. No trial has come to you

but what is human. God is faithful and will not let you be tried beyond your strength; but with the trial he will also provide a way out, so that you may be able to bear it."

The world around us also contributes to provide us with temptations, but the things of the world become sources of temptation only when they fit in with some desire in ourselves. One woman with a quick temper may "fly off the handle" when one of her children asks "Why?" for the third time, while a more placid woman might take little notice of that yet find it easy to spend more than she should on an especially pretty dress, or another person might be inclined to envy the better salary and more expensive car of a co-worker.

"The flesh" in the form of our own inclinations and desires can provide us with more than sufficient temptations, "the world" enticing us according to those inclinations, so let us not attribute too great a part to the devil while our own appetites can draw us away from God's will without much, if any, additional "help." Usually it serves no purpose to examine whether our temptations come from the devil or from our ordinary tendencies and from the influence or attraction of some persons, places, or things in our surroundings.

The Church recognizes, however, that some temptations can come directly from the action of the devil, while some seemingly ordinary temptations can come our way with a little help from the devil. So we need to pay attention to the words of St. Peter:

> "Be sober and vigilant. Your opponent the devil is prowling around like a roaring lion looking for [someone] to devour. Resist him, steadfast in faith, knowing that your fellow believers throughout the world undergo the same suffering" (1 Pt. 5:8-9).

Infestation and/or Obsession

Keeping in mind the picture of the Palestinian house as we begin to examine temptation, infestation/obsession, and possession, a few remarks from Rev. Adolph Rodewyk, S.J. may be helpful:

> "To understand what happens in such cases, we should define what is meant by the concepts of 'possession' and 'obsession' in their specific religiotheological meaning. Both words have Latin origins that

compare them to a city being attacked by an enemy. *Possessio* means that the enemy, in this case the Devil, has conquered the city and is in control of it from its internal strongholds; *obsessio* means that the enemy has the city under siege and is able, by external assaults, to create severe disturbances and chaos within the city" (*Possessed by Satan, The Church's teaching on the devil, possession, and exorcism*, New York, Doubleday & Company, Inc., 1975, p. 179).

Adolph Rodewyk, a German Jesuit, is an international authority on the phenomena of demonic possession. After his theological studies, he was rector of a school, and then during World War II was a hospital chaplain.

One of the major difficulties in dealing with this topic is that theologians do not always agree about the terms we shall be using. What we mean by "temptation" at one end of the scale and "possession" at the other end is comparatively clear. The terms "infestation" and "obsession" are applied to intermediate conditions. Father Rodewyk explains that using the two terms "obsession" and "possession" to distinguish two phases of diabolical activity began only during the eighteenth century, so there is some excuse for the fact that the terminology is still in flux, as Monsignor Balducci states:

"There is no uniformity among theologians as regards the terms used to describe the various types of diabolical activity. Many authors restrict the word 'infestation' to diabolical activity on a given place or locality, and use such terms as 'obsession' and 'possession' to designate the devil's influence on human beings. In English, the terms used are 'diabolical temptation,' 'local infestation,' 'obsession and possession.' "The phrase 'personal infestation' seems to be more accurate than 'obsession,' however, because the latter term has a personal and subjective connotation, as when the psychiatrist speaks of an 'obsessive idea' or simply an obsession. But when we speak of diabolical influence on a person, we are referring primarily to the devil as the agent of that particular activity; . . . For that reason we prefer to use the division into diabolical temptation, local infestation, personal infestation (what others call diabolical obsession), and diabolical possession" (Balducci, op. cit. p. 94).

Rodewyk acknowledges that modern psychology "uses 'obsession' for a neurotic condition in which there is emotional overinvolvement with an act or idea; . ." (Rodewyk, op.cit. p. 179).

Nevertheless, this author continues to use the word "obsession." Making due allowance for the differences of opinion about terms, let us examine some of these activities of the devil.

1) Monsignor Balducci passes briefly over what he terms "local diabolical infestation," quoting the parapsychologist S. Conti:

> ". . . a mysterious phenomenon that occurs over a period of time in a specific place or locality, whether inhabited or uninhabited. It can be recognized by the strange and sometimes frightening manifestations that indicate a diabolical presence: sounds and noises whose origin and nature cannot be explained; the sound of footsteps; groans or screams; bursts of laughter; sudden movements of objects; pleasant or unpleasant odors; gusts of cold air when there is no wind; the appearance of ghostly figures" (Balducci, op. cit. pp. 109-110).

It is interesting to note that these phenomena are precisely the kind which are attributed to poltergeist (German for "noisy spirit") activity by many investigators of occult phenomena and also by the Rev. Herbert Thurston, S.J. (1856-1939), who became something of an expert on the subject. In the Preface to *Ghosts and Poltergeists*, a collection of his articles on the subject (edited by J. H. Crehan, S.J., published in London, Burns Oates, 1953), Thurston is quoted:

> "That there may be something diabolical, or at any rate evil, in them I do not deny, but, on the other hand, it is also possible that there may be natural forces involved which are so far as little known to us as the latent forces of electricity were known to the Greeks. It is possibly the complication of these two elements which forms the heart of the mystery" (op. cit., p. vi).

In an appendix to that collection of Thurston's articles on poltergeist phenomena is his article dealing with the matter of exorcism for such. He says that for a long time he thought that the

Church had never made provision for such infestation of places or things except for the customary blessings of houses, of fields, etc. In the solemn consecration of a church and the solemn blessing of a graveyard, the ceremonies begin with what could be called a form of exorcism, since the site is sprinkled with holy water, which has been blessed with the express intention to banish the powers of darkness from whatever it touches.

No specific ritual, however, had been found for putting an end to what could be called the minor annoyance of poltergeist activity until, at last, Father Thurston stumbled upon a document in an appendix to an edition of the *Rituale Romanum*, published in Madrid in 1631, with the heading "The exorcism of a house troubled with an evil spirit" (op. cit. pp. 204-208).

This is, admittedly, a very minor bypath in the topic under consideration, but it needed to be addressed, if only briefly.

The primary purpose of exorcism, however, is to free *persons* who are afflicted.

2) Personal infestation, Monsignor Balducci's term, or diabolical obsession

> ". . . occurs when the devil focuses his power on a person in order to gain control of the individual. But it never reaches the point of a total invasion of the individual, as happens in diabolical possession . . . the devil's activity is extrinsic to the person; it does not impair the use of reason and free will. Nevertheless, the devil attacks the individual in a manner that is so intense and sensible that there can be no doubt of his presence and activity. . . . Although it is an extraordinary diabolical activity and therefore a rare phenomenon, it is nevertheless more frequent than local infestation or diabolical possession" (op. cit. p. 110).

Sometimes it is difficult to determine where simple temptation ends and true obsession begins. Through external obsession the evil spirit acts on the person's senses; it is, therefore a diabolical action extrinsic to the person who suffers it. Rarely, however, is obsession only external, since the devil is intent on disturbing the person's peace of soul. In obsession, the person is aware of his or her own vital activities (which is not true of persons who are possessed), but also clearly aware of the presence and activity of Satan, who uses incredible violence on the person's internal faculties, especially the imagination, attempting to lead the soul to evil.

To express this condition in terms of the Palestinian house, the enemy, the devil, has broken the gate and is trying to reach the inner courtyard; the battle is being fought, not in the house itself, but in its entrance hall: in the case of persons, our senses and their internal counterpart, our imagination or feelings, inexplicable emotions of anger, sentimental love, despair, seductive scenes in the imagination to allure the person to sin, or very frightening scenes, sudden severe pain for no apparent reason.

Can I become obsessed or personally infested? Any discussion of this subject is sure to bring forth such a question.

The answer is: Most likely not. The devil is generally content to persecute ordinary folks with ordinary temptations. Both Monsignor Balducci and Father Jordan Aumann agree that obsession or personal infestation is more likely to happen to "souls that are far advanced in virtue." (Jordan Aumann, O.P., *Spiritual Theology*, Westminster, Md., Christian Classics, 1987, p. 406) In fact, many of the Saints have suffered from severe diabolical attacks, including the Curé of Ars, St. Jean Vianney. Balducci states:

> "The purpose of the diabolical activity is to attack by every means possible their goodness, fidelity, and love of God. . . . With God's permission, the devil may wage a vendetta against them, but it can all be turned to good use by way of expiation, propitiation, and merit" (op. cit. pp.111-112).

Possession

In the case of demonic possession, the enemy, the devil, has entered the central courtyard of the house, from which he can control the entire household from within; he can govern it like a despot.

While it is usually holy people who suffer obsession or personal infestation, possession is suffered by some innocent people for reasons which are not always clear, but more commonly it results from a person dabbling in the occult or even from deliberately giving oneself to the devil. Nevertheless, during possession, the person is not aware of his or her actions, and is, therefore, not responsible for those actions, however outrageous or wicked they may be. The person would be responsible for the initial action or actions which put him- or herself under the control of the devil.

Why does God permit persons to become possessed? Monsignor Balducci gives five reasons.

Divine providence, restricting and controlling the devil's activity, even in possession, so that he can do only what God allows; the goodness of God, who gives the Church and her ministers power over the evil spirits; the justice of God, allowing sinners who have given themselves to evil to suffer in this world where they can be helped and so come to repentance; God's wisdom, which brings good out of evil; all of these show forth God's glory.

The Church Fathers and contemporary missionaries state that the power of exorcism to release persons from the power of the devil through exorcism is strong evidence for the Christian faith.

Another reason why God permits the devil to take possession of a person is the spiritual benefit of the individual. Bearing this trial with resignation to God's will develops the virtues of patience, humility, and love of God, increasing that person's merit, while suffering enables the person to atone for past sins.

Those who witness diabolical possession and exorcism, if they are Christians, are generally moved to examine their own lives and to turn more fervently to God. Unbelievers are generally moved to admit the existence of spiritual reality and to examine their belief systems, even to turn to religion as a result of their experience.

Finally, the words of St. Paul regarding a scandalous sinner of Corinth may shed light on another reason why God allows possession, that God permits the evil spirit to afflict a serious sinner in this life so that he or she may be converted before dying in sin. This would seem to be a strange act of God's mercy, but only if we think according to the standards of this world:

> "I hand him over to Satan for the destruction of his flesh, so that his spirit may be saved on the day of the Lord" (1 Cor. 5:5).

What Can Bring About Infestation/Obsession and Possession?

Anyone who dabbles in the occult: using ouija boards, tarot cards, taking part in fortune telling, séances, channeling, invoking or inviting spirits (spirits of the dead or any other spirits) is opening an entry point through which evil spirits can enter oneself.

Some patterns of behavior such as repeated, unrepented, serious sins, such as consenting to feelings of or expressing that consent in acts of pride, envy, anger (particularly if one wishes harm to another), lust, or uncontrolled sexual activity can open a person to Satanic activity. When a person continually chooses to act contrary to God's express will (the Commandments, for example), one has crossed over into the devil's territory.

Finally, wounded human emotions can mislead a person into believing that he or she is being victimized by evil spirits. Repeated hurts, physical or sexual abuse, low self-esteem, fear — such conditions call for loving care, counseling, and particularly for the kind of counseling which leads the person to a healthy search for God through spiritual discipline in the teaching and prayer life and loving community of the Church, away from any morbid search through the underbrush of the occult.

Some Cautions

Recently some charismatic prayer groups have conducted seminars on demonic deliverance for lay persons. This "deliverance ministry" emphasizes casting out evil spirits by rebuking them in the name of Jesus Christ. Some disturbed persons have become hysterical as demons were supposedly cast out. Serious damage can be done to a fragile psyche by such a ministry.

The Catholic Church has always exercised extreme caution through a most careful testing and discernment process before judging that a person is obsessed or possessed. Only a priest exorcist appointed by the bishop has the authority to cast out the demonic by the rite of exorcism. The bishop gives such authority only after all possible medical and psychological causes for the possible demonic activity have been eliminated. No one should undertake the use of the rite of exorcism or attempt an actual exorcism on one's own authority.

Anyone, however, may pray for persons who are suffering from what seems to be demonic interference to be delivered from that by God's merciful power. Prayer for God's help is not a formal "casting out." The person suffering and the sufferer's friends should pray, as we are told, "without ceasing." The prayer should take the form of praise of God's power and infinite goodness, thanks for His mercy, repentance for sins, and petitions for perseverance and final release.

But Do We Still Believe in Satan and Demons?

Before leaving this topic, it is important to call to the attention of our readers that the liturgical changes implemented after the second Vatican Council included the omission of the prayers which we formerly recited at the end of "Low Mass" by order of Pope Leo XIII, which included a prayer to the Archangel Michael. The purpose of the omission of these prayers was, however, to cast clearer light on the liturgical action of the Mass and in no way indicated any lessening of belief in the reality of angels and/or demons on the part of the Council Fathers. Proof of this can be found, if it should be needed, in some of the Vatican Council II documents:

"In order to establish a relationship of peace and communion with himself, and in order to bring about brotherly union among men, and they sinners, God decided to enter into the history of mankind in human history in a new and definitive manner, by sending his own Son in human flesh, so that through him he might snatch men from the power of darkness and of Satan (cf. Col. 1:13; Acts 10:38) and in him reconcile the world to himself" (*Ad Gentes, Decree on the Missionary Activity of the Church*, #3)

[With reference to the catechumenate and the reception of the sacraments of initiation] ". . . having been freed from the powers of darkness by the sacraments of Christian initiation (cf. Col. 1:13). . ." (ibid. #14; see also footnote to this text #5: "On this deliverance from the slavery of the devil and of darkness in the Gospel, cf. Mt. 12:28; Jn. 8:44; 12:31. Cf. I Jn. 3:8; Eph. 2:1-2. On the Liturgy of Baptism, cf. Roman Ritual).

". . . man's swelling power at the present time threatens to put an end to the human race itself.

"The whole of man's history has been the story of dour combat with the powers of evil, stretching, so the Lord tells us, from the very dawn of history until the last day [footnote: Cf. Mt. 24:13; 13:24-30 and 36-43]. Finding himself in the midst of the battlefield man has to struggle to do what is right, and it is at great cost to himself, and aided by God's grace, that he succeeds in achieving his own inner integrity" (*Gaudium et spes, The Pastoral Constitution on the Church in the Modern World*, #37).

"The miracles of Jesus also demonstrate that the kingdom has already come on earth: 'If I cast out devils by the finger of God, then the kingdom of God has come upon you' (Lk. 11:20, cf. Mt. 12:28)" (*Lumen Gentium, Pastoral Constitution on the Church*, #5).

"They [the faithful, the laity] show themselves to be the children of the promise, if, strong in faith and in hope, they make the most of the present time (Eph. 5:16; Col. 4:5), and with patience await the future glory (cf. Rom. 8:25). Let them not hide this their hope then, in the depths of their hearts, but rather express it through the structure of their secular lives in continual conversion and in wrestling 'against the world rulers of this darkness, against the spiritual forces of iniquity' (Eph. 6:12)" (ibid. #35).

". . . though we have not yet appeared with Christ in glory (cf. Col. 3:4), in which we shall be like to God, for we shall see him as he is (cf. I Jn. 3:2), 'while we are at home in the body we are away from the Lord' (2 Cor. 5:6) and having the firstfruits of the Spirit we groan inwardly (cf. Rom. 8:23) and we desire to be with Christ (cf. Phil. 1:23). That same charity urges us to live more for him who died for us and who rose again (cf. 2 Cor. 5:15). We make it our aim, then, to please the Lord in all things (cf. 2 Cor. 5:9) and we put on the armor of God that we may be able to stand against the wiles of the devil and resist on the evil day (cf. Eph. 6:11-13)" (ibid. #48).

It is very clear from these quotations from the documents of the second Vatican Council that the traditional teaching about the activity of the devil or Satan in the lives of Christians, attempting to lead them away from God, was strongly reiterated.

Postconciliar documents also restate this constant teaching.

". . . when speaking recently of evil as this 'terrible reality, mysterious and frightening,' His Holiness Paul VI could assert with authority: 'It is a departure from the picture provided by biblical and Church teaching to refuse to acknowledge the Devil's existence; to regard him as a sustaining principle who, unlike other creatures, does not owe his origin to God; or to explain the Devil as a pseudo-reality, a conceptual and fanciful personification of the unknown causes of our misfortunes' (address to a general audience, Nov. 15, 1972). Exegetes and theologians should not be deaf to this warning" (*Christian Faith and Demonology*, a paper commissioned by the Sacred Congregation for the Doctrine of the Faith, June 26, 1975, English translation courtesy of *The Pope Speaks*).

Similar statements can be found scattered throughout other speeches of Pope Paul II and the speeches and writings of Pope John Paul II.

In regard to the words of the popes and of the ecumenical councils, there is an interesting incident related in the Gospel of St. Luke (10:1-20).

In the opening verse of Chapter 10, Jesus is shown appointing seventy-two disciples and sending them on ahead into the towns and places He intended to visit, giving them directions for what might be called their apprenticeship as missionaries. They were to take whatever shelter, food, and drink would be offered to them, saying "Peace be to this house." They were to cure the sick and to say "The kingdom of God is very near to you." In the Gospel of St. Matthew, the Apostles sent out on similar journeys are told also to raise the dead, to cleanse lepers, and to cast out devils (Mt. 10:8). The words of Jesus, as He sends out His disciples, can apply to us with regard to the teachings of the Church: "Anyone who listens to you listens to me; anyone who rejects you rejects me, and those who reject me reject the one who sent me" (Lk. 10:16)

The power of their faith in Jesus and their obedience in faith is shown when the disciples returned to Jesus rejoicing, saying, "Lord . . . even the devils submit to us when we use your name." Jesus replied, "I watched Satan fall like lightening from heaven. . . . Yet do not rejoice that the spirits submit to you; rejoice rather that your names are written in heaven" (Lk. 10:17, 18, 20).

Infestation, Obsession, Possession: Suggested Reading

In a certain sense, this bibliography supplements and continues the bibliography on Satanism, below in Chapter 11. While that chapter deals with the cult of devil worship, this chapter is concerned with the possible effects of diabolical attacks of greater or lesser severity on persons who usually are not inclined to worship the devil, although some may have dabbled in various cultic practices. For this reason, although the basic bibliography on Satan and Satanism is not repeated here, it is presupposed and a prerequisite for understanding and using the books listed here.

Balducci, Corrado, *The Devil ". . .alive and active in our world,"* New York, Alba House, 1990 (Preface by Cardinal John J. O'Connor) [Deals with the tradition and theology of the devil, "Does the devil exist?", the question of diabolical possession, diabolical presence and activity, "Diagnosis of extraordinary diabolical activity," and finally preventive therapy, i.e., prayer, reception of the sacraments, curative therapy (i.e., exorcism), and practical suggestions.]

Bruno de Jésus-Marie, O.C.D. (editor): *Satan*, London and New York, Sheed and Ward 1951 [A collection of essays by authoritative writers, full references.] *Soundings in Satanism* (F.J. Sheed, editor), London and Oxford, Mowbray's, 1972 [A new edition of the above, one third the length of the earlier book, and "not about Satan but about Satanism." It contains two essays pertinent to obsession and possession: one by Jean Vinchon and one by Jean Lhermitte, as well as an essay by F.X. Marquart with a postscript by Joseph de Tonquédec.]

Corte, Nicolas (pseudonym of Msgr. Leon Cristiani), *Who Is the Devil?* (transl. by D.K. Pryce), New York, Hawthorn Books, 1958

Cristiani, Msgr. Leon, *Evidence of Satan in the Modern World,* New York, Macmillan, 1962 [Careful documentation of the continuing presence of diabolical infestation and possession in the modern world and the influence of Satanic temptation in society.]

Harris, Charles, C.S.C., *Resist the Devil, A Pastoral Guide to Deliverance Prayer*, South Bend, Ind., Greenlawn Press, 1988 [Clearly distinguishes between psychiatric disorders and diabolical activity.]

Lhermitte, Jean, *True and False Possession*, New York, Hawthorn Books, 1963 [The author is a neurologist and a member of the French Académie Nationale de Médecine.]

Rodewyk, Adolf, S.J., *Possessed by Satan, The Church's Teaching*

on the Devil, Possession, and Exorcism, Garden City, N.Y.,
  Doubleday & Company, Inc., 1975
Thurston, Herbert, S.J., *The Physical Phenomena of Mysticism*,
  London, Burns & Oates, 1951 [This book includes data pertaining
  to mystical phenomena of apparent divine origin as well as
  counterfeit phenomena of diabolical origin and also similar
  phenomena caused by psychic disorders.]
Volken, Laurent, *Visions, Revelations, and the Church*, New York,
  P.J. Kenedy & Sons, 1963 [The author has served as professor of
  theology at Tournai and as rector of the LaSalette Seminary in
  Fribourg and in Rome, as well as president for the section on
  Protestantism of the international ecumenical association *Unitas*.
  He shows how the findings of psychiatry supplement the wisdom
  of theology.]
Wiesinger, Alois, O.C.S.O., *Occult Phenomena in the Light of
  Theology*, Westminster, Md., The Newman Press, 1957 [Excellent
  analysis of various phenomena from the viewpoint of theology
  and psychology, more analytical than Thurston's book, the style
  of which is more narrative history.]

NOTE: It is important to emphasize that there are numerous books
on possession and exorcism available on the shelves of secular stores
selling both new and used books. I have not listed any of them. All
of the books listed above are by accepted theologians and/or
exorcists who work or who have worked with the approval of their
bishops. Any other books show varying degrees of accuracy, with
serious lacunae, and their authors often show a too avid interest in
the bizarre, with the resulting warp in their treatment of the subject.

10.

Witchcraft

Donald H. Thompson

Witchcraft, is it real?

WE have the right (and we owe it to ourselves) to ask: is witchcraft real? But before we can answer that question, the question itself must be broken up into three questions:

1. Does the person who practices the occult rituals that are called "witchcraft" believe that he/she has the power to affect/move/change the people and the world around us by means of these rituals? — that is, is witchcraft "real" to the practicing witch?

2. Do the people who consult a witch believe that the witch can effect changes in persons or in events through the practice of "the craft"? — that is, is witchcraft "real" to its clientele?

3. Regardless of the belief of the witch or of the client, can the rituals of witchcraft affect things or people for good or ill? — that is, is witchcraft a "fact"?

The law makes clear, as we shall see when we skim superficially over a very short history of witchcraft in Western Europe, that some of what appears to be the practice of witchcraft is simply fraud: for example, people who are very clever at discerning areas of concern in the lives of others using cards or crystal balls or dates of birth around which to build histories of past events and "predictions" of the future. In some such cases, the apparent witch may have a modicum of belief in the ancient gods or the spirits of the dead, but mingled with a cynical dependence on the greater or lesser belief in those powers as well as curiosity on the part of the one who seeks answers.

As we look at the history of witchcraft, we shall discover that these questions are not at all exclusive to our generation, but they are questions which demand careful examination and thought.

What Is Witchcraft?

Not all witches are old hags, nor are they young, beautiful fairy-tale damsels, nor are they exclusively female, nor do they meet in remote woods.

Expressing the beliefs of some modern witches, Lady Olwen made this statement to a British newspaper in 1979: "We are celebrating life. . . . We believe in two major forces in life, one male, the other female, and we worship these forces as a god and a goddess" (from Eric Ericson, *The World, the Flesh, the Devil: A Biographical Dictionary of Witches*, New York, Mayflower Books, 1981, p. 8).

Witchcraft as a belief system encompasses a magical view of the world. It is avowedly *non-*, not *anti-*, Christian, according to those who express belief in witchcraft in our period of history. But is it a religion?

Ancient societies, for example, did not distinguish, as does the modern world, between astronomy (the science) and astrology (the belief that human affairs are influenced, even controlled, by the stars), nor did ancient society distinguish between the stars as real, material things and the stars as gods, goddesses, or heroes raised to some preternatural form of existence.

> "The essence of the magical world view is belief in a homocentric universe . . . all things — stars, herbs, stones, metals, planets, the elements and elementals — mesh with man, his longings, his lusts, his desires, his fears, and even his physical appearance and health. Each natural object and natural phenomenon has a direct influence upon some aspect of man's body or psyche, and man's actions can in turn affect the elements" (Jeffrey Burton Russell, *Witchcraft in the Middle Ages*, Ithaca, N.Y., Cornell University Press, 1972, p. 5).

The distinction made in contemporary witchcraft between "white" and "black" magic ". . . is the creation of modern writers, mainly occultist, and seldom appears in the history of world magic." writes Russell (ibid. p. 6). He distinguishes between "high" magic, an attempt to understand and ultimately to control the universe through occult knowledge, and "low" magic, which is an attempt to obtain immediate effects in the practical order, e.g., to cause rain or to harm crops, to influence a lover in one's favor or to harm a rival. In brief: magic (centered on self) attempts to possess or to control or to compel the world in which we live; while science (religiously neutral) attempts to understand the world around us, whether that understanding will enable us to manage our surroundings better for our own use or according to the will of God; and religion (pagan, Judeo-Christian, Islamic, or Oriental) responds to the ultimate power in an attitude of trust, submission, supplication.

> "Magic is traditional and science, experimental; magic seeks to control and science, to learn: explanations in science are material as opposed to spiritual, for magic often calls in supernatural forces" (Russell, op. cit., p. 12).

European witchcraft is very similar to the shamanism (or the way of the shaman) of the people of the Arctic, the people of northern Asia, and the so-called "medicine men" of Amerindian tribes. Jeffrey Burton Russell (op. cit., pp. 13-15) lists over fifty motifs found in the folklore of other societies which are very similar to the folklore relating to European witchcraft, some of which are: strange weather patterns attributed to witches, witches changing themselves into animals, certain animals considered pets or "familiars" of witches (such as crows or black cats, lizards, toads, frogs, and owls), the color black as special to witches (also green, the color of fairies in Britain, as in the old song "Greensleaves"), the evil eye, reincarnation, the reported ability of witches to become invisible or to travel by "flying" by night (magic wands are common to the notion of magic in all societies, but riding on sticks seems to be mainly European).

Sorcery, the power to cast spells through the aid of evil spirits, is neither the same as witchcraft, although it is part of "black" magic, but in literature about witchcraft the two words are often used as synonyms. Sortilege is another word which appears somewhat similar, but it means casting lots, fortune telling by means of dice or cards. All attempts to foresee the future or to learn what is happening at a distance by means of crystal balls, cards (regular playing cards or the Tarot deck), numerology, palmistry, astrology, are called "divination" in Holy Scripture, i.e. a kind of "playing God," and are explicitly forbidden since they violate the first Commandment.

Is There a Link Between Witchcraft and Satanism?

When we think about witchcraft today, most Americans think of the trials in Salem, Massachusetts, in 1692, during which thirty-one persons were tried for witchcraft, twenty of those convicted were hung (not burned at the stake, by the way), and two others died in prison.

In 1603, the learned King James VI of Scotland, who had authored a book, *Daemonologie*, printed in Edinburgh in 1597, succeeded Queen Elizabeth to the throne of England as James I. In the following year, 1604, King James I convened a conference to prepare for a new translation of the Bible into English, which ultimately issued in 1611 that translation now known as the "Authorized Version." In that same year of 1604, in response to the demand of King James I, a comprehensive act against witchcraft was passed, making the practice of witchcraft a capital crime, whether or not the witch could be shown to have harmed anyone.

The judges who sentenced the reputed witches of Salem to death or imprisonment, and the people of Salem, Massachusetts, who joined their religious leaders in denouncing witchcraft, really believed that the practice of witchcraft was a serious sin and a crime against the good order of the community. They were complying with the intention and the express law promulgated by King James I, and England was not alone in prosecuting witches and the practice of witchcraft. In the sixteenth and seventeenth centuries, most of the continental European countries also had strong laws against witchcraft.

What connection can we make between the obvious zeal for religion of James I and the equally evident zeal to prosecute witchcraft?

In the early Middle Ages, benevolent traditional healers, persons who knew which herbs would cure various ills, were often overlooked by the Church. In theory, however, since medicine as a science had not as yet developed out of herbalism, many clergy viewed "herb women" as attempting to control supernatural forces, and since neither God nor the good angels are subject to control, the forces (sometimes actually invoked by the "healer") must be demonic. Therefore there was no "good" magic.

(It is important to note that most homeopathic herbalists, known today as "herb ladies" or "granny witches" in some parts of the United States, are more often Christian than not but are simply trying to use their knowledge of local plants to help their neighbors. Some, however, use "poems" or "prayers" the meaning of which they do not know, but which have been "passed down in the family," perhaps by a grandmother or aunt or uncle who may not know the origin of the words of power which may be centuries old.)

Since many of the persons practicing various forms of traditional "magic" in the Middle Ages were holding on to pre-Christian beliefs, in spite of the presence of Christianity in their locality, in the High Middle Ages many of the witches questioned did not hesitate to say that they were adherents of the devil.

It is this process of reasoning, including the testimony of many witches themselves, together with biblical strictures against "divination" (fortune telling), astrology, or calling on spirits, which brought about the condemnation of witches as Satanists in the twelfth through seventeenth centuries.

In addition to this kind of reasoning, however, there was a kind of fear of anyone practicing witchcraft, stemming partly from the secrecy involved, partly from lack of understanding of exactly *how* the so-called magic "worked," and partly from the fact that pre-Christian societies in Europe, whether Celtic or Teutonic, practiced some form of human sacrifice.

In this period at the end of the Middle Ages, however, some persons, both Catholic and Protestant, began to publish books expressing their questions about whether everyone really was a witch who professed to be a witch or who confessed to the practice of witchcraft when questioned. In *De Praestigiis*, published in 1513, Johann Wier theorized that some of the diseases believed to be caused by spells were quite natural in origin and that so-called witches were really deluded, concluding that witchcraft should be studied and treated more by physicians than by theologians and magistrates. Nevertheless, he stated that those who thought of themselves as witches and used rituals with the intention of doing evil should be punished.

Reginald Scot, publishing *Discoverie of Witchcraft* in 1584, declared that many witches achieved their results by poison (in the cases of pretending to cause sickness) or by fraud. Even though he and Wier believed in demons, he wrote that little was known about them and that most strange events were susceptible of quite natural explanation.

Friedrich von Spee, a German Jesuit, in his *Cautio Criminalis*, likewise protested against indiscriminate accusations of witchcraft and the trials which followed, concluding that although sorcery was possible, and that some persons really practiced witchcraft, not all were in fact witches who were tried as such. He strongly condemned the superstition, gossip, and slander which were engendered by the trials.

King James I himself was strongly skeptical, stating plainly that credulous persons could be easily deceived and urging judges to be very cautious in dealing with evidence presented by persons alleged to have been bewitched.

What happened to the act of James I against witches and witchcraft? It was repealed in 1736, during the reign of George II. Witchcraft was no longer a capital offense, but still illegal, with this difference: reflecting the influence of rationalism and skepticism toward anything preternatural or supernatural, anyone *pretending* to practice witchcraft could be punished by imprisonment. The Vagrancy Act of 1824 decreed that Spiritualist mediums could be prosecuted, making any séance illegal.

This was the legal status of witchcraft in England until 1951, when the old Witchcraft Act was repealed and replaced by the Fraudulent Mediums Act, which legally acknowledged the possibility of genuine mediums. Considerable persuasion by Spiritualists had brought this act to final passage.

All of that seems so long ago and, even to persons living in the Bay State, so far away, because it really is foreign to many of our interests, quite alien to our thinking, even something not to be treated seriously, fun for the children at Halloween. It is difficult to imagine how people of the seventeenth century could take seriously even the possibility of other persons casting spells *effectively*. It is still more difficult for us to imagine a court convicting and sentencing to death someone reported to have done that. No Christian today wants persons who believe in witchcraft and who consider themselves to be witches to be prosecuted for their beliefs, much less executed for their beliefs. We respect their right to believe as they do, only asking that they, in turn, respect the personal rights and property rights of others.

Nevertheless, anyone who finds it hard to believe that witchcraft is a belief system expressed in ritual and practice today needs only to recall the many years that Haiti was controlled by "Papa Doc" and then his son "Baby Doc" Duvalier, both admitted "doctors" of Voodoo, the Haitian form of witchcraft.

Reference to the Duvaliers recalls us to the question of "white" magic and "black" magic, and the oft-proclaimed statement of witches that they are "not Satanists" since they belong to "the Old Religion," i.e. pre-Christian, and therefore do not believe in a devil. It is worthwhile to reflect on Aleister Crowley, who began as a practicing witch, but astrology, card-reading, and herbal healing were perhaps not sufficiently "interesting" (or "exciting") for his restless mind. So he began to experiment with incantations ("calling up" demonic spirits), then went on to using drugs and into deeper association with the demonic, ending at last as a Satanist.

Because witchcraft does not recognize an all-good Creator God, its belief system does not contain an Authority who has the right and the power to forbid such aberrations which lead to such descents into evil.

The revival of interest in the culture of the Middle Ages at the beginning of the nineteenth century led to a parallel interest in the occult, so that by the beginning of the twentieth century, persons such as Aleister Crowley (to whom we have referred above) and Magregor Mathers had a certain following. But "Wicca" as a belief and witchcraft as a practice did not gain a popular following in the United States until Sybil Leek, a professed witch from England's New Forest, with her jackdaw (an English term for black crow), appeared on the Today Show with Hugh Downs and Barbara Walters. Sybil Leek made witchcraft seem harmless and interesting to persons looking for new answers to their questions about life and its problems.

In contemporary American life, witchcraft, if we understand the term as covering some forms of the belief systems of the older religions of various peoples with their specific rituals, includes not only the "old religions" of Europe, but also the traditional religions of the native peoples of Central and South America and various African religions. In many cases, elements of each of these forms of older native religions are combined by the choice of the leader or the members of a group or coven into a new eclectic form of witchcraft, to which various other new beliefs or rituals can be added or from which some present beliefs or rituals can be dropped according to the changing interests of the members.

Many contemporary students of the history of witchcraft accept the theories of Professor Margaret Murray of Oxford, author of *The Witch Cult in Europe* (1921) and *The God of the Witches* (1933), in which she attempted to demonstrate that European witchcraft was the persisting survival of an ancient fertility religion from pre-Christian times through the seventeenth century.

One of the most knowledgeable of contemporary historians, Jeffrey Burton Russell, in his monumental study, *Witchcraft in the Middle Ages*, from which we have previously quoted, points out:

> ". . . Murray's use of sources in general is appalling. Not only did she force evidence to fit her theory, but she ignored vast bodies of materials, particularly for the Middle Ages, that were readily available to her and that, ironically, in some instances even would have fortified her position. . ." (op. cit., p. 37)

Russell states that Murray "read back into the entire history of witchcraft . . . practices which were peculiar to certain times and places. . ." naming such Scottish customs of the fourteenth century as the coven and the French custom of the sabbat, ". . . which she makes the center of her fertility cult but which is not mentioned in any of the sources before the late fifteenth century" (ibid., pp. 36-37).

In her favor, Russell mentions that as a valuable historic insight, Murray emphasizes that pagan folk beliefs and practices, Greco-Roman, Teutonic, and Celtic, did not die out when

Christianity entered the scene, ". . . but rather remained and constituted the fundamental substratum of witchcraft" (ibid.).

These views of Margaret Murray are important, in spite of the existence of many other, possibly less biased, historians of witchcraft, because her views and those of Jules Michelet (*La Sorciére* [1863], published under the title *Satanism and Witchcraft*, trans. by. A. R. Allinson, New York, Dell Books, 1939) are apparently the most influential on popular thinking. Michelet saw witchcraft as a form of rebellion against the prevalent social ills of feudalism, war, and the physical problems of poverty and the Black Death in the fourteenth century.

The religious revival of ancient paganism is snowballing among all social and economic levels of society. The movement is known as Wicca or the Craft, a nature religion taken from pre-Christian European religions.

Witches across the nation are trying to recapture the Craft as designed by its creators. It is no longer an underground religion but an open religion practiced by tens of thousands of individuals. Individuals dedicated to nature, magic rituals, and potions.

The witches that I have had the opportunity to deal with openly referred to themselves as pagans, from a Latin word meaning "peasant" or country dweller. These witches openly discussed their religious belief system, always emphasizing that they are not Satanists. They go to extremes explaining that Satan absolutely has no place in their Craft.

In a lot of my lectures, it is not unusual to see individuals who identify themselves as witches wearing buttons stating "Witches against Satanism." I believe most attend to monitor what I am telling the public about their Craft.

The witches belonging to covens or circles are usually comprised of thirteen people, and contrary to most belief, men are very much a part of these covens.

The covens are governed by a high priestess and a high priest, with the high priestess being the leading figure in the coven. Their purpose is to guide members to achieve a nature-based attitude and to instruct them in the ways of the Craft, with its rituals and initiations. The high priestess also may single out an assistant referred to as a maiden. The maiden's purpose is to assist the high priestess in rituals.

Rituals are numerous in this religious sect. There are rituals for initiation, rituals for healing and protection, rituals for the sun and the sea, and it goes on and on. You can look at witchcraft as a religion expressed in rituals.

These covens meet to practice their belief. These rituals are held in a home or building or out in the open, in field or forest. Some perform the rituals being "skyclad," a term used for being totally nude. They believe it is totally natural to be nude, that they can achieve a greater understanding of the male and female power when the are "skyclad." They are always seeking power to develop themselves mentally, spiritually, and emotionally. They believe it is easier to raise psychic power being nude, making it easier to exchange unconscious information, but more importantly, doing rituals "skyclad" leads to self-realization.

Most Wiccan witches believe in reincarnation, that at the time of death the soul is reborn. They believe this is possible over and over again to increase their mental powers.

Most witches also practice clairvoyance and divination, usually starting with tarot cards; however, crystal balls (the larger the better), flasks, and black mirrors all become part of the rituals to develop clairvoyance and divination.

One of the more startling aspects of the Wiccan belief system is astral projection. They believe when the body is relaxed, astral projection takes place. Some sit in a chair in front of a full-length mirror. They relax the body and concentrate on their heartbeat and body points touching the chair, believing that this mentally transfers their conscious mind to the air around them.

While all this may seem absurd to many of us, let me assure you that these powers are possible to achieve, and many have succeeded in obtaining these powers and having out-of-body experiences. Where does the power come from? Does it come from the development of your mind through rituals to connect you with the powers of the universe that these individuals have tapped into? Does it come from powers of evil? I adhere to the Christian belief system, for I am reminded that God has set down in his Word, in Deuteronomy 18:9-12, that "there should not be any among you who

. . . uses divination or an observer of times or an enchanter or a witch . . . for all who do these things are an abomination unto the LORD". This answers those questions for me.

In 1974, the Council of American Witches met in Minnesota and made public the tenets of their belief system. The following is what the Council agreed upon:

> "1. We practice rites to attune ourselves with the natural rhythm of life forces marked by the phases of the Moon and the seasonal Quarters and Cross-Quarters.
>
> "2. We recognize that our intelligence gives us a unique responsibility toward our environment. We seek to live in harmony with Nature, in ecological balance offering fulfillment to life and consciousness within an evolutionary concept.
>
> "3. We acknowledge a depth of power far greater than is apparent to the average person. Because it is far greater than ordinary, it is sometimes called 'supernatural,' but we see it as lying within that which is naturally potential to all.
>
> "4. We conceive of the Creative Power in the Universe as manifesting through polarity as masculine and feminine and that this same Creative Power lives in all people and functions through the interaction of the masculine and feminine. We value sexuality as pleasure, as the symbol and embodiment of Life, and as one of the sources of energies used in magical practice and religious worship.
>
> "5. We recognize both outer worlds and inner, or psychological worlds — sometimes known as the Spiritual World, the Collective Unconscious, the Inner Planes, etc. — and we see in the interaction of these two dimensions the basis for paranormal phenomena and magical exercises. We neglect neither dimension for the other, seeing both as necessary for our fulfillment.
>
> "6. We do not recognize any authoritarian hierarchy, but do honor those who teach, respect those who share their greater knowledge and wisdom, and acknowledge those who have courageously given of themselves in leadership.
>
> "7. We see religion, magic, and wisdom-in-living as being united in the way one views the world and lives within it — a world-view and philosophy-of-life which we identify as Witchcraft, the Wiccan Way.
>
> "8. Calling oneself 'Witch' does not make a Witch — but neither does

heredity itself, or the collecting of titles, degrees, and initiations. A witch seeks to control the forces within him/herself that make life possible in order to live wisely and well, without harm to others, and in harmony with Nature.

"9. We acknowledge that it is the affirmation and fulfillment of life, in a continuation of evolution and development of consciousness, that gives meaning to the Universe we know, and to our personal role within it.

"10. Our only animosity toward Christianity, or toward any other religion or philosophy-of-life, is to the extent that its institutions have claimed to be 'the one true right and only way' and have sought to deny freedom to others and to suppress other ways of religious practices and belief.

"11. As American Witches, we are not threatened by debates on the history of the Craft, the origins of various terms, the legitimacy of various aspects of different traditions. We are concerned with our present, and our future.

"12. We do not accept the concept of 'absolute evil,' nor do we worship any entity known as 'Satan' or 'the Devil' as defined by Christian Tradition. We do not seek power through the suffering of others, nor do we accept the concept that personal benefits can only be derived by denial to another.

"13. We seek within Nature for that which is contributory to our health and well-being."

All who seek to identify with the Wiccan Witchcraft movement must accept the thirteen principles, as in all religious movements the Wiccan Witches celebrate holy days they refer to as sabbats starting with:

February 2: Candlemas — Feast of Lights
March 21: Spring Equinox — Solar Festival
April 30: Beltane/Bealtine — May Day — Fire Festival
June 22: Summer Solstice — Fire and Water Festival
July 31: Lammas — Solar Festival
September 21: Autumn Equinox — Solar Festival
October 31: Samhain — Halloween — Fire Festival
December 22: Yule — Death and Rebirth of Sun God

Great preparation is taken to celebrate each of the eight Sabbats, much the same way a Christian would prepare for Christmas. The rituals celebrated on these days are very elaborate, calling for the use of certain tools associated with the Wiccan belief system — such tools as:

The Athome — knife/ritual tool.
The Sword — represents fire.
The Wand — represents air.
The Chalice — represents water.
The Pentacle — represents earth.
The Censer — represents air.
White-handled knife — working tool.
The Scourge — symbolic.
Cords — usually three of different colors.
Broomstick — symbol of the craft.
Cauldron — used with water, fire, incense.
The Necklace — represents rebirth.
The Garter — represents magical object or rank in a coven.

While these are the thirteen main tools used, you will also find candles, flowers, robes, and herbs in many rituals as well.

While the Wiccan Witches movement believes, "Do what thou will but harm no one," it is also important to mention that other Witchcraft movements do not adhere to this belief. There are some groups who deal strictly in the black arts, calling up demons by doing sacrifices. They refer to themselves as emissaries of the devil. This is a close-knit group, very secretive, and a high degree of loyalty is common. This group seeks power for personal gain, following many Satanic rituals but again denying that they are Satanists. The number of these groups is unknown, and is thought to be small in number. However, these groups are dangerous and will go to extremes to reach their goal and to accomplish their task.

11.

Satanism

Donald H. Thompson

PARENTS, teachers, police, and clergy are seeing evidence throughout the United States which suggests that our society is now facing a phenomenon that could be one of the most challenging problems we have ever had to confront. The problem is Satanism and the occult. The word Satanism alone causes a myriad of thoughts in people's minds, from images of a cartoon character dressed in a red suit with a pitchfork to sacrificed animals and humans as a part of religious worship. As a police officer for twenty-one years, I want to share with my readers information I have learned and experienced firsthand, so that all of us may see at least one aspect of what society is now facing and possibly what the future may hold.

Satanism for the most part is the worship of the Devil as a deity, using rituals and specific ceremonies that have been passed down in writings or by word of mouth. Through years of interviewing youths involved in Satanic and occult activities, I have found that they defined these activities as rites and rituals that go beyond human understanding in an attempt to bring supernatural forces under their control, to acquire simple power, power to do things others are unable to achieve. This seems to be one of the main attractions of this religion among youth.

Satanism is a religion, and as such it is protected by this nation's laws. The individuals involved go beyond the laws and boundaries of freedom of religion and commit crimes to obtain supernatural experience. At this point, law enforcement and society can object to the actions of those who practice this religion. What we are seeing now is not crime for crime's sake but crimes for the sake of religion. Crimes with Satanic overtones are occurring in every state in the United States on a continuing basis. Police reports continue to be processed reporting ritual killings, ritual abuse, grave robbing, animal sacrifice and destruction of property, all in the name of religion, Satanism.

> Indiana: Fifteen corpses were stolen from grave yards, then sold to be used in Satanic rituals.
>
> New York: Teenagers beat and stab another teenager until he dies, then removed his eyes, all in the name of Satan.
>
> Texas: Awaiting execution, an inmate tells of the mutilation of children and adults who were used in rituals.
>
> California: Teenagers put together a manual of how to dispose of their parents, how to sacrifice them to the family dog, and then how to sacrifice the family dog to Satan.

These are but a few of the hundreds of police reports that continue to be processed each day, and yet I hear other professionals saying that this phenomenon is being blown out of proportion or that the problem doesn't exist. One only has to remember Tommy Sullivan, the fourteen-year-old boy who was involved in Satanism for eight weeks; who killed his mother, then committed suicide, leaving behind his diary with a pledge to Satan to kill his family; or the story of Matamoros, Mexico, where Mark Kilroy, a premed student, was kidnapped and sacrificed along with fourteen other men and boys, all for power and religion — and I ask you to judge who is covering up what.

Individuals involved in Satanism have told me that there are no laws in Satanism. "Do what thou will" is the whole of the law. The laws are established by the individual or the group you belong to. Basically, if it feels good, do it. Everything is okay. With this philosophy, it is easy to understand why society experiences these types of crimes and why certain individuals become involved. You can excuse a lot of bizarre behavior and fetishes that society says are wrong but a religion or group says is okay.

To most of those involved, Satanism condemns whatever society stands for as being right and just. Satan now represents good, and

God is now the God of evil and of the weak individuals who are followers of silly church teachings. Biblical principles and values as you know them have no place in this religion, which reverses our biblical standards and threatens the peace and safety of our society.

While giving numerous lectures in Catholic and private schools, I have found that many youths, whether or not they were involved in Satanism, know the Satanic Bible, the Black Mass, and dominant figures in the Satanic religion. Most know people who have experimented or are involved with Satanism. Chances are that your teenagers know more about this movement than you do.

When I have an auditorium of students without the presence of teachers or parents, I have found that the students will tell me anything I want to know about the occult or Satanism. When parents or teachers are present, only a few brave youths will share information. The expression on the face of the teachers and parents is one of shock, horror, and unbelief. How may parents have asked their children if they have ever seen the Satanic Bible, or if the children know someone involved in occult activities? When speaking in a non-condemning way, seeking answers, I have found that most youths will share learned information. But when your body language and tone of voice show a condemning point of view, most children will not participate in the discussion. Parent-child communication is an important learning tool.

To understand the "why" and "how" of youth who become involved in Satanism, it is first necessary to understand some of the practices involved. Always keep in mind, it's not so much what you personally believe but what those involved in Satanic activities believe they can achieve. The group in Matamoros who sacrificed fifteen humans in bizarre rituals believed that by doing these sacrifices they could obtain more drugs, the police would not be able to arrest them, and that police bullets would not hurt them if they were shot. Throw logic out the window and remember that most of those involved are attempting to control supernatural power.

Youth involved in Satanism are usually referred to as experimental Satanists, starters, dabblers, or self-styled Satanists. Whatever name is used, this group is composed of individuals ranging in age from twelve to twenty. They are learning about Satanism, gathering information from books available at the public library, or from videos available at neighborhood video stores. For this group, however, most information comes from friends in school who have studied the Satanic prayers, doctrines, and dogma of their newfound interest. I have found that as youths study and learn, they are drawn deeper and deeper into the area of black magic and Satanic worship.

They will learn spells and incantations with special prayers and chants, all laid out in occult literature. They will practice these rituals hoping to achieve the Satanic magic. One type of magic can be conjured for sexual freedom and success, in which the apprentices are instructed that spell-casting can summon a partner to satisfy their sexual desires. There are rituals for success, destruction of enemies, and sacrifices to Satan. Basically, if there is a need or want, there is a ritual designed to achieve that desire.

With the newfound information, youths will learn the need to establish an altar or a specific area where rituals can be conducted. It can be as crude as two cinder blocks with a board across, or as elaborate as a church altar. Special clothing must also be worn for the serious worshiper. Black robes or dark clothes are worn, symbolizing the power of darkness. Black and white candles will be used, but no more then one white candle is to be lit during a ritual. The black candles represent the light and wisdom of Satan, and the white candle represents the followers of Christ and is used for their destruction. The chalice or cup is another item needed, all types are acceptable except gold, because gold represents Heaven and they do not want to have anything to do with that. Now what good is a chalice if there is nothing in it to drink? Anything can be drunk out of the chalice if it can intensify your feelings; therefore, alcohol and drugs are usually used by youth. The next item is the sword or knife, which symbolizes force. Now that the altar is set, the ceremonies can begin.

One family whose son committed suicide was devastated to find a makeshift altar draped in black on the floor of his closet. They never realized that he was involved in this type of activity until it was too late.

The most intriguing ritual for youths seems to be the animal sacrifice, the spilling of blood, drinking of blood, and eventually the eating of animal parts, all to gain supernatural power.

They will be taught that the life forces are contained in the blood, and that these forces can be taken into their bodies by consuming blood or eating specific body organs, such as the heart. Writings also explain that energy will be released into the air by torturing. Screams and cries release energy that can be absorbed into their own bodies, and they can become stronger and more powerful. The convert will be instructed that his new god demands sacrifices for the rituals to work.

The first time they experience a sacrifice they may become scared or fearful of the experience, but this soon passes as they quickly become desensitized, hopeful that they will become more than they already are.

The more they learn, the deeper they become involved — until they are ready to make a pact with Satan himself, total commitment, or a blood oath selling their soul to the devil and promising to follow all the teachings, holding all things secret. I have seen youths write pacts to Satan selling their souls and promising allegiance forever, then cutting their finger to sign their names in blood. The oaths are usually written in a diary called the Book of Shadows, Witches' Cookbook, or a host of other names. Such a diary is kept by all involved in the black arts. It is usually a composition book or a steno book, and it will contain rituals, prayers, and ceremonies with personal notes and pacts to Satan. This is a very useful book for parents if it is found. It can indicate the degree of involvement of the youth. As this book is so important, it will always be hidden out of the reach of parents.

Parents will also see increased interest in "punk rock" or "heavy metal" music. Music has a heavy influence on today's youth. They wake up to music played on clock radios, get dressed by it, hear it on most school buses, and do homework by it. Then at day's end they fall asleep to the music. All one has to do is walk into a record store and look at the album covers of some of the "heavy metal" groups to clearly see death's-heads and occult symbols blatantly displayed on album covers. While some "heavy metal" groups admit to being involved in the black arts, others who are not involved still write music with Satanic overtones because they realize that this sells and sells big in the United States. Some groups set Satanic rituals to music so youths can hear, learn, and most importantly, remember.

Parents should check to see what type of music their children are listening to and analyze it, to see how the music is affecting and persuading their children. Some "heavy metal" groups have been sued by parents because of the serious negative effects the music has had on their children. For instance, some children have committed suicide while listening to music.

Another avenue of interest is occult games such as ouija boards, tarot cards, and fantasy role-playing games such as Dungeons and Dragons. These all seem to add to the excitement of the occult magic and obtaining of supernatural power.

Youths who have become involved in this activity will start to show personality changes and begin to withdraw from family and friends, maybe acquiring new friends with similar interests. They will become secretive about their activities and ignore normal household tasks, schoolwork, and family moral values. Their style of dress my change, wearing all-black or dark clothing, occult jewelry such as pentagrams and upside-down crosses, and occult symbols tattooed on their bodies to show their friends that they are serious. Parents for the first time may see signs of alcohol or drug abuse causing changes in their children's personality and their relationship with family members.

In the downward spiral, connected with their newfound religion, crime usually becomes a way of life. It is these youths who are responsible for damaging attacks on cemeteries, spray-painting occult symbols on churches, synagogues, private yards, homes, and bridges, all in the name of Satan.

As their lifestyle and moral values change, suicide also seems to be a growing problem for individuals involved in Satanism. I have interviewed youths in mental hospitals who were involved in Satanism. All have thought about taking their own lives. Some, even though under treatment, willfully succeed in taking their own lives so they can live and reign with their father, Satan, for eternity. They leave behind suicide notes expressing how they could no longer stand being away from their master and wishing to join him — while others leave notes stating that they just wish to end it all, having failed to achieve a position in Satanism.

The use of drugs, alcohol, and "heavy metal" music lyrics seems to add to the suicide rate among young apprentice Satanists. This influence seems to stimulate faulty thinking and opens their minds to demonic forces and supernatural powers, which end up destroying them in one way or another.

Although I have been discussing youth who became willfully involved in Satanism, it is equally important to mention youths who have been recruited into it without understanding what is actually happening.

Youth involved in Satanism have successfully recruited unknowing youths into their ranks. Some have told me that they wait outside a counseling center knowing the youth inside are vulnerable and usually are having trouble with their parents or have an alcohol or drug problem. They stated to me that most youths have appointments at the same day and at the same time. The "recruiters" wait outside for the youth to leave the center, and then they will start talking to the other youth, gaining his confidence, and in this conversation the recruiter tells the other youth that there is a way to gain control over his own life as well as controlling others.

Some recruiters go to bus depots, train stations, and resort areas looking for runaways. They know these runaways are scared and need food, shelter, and most of all companionship. Some recruit at college campuses making friends with freshman who have come from out of state who are unsure in their new surroundings, hoping to fit in with their peers and to make friends.

However, most recruiting occurs in high schools. A group of Satanists will single out students who do not fit in with the crowd, do not have close friends, or do not participate in school activities. The recruiter refers to this type of individuals as nerds or loners. They befriend these individuals by talking to them before school, between classes, or after school. They will eat lunch with these new friends and maybe help them do homework, gaining the confidence and friendship of the individuals.

The unknowing students may feel for the first time that they have individuals who seem to really enjoy their company and care about them. They think they have fit in at last. When confidence and trust have been gained, the unknowing students are likely to be asked to attend a special party where drugs and alcohol are free if they care to indulge. The people at the party will seem to be very friendly and caring. At these parties nothing about Satanism will be mentioned.

He or she may be invited to quite a few of these parties so that the recruiters may gain as much information about the individual as possible and so that the potential recruit may become comfortable with them. There will come a time when the group will ask the individuals to join their club. If the individuals agree to attend a club meeting, a light Satanic service will be performed for their benefit.

Satanism draws youth because of the secretiveness and the mystery surrounding it. It seems everyone wants to know a secret, and by the recruiters' keeping the service mysterious and secretive, the potential recruits want to learn more and do not want to offend their newfound acquaintances who have been so friendly.

The candidates will be asked if they would like to join the club and learn more, and usually without hesitation the answer is in the affirmative. However, before an initiation can begin, the recruited one is required to commit a crime, then return to the group and report exactly what has been done. It need not be anything big, maybe to set fire to the dumpster behind the shopping center, or spray paint symbols on a church, or knock over tombstones in a local cemetery. Sanctioned members of the group will accompany the candidate to assure a crime has actually been committed.

When a crime has been performed, a report is made to the group by the candidate, who will be welcomed by each member as a brother. From now on this individual will be indoctrinated into the belief system in a gentle manner, the older members being watchful of the reactions of the inductee.

At a certain point, the group will tell the recruit it is now time to show him or her the deeper side of this new religion, and they will ask the individual to steal an animal, maybe a neighbor's cat, in order to take part in animal sacrifice. Most youth will now start to have second thoughts about what they are involved in, maybe even wish to leave the group and refuse to participate in this activity. If this happens, the group will put pressure on the individuals and tell the recruits that they will call the police and report the crimes they committed, or the group will show the recruits pictures taken at the so-called innocent parties, including pictures of the individuals taking drugs or engaging in sexual activities. The group threatens to send these pictures to the individuals' parents, church, and school.

Sometimes the group will threaten the lives of the individuals' families or threaten to burn down their houses.

The individual is now forced to stay in the group through fear and intimidation. Most will not tell their parents of their problem for fear of retaliation or embarrassment. These individuals are now on their way to being abused by the group until they are so desperate that they tell their story, hoping someone will believe.

By now the damage has usually reached the point that professional counseling is necessary to restore the individual to a normal, stable social life, or maybe even hospitalization in a mental facility to reverse destructive behavior or thoughts. I have interviewed youth in mental hospitals who have explained in detail the supernatural powers they achieved or experienced, powers such as levitation, supernatural strength, and seeing images of creatures they have called up in rituals. It is important to know that it is possible to obtain such powers. In the years I have dealt with the occult, I have also seen levitation and supernatural events, and it's enough to make the hair stand up on your arms. In front of twenty-four people, one individual raised himself up from a sofa and hovered in the air. He then slowly moved to the other end of the sofa and lowered himself. I have seen people of small frame pick up individuals twice their size and throw them across the room. I assure you the power is there, it's real and it exists, but everyone who obtains this power pays the price.

Most youth who become involved in Satanic activities are not the underprivileged or poor but the intelligent and curious. They are almost always white males (although females also can be involved) from a middle- to upper-middle-class family. Most seem to be rebelling against society and its moral values, while almost without exception a negative self-esteem problem is always present.

Parents, teachers, and all who deal with youth should be familiar with warning signs associated with occult influence:

> Withdrawal or alienation from family or friends;
> Sudden loss of interest in church or church activities;
> Wearing black or dark clothing with occult jewelry;
> Increased rebellion and aggressive behavior;
> Negative change in moral behavior;

Sudden drop in grades at school;
New interest in occult literature;
Fascination with death;
Constant viewing of occult movies;
Occult posters and records in rooms;
Collection of occult items (skull, bones, ritual knives, and candles);
Threats of suicide;
Frightening nightmares.

If youth show any of these danger signals, parents should recognize this as a warning for more parental investigation. Teenage Satanism is fast becoming an accepted reality. Any teenager or parent who has not been educated about Satanic cult methods and tactics can be unknowingly in danger. It is necessary to educate yourself about these recruiting methods to protect yourself and, most important, your children. It is my sole intention that this chapter may cause you to become more aware of Satanism as a fact in contemporary society.

Suggested Reading: Witchcraft, Satanism

For the sake of clarity I wish to stress that combining the bibliographies for these two chapters in no way indicates failure to distinguish between witchcraft and Satanism. Most acknowledged witches state that since they do not believe in the God of Jews and Christians, they also do not believe in Satan or devils, fallen angels. Just as not all professing Christians obey all of the Commandments of God all of the time, and just as some professing Christians even turn away from the practice of their religion temporarily or even permanently, some practitioners of witchcraft turn to Satanism, mingling it with witchcraft or turning to it altogether. For this reason as well as for the reason that witchcraft was considered Satanic in the late Middle Ages, and also because many books treat of both subjects, the two topics are combined here.

A further clarification is needed with regard to authors. Witchcraft and Satanism have been peripheral subjects for most serious scholars. Until recently they were considered "seasonal" topics or topics inviting sensational treatment by journalists. For this reason, most dedicated serious scholars avoided research on these topics or pursued the topics as tangential to their main subject of research. Many of the books which are considered the results of strongly focused study come from persons who became almost infatuated with the subjects, e.g., Jules Michelet in France and Montague Summers in England. Their work reflects their simultaneous attraction-repulsion, and certainly in the case of Montague Summers that strong attraction to the occult caused serious defects in his scholarship. I have, therefore, refrained from listing books by either of those authors. The works listed are clearly as unbiased as could be found, or are plainly listed as authored by members of the cults.

de Rougemont, Denis, *The Devil's Share, An Essay on the Diabolic in Modern Society*, New York, Meridian Books, 1956 [From the rear cover: an ". . .analysis of the dislocations and confusions of modern society . . . the curious contradiction of a world that still officially claims to believe in God and yet denies the Devil."]

Johnston, Jerry, *The Edge of Evil, The Rise of Satanism in North America*, Dallas, London, Word Publishing, 1989

Kahaner, Larry, *Cults that Kill: Probing the Underworld of Occult Crime*, New York, Warner Books, 1988 [Both of these books treat the topic of Satanic crimes, particularly such subjects as mass murderers or murders committed by Satanists who are involved in or leaders in drug trafficking. Both touch on many of the same crimes or on the same topics as are found in Carl Raschke's book, although from slightly different perspectives.]

Leek, Sybil, *Diary of a Witch*, New York, Prentice Hall, 1968 (pb Signet Books, 1969); *The Complete Art of Witchcraft*, New York, Thomas Y. Crowell, 1971 (pb Signet Books, 1973) [In the 1950s Sybil Leek moved from her home in the New Forest in England, where her family had lived and had practiced witchcraft for many generations, to the United States. For several years she was interviewed on many radio and TV shows, which resulted in much of the public viewing witchcraft as acceptable, legitimate. These books are listed here because they provide an "insider's view" of that moment in history when witchcraft had been practiced "underground" and then became legal. She is professedly a "white witch."]

Levin, Harry, *The Power of Blackness: Hawthorne, Poe, Melville*, New York, Random House, 1958 [A study of the attraction to and fascination with dark forces on the part of three authors of American literary classics.]

Nugent, Christopher, *Masks of Satan: The Demonic in History*, Westminster, Md., Christian Classics, 1989 ["Dr. Nugent writes as a professional historian, from an avowedly Catholic-Christian and theologically informed viewpoint, about the demonic in its context — that is, in its actual manifestations in human, and specifically in Western, history" — from the cover.]

Pulling, Pat, *The Devil's Web: Who is Stalking Your Children for Satan*? Lafayette, La., Huntington House, 1989 [Experienced investigator and authority on occult-related crime, Pat Pulling conducts law enforcement seminars and lectures to mental health professionals, school systems and church groups, since her own son committed suicide after a brief involvement with the occult. This book explains how the violent underworld of the occult operates, how it recruits children, youth and young adults, and how we can protect our children. No index, but excellent appendices, which include signs and symbols of the occult, of interest not only to police but also to parents, teachers, and youth leaders; glossary of occult terms; names and addresses of persons and organizations that can supply information or professional help to persons or groups needing help for themselves or for young persons for whom they are concerned; also a good bibliography.]

Raschke, Carl A., *Painted Black: From Drug Killings to Heavy Metal — The Alarming True Story of How Satanism is Terrorizing Our Communities*, New York, Harper and Row, 1990 (no index) [Carl Raschke, Ph.D., is director of the Institute for Humanities and professor of religious studies at the University of Denver. It is by no means superficial, although it covers a wide range of topics, each in sufficient depth to provide a good working knowledge of the subject, and extensive bibliography for those who desire additional information. Topics: the Satanic crime scene, with excellent in-depth research, the occult underworld, Satanism, Satanism as licensed and accepted religion, heavy metal music, theater of cruelty, e.g., "slasher" and "snuff" films, fantasy role-playing games, devil's contracts, child pornography, child sacrifice, skinheads and neo-Nazis. Solid research, well documented.]

Russell, Jeffrey Burton, *The Devil: Perceptions of Evil from Antiquity to the Middle Ages*, Ithaca, N.Y., Cornell University Press, 1977; *Witchcraft in the Middle Ages*, Ithaca, N.Y., Cornell University Press, 1977 [Probably the most thoroughly researched and unbiased treatment of these subjects available at the present time. For the average reader, probably "more than you ever wanted to know" about the subjects, but for anyone working in this field in a professional capacity, these books are essential tools.]

Soundings in Satanism, assembled by F. J. Sheed, London and Oxford, Mowbrays, 1972 ["Twenty years ago we published *Satan*, a translation of a volume of the same name . . . edited by Father Bruno, O.C.D. The present book is not about Satan but about Satanism. . . ." from Assembler's Note, by F.J. Sheed. Note: *Satan*, published by Sheed and Ward, N.Y., 1952, is considerably longer than this book, in addition to its different focus, but is not readily available except in seminary and a few university libraries.]

Starkey, Marion L., *The Devil in Massachusetts: A Modern Inquiry into the Salem Witch Trials*, New York, Time, Inc. 1963 (original copyright, 1949)

Valiente, Doreen, *An ABC of Witchcraft Past and Present*, New York, St. Martin's Press, 1973 [The author is a professed witch. "By 'witchcraft' I mean the remains of the old religion of Western Europe, driven underground by the rise of Christianity and compelled to organize itself as a secret cult in order to survive. . ." The author does not write of the 'witchcraft' of any other continents. She distinguishes between 'witchcraft' and 'magic' which she defines as the use, or misuse, of occult powers.]

Woods, Richard, O.P., *The Occult Revolution, A Christian Meditation,* New York, Herder and Herder, 1971; *The Devil,* Chicago, The Thomas More Press, 1973 [Two well-written studies for the average reader, situating the growth of interest in the occult in modern society, growing out of the breakdown of many previously accepted cultural and social norms. Together, they constitute a good introduction to witchcraft and Satanism at present, but perhaps in attempting to avoid sensationalism, the signs of which might indicate involvement area not mentioned. For this reason, these two books are recommended as excellent background reading, but more detailed reading is indicated for parents, teachers, and particularly for youth group leaders.]

The Relationship Between the Entertainment World and the Occult:
Gore, Tipper, *Raising PG Kids in an X-Rated Society*, Nashville, Abingdon Press, 1987 (pb, New York, Bantam Books, 1988) [Exposé of the destructive messages delivered to children and youth by records, tapes, TV programs, and movies; how some of these actually promote violence, drug abuse, sexual promiscuity, Satanism, and suicide. What parents, teachers and youth leaders can do to counteract these influences. Slightly dated because of the constant changes in styles of entertainment, but *almost necessary reading for anyone working with youth*. Almost all of the records, tapes and programs cited in this book are outdated now, but it is still an invaluable reference for background on popular entertainers and very enlightening for parents who might think their children are "only going through a phase."]
Harry Shapiro, *Waiting For the Man: The Story of Drugs and Popular Music*, New York, William Morrow and Co., Inc., 1988

Special Category:
LeBar, Rev. James J., *Cults, Sects, and the New Age* (Introductory comments by Cardinal John J. O'Connor and Cardinal John J. Krol) Huntington, Indiana, Our Sunday Visitor, Inc., 1989 [This book is in a special category because it is a single-volume source of information: defining the characteristics of a cult; discussing the reasons people, especially youth, join cults; examines the most widespread cults, including the Satanist movement, outlines plans for countering cults, and includes various official statements of bishops regarding specific cults and the Vatican document on sects or new religious movements.]

12.

Syncretism

Father Lawrence J. Gesy

A FTER visiting India for the first International Eucharistic Congress, December 2-5, 1964, Pope Paul VI commented at his first general audience upon his return to Rome on the impression he had received of the good in "the heritage of moral and religious values" possessed and preserved by the people of India. But he cautioned that "it is an impression that is not reducible to irenicism or syncretism. . ." (*The Pope Speaks*, vol. 10, no. 2, 1965, p. 160).

Irenicism?

Syncretism?

What do those words mean? And, more especially, how do they concern us?

Pope Paul VI had visited Bombay for four days in early December, just two weeks after the third session of the Second Vatican Council had formally closed on November 21. On November 20, the day prior to the closing, the Council Fathers had voted approval of the declaration on non-Christians, which Cardinal Bea described as similar to the mustard seed "in that it has grown from a brief statement on the Jews into a treelike document in which all non-Christian religions are finding their place" (*Council Daybook*, Vatican II, Session 3, p. 296).

After the various commentaries on the document had been studied and the document was given final form, the final vote of the Council Fathers on the document on the relation of the Church to Non-Christian Religions was cast on October 14, 1965, and the declaration was proclaimed by Pope Paul VI at the session of October 28, 1965.

Cardinal Bea, president of the Secretariat for Promoting Christian Unity, said of the Declaration: "Here in fact the Church itself, for the first time in history, proposes brotherly dialogue with non-Christian religions" (op. cit., Session 4, p. 197).

Previously he had said, "For the first time in the history of ecumenical councils, the principles dealing with non-Christians are set forth in solemn form. The Church has a serious obligation to initiate a dialogue with the one billion . . . who do not know Christ or His work of redemption, . . . It is the task of the Church to assist them in reaching a full share in the riches of Christ. . ." (reported by James C. O'Neill, ibid., Vatican II, Session 3, p. 296).

* * * * *

A short digression into history will enable us to understand why Cardinal Bea used such apparently extravagant language, ". . . for the first time. . . ."

On some of the maps drawn in the Middle Ages and in the early Renaissance, the Atlantic Ocean would be shown to a distance of perhaps a hundred miles beyond the coastline of Europe and the British Isles, then there would be drawings of strange fish and birds and the caption: "After [or 'Beyond'] this be dragons." In similar fashion, the lands east of European Russia were indicated by these or similar words: "The lands of Prester John." Below the Mediterranean rim of North Africa, the map-makers had only to write, "Desert."

Muhammad was born in A.D. 570. From the time of his death in A.D. 632, Islam had spread by conquest to include present-day Iran, western Pakistan, Afghanistan, the southern tier of Siberia (the present independent Muslim, former Soviet, Republics), Armenia, Syria, Palestine, Egypt, present-day Libya, Morocco, and Spain (conquered between 711 and 713).

Thus was effectively ended direct personal knowledge of the Oriental world by the people of Europe. A few exceptionally hardy sailors dared the Atlantic and became the subjects of myth and legend, but if they learned anything about the religious beliefs of the natives of North America, they communicated none of it to their

226

European contemporaries. Even fewer, dared the land route to China, the best known being "Prester John." Egypt, Ethiopia, and sub-Saharan Africa were the subjects of imaginative speculation. Until ships with movable rudders were developed in the Portugal of Prince Henry the Navigator, it was impossible to explore the Atlantic coast of Africa below Morocco.

In the late fifteenth and sixteenth centuries, exploring past the horn of Africa and up through the Indian Ocean to the subcontinent of India opened those areas to trade. A few hardy missionaries, such as St. Francis Xavier, accompanied the traders, but centuries of isolation on the other side of the world had poorly prepared either the merchants or the missionaries to relate to the religions of the East with understanding. Moreover, shortly after Xavier, the Japanese closed their borders to all contact with the West and began systematic persecution of all Japanese who had converted to Christianity. China was not much more open. It can be argued rather effectively that when Matteo Ricci, S.J., was able to open apparently effective communication with the Chinese Court, the almost total lack of understanding in Europe of cultures and languages other than their own doomed the Chinese mission to failure.

Even though travel to the Orient had become possible by the end of the sixteenth century, it remained difficult until the twentieth century, so the civilizations and the religions of the peoples of the Near and Far East remained objects of sentimental speculation. Madame Blavatsky and *The Rubaiyat of Omar Khayyam*, translated by Edward Fitzgerald, as well as the fascination of some branches of Masonry with Islamic names and symbols, are part of the late-nineteenth-century sentimental interest in a part of the world newly discovered.

One need only contrast James Hilton's *Lost Horizon*, published in 1933, with the published interviews with the "hippies" and "flower children" of the 1960s who trekked to India and Tibet in search of "wisdom." Not only was Hilton's *Lost Horizon* a sentimental, deliberately unrealistic novel or allegory; it could be written in that vein with almost the assurance that western readers could lose themselves in a novel about a monastery in the Himalayas where persons could seek wisdom, while little or no knowledge of the real religion and way of life in that part of the world would intrude to break the spell.

Even some, perhaps many, *National Geographic* articles were written by travelers who viewed the people and the countries they visited through Western eyes, and the editorial staff carefully excised many of the harsher realities from their accounts of life in the Orient.

The Europeans who lived in or served as colonial administrators in the eighteenth and nineteenth centuries often so despised the "natives" that most gave little or no respectful consideration to the religions of the "natives."

But, of course we sent missionaries to the lands difficult for ordinary folks to visit. Undoubtedly some achieved excellent rapport with the people they served. Others, however, worked for years with the handicap of "Western eyes." This, too, is addressed in some of the documents of the Second Vatican Council.

It is almost impossible for someone living in the last decade of the twentieth century, with television and radio bringing the whole world into our living rooms, to imagine the limited knowledge of the world which restricted the thought processes of the people of the Middle Ages, even the limited knowledge of our parents and grandparents. How different is reading about India in a book from seeing the teeming millions jostling through incredibly crowded streets, stepping over dead or dying beggars, seeing and hearing Mahatma Gandhi!

Another element contributing to our sense of familiarity with other parts of the globe is the fact that thousands of young men from Europe and North America became acquainted with the countries of the Near and Far East during the second World War and the later campaigns in Korea and Vietnam.

It is this explosion of knowledge in our lives and in our living rooms which has contributed to the problem, mentioned briefly by Pope Paul VI, which is the topic of this chapter.

* * * * *

The document of Vatican Council II "Declaration on the Relation of the Church to Non-Christian Religions" (*Nostra Aetate*, October 28, 1965) states:

"The Catholic Church rejects nothing of what is true and holy in these religions. She has high regard for the manner of life and conduct, the precepts and doctrines which, although differing in many ways from her own teaching, nevertheless often reflect a ray of that truth which enlightens all men. Yet she proclaims, and is in duty bound to proclaim without fail, Christ who is the way, the truth, and the life (Jn. 14:6). In him, in whom God reconciled all things to himself (2 Cor. 5:18-19), men find the fullness of their religious life.

"The Church, therefore, urges her sons to enter with prudence and charity into discussion and collaboration with members of other religions. Let Christians, while witnessing to their own faith and way of life, acknowledge, preserve and encourage the spiritual and moral truths found among non-Christians, also their social life and culture" (N.A. #2).

Many problems have arisen from this document, not because it contained error, which would not be found in a document of an ecumenical council approved and promulgated by a Pope. Nevertheless, this would not be the first time in the history of the Church that a council issued a statement which lacked something in clarity and precision, all the more to be expected when the issues were being addressed for the first time in centuries.

What was meant by "true and holy" elements in non-Christian religions?

A second problem was raised by encouraging dialogue with persons of other religions in which those persons would be encouraged to "preserve and encourage the spiritual and moral truths found among non-Christians."

It is obvious that by these expressions the Council Fathers intended to show respect for those believers who do not know the Trinity and the Incarnate Word, the Savior, as do Christians. Here we meet the principle which is expressed in the word "irenicism" which comes from a Greek word meaning "peace." We are to meet those of other religions in a spirit of peace and charity.

". . . the spiritual and moral truths found among non-Christians" was a very broad term. What "spiritual and moral truths"? The Council Fathers no doubt knew what they meant by that expression, and did not, could not, intend Christians to embrace, by *syncretizing* with Christianity, the polytheism, idolatry, and pantheistic beliefs and practices of Hinduism and Buddhism.

"Syncretism" is an interesting word. The Greek word, *synkretismos* (many theological terms come from Greek roots) means a union of Cretans, who were well known for fighting each other, to form an alliance against a common foe, in spite of their differences, even opposition, to each other.

The Council Declaration and all of the subsequent documents which develop the ideas contained in it and provide guidelines for its implementation indicate that "irenicism," peaceful and respectful dialogue to gain deeper insights into non-Christian religions while presenting to the non-Christians the beliefs of Christianity, is only the first step. The second step: going beyond knowledge of each others' beliefs to a joint search for truths held in common. This step cannot be syncretism, because that would be grave disrespect for the truth to which those in dialogue are presumed to be dedicated. However hard it may be for one to present the truth in a way to which those of another culture can relate and which they can understand in terms of their own previous history, however hard it may be for those of the other culture to open their minds and hearts to some truth their culture may have dimly perceived in the past, and however hard it may be for western minds and hearts to see good and desire for truth in those of a very different culture from ours, this hard journey cannot be shortened by the "quick fix" of syncretism.

How did these principles come to be considered during the discussions of the Second Vatican Council?

In the presentation of the draft proposal "On the Nature of the Church," September 30, 1963, Archbishop Ngo Dinh Thuc "complained that the schema does not provide an adequate presentation of the Church for non-Christians. The result, he said, is that the Church would remain for non-Christians an almost unintelligible organism. He made a strong recommendation that heads of non-Christian religions be invited to the council as observers" (*Council Daybook*, Vatican II, Session 2, p. 151).

On October 2, 1963, during the continuing discussion of that topic, Bishop William Brasseur, C.I.C.M., Vicar Apostolic of Mountain Province, Philippines, questioned whether the traditional arguments concerning the salvation of non-Christians and the requirements for sharing the Christian faith had reached the stage of clarity necessary to become the subject of a solemn council declaration. He asked for some expression which would emphasize the fact that — in a spirit of universal charity — the Church opens her heart to all men (op. cit.).

Father Georges Tavard, A.A., of Pittsburgh, commenting on Bishop Brasseur's statement, pointed out that the bishop was certainly not questioning that non-Christians can be saved, but that "the arguments on the manner of their salvation have not yet matured sufficiently for a conciliar declaration. . ." (ibid., p. 158).

During that Second Session of the Ecumenical Council (Vatican II), Pope Paul VI directed that Catholic laity be admitted and that non-Christian as well as non-Catholic observers be admitted. The letter of invitation stated that the Pope had already "called to the ecumenical council observers of Christians separated from the Apostolic See and sought to increase the number [of them]. Moreover, it has seemed opportune for us to extend the efforts of the Secretariat [for Promoting Christian Unity, headed by Augustin Cardinal Bea] previously established also to those who are members of non-Christian religions" (letter of Pope Paul VI to Eugene Cardinal Tisserant, dated Sept. 12, 1963, from *Council Daybook*, Vatican II, Session 3, pp. 133 and 135).

On November 18, 1963, discussion of the draft proposal or schema on ecumenism began. It was composed of five chapters:

I. The Principles of Catholic Ecumenism
II. The Implementation of Ecumenism
III. Christians Separated From the Catholic Church
IV. The Attitude of Catholics Toward Non-Christians, and Particularly Toward the Jews
V. Religious Freedom

At a press conference arranged by the German bishops, before the discussion of the schema on November 18, 1963, Father Edward Stakemeier, faculty member of the Ecumenical Institute of Paderborn, Germany, and of the Paderborn Archdiocesan Seminary, noted that no previous ecumenical council had ever dealt with the topic of ecumenism. "That a draft proposal on ecumenism could be presented to the Second Vatican Council is in itself an event of transcending importance" (op. cit., p. 273).

Nov. 20, 1963: Bishop Angelo Jelmini, Apostolic Administrator of Lugano, speaking in the name of the Swiss Bishops, "urged the Council to take up not only the question of the Jews but also of Muslims, saying that 'in these days of atheism we should consider all who believe in God because the Church must present herself as the friend of all believers. Without a firm stand on religious liberty there can be no ecumenism' " (ibid. p. 286).

Speaking on the schema on ecumenism in general and in particular on the section in Chapter IV on the Relationship of Catholics with Jews, Coadjutor Bishop Michael Rodrigues of Belgaum, India, stated:

> "No matter what precautions we take, it is inevitable that this council text will be misinterpreted for political reasons. It will cause trouble in Arab nations and in Asiatic countries which have very ancient religions not mentioned in the schema. Either Chapter IV should be eliminated completely or further chapters should be added on Hinduism. Islam, and so on" (op. cit., p. 293).

Bishop José Pont y Gol of Segorbe, Spain, also opposed the inclusion of Chapters IV and V, recommending that Chapter IV be turned over to the secretariat for non-Christian religions which is to be set up in the future (ibid.).

Archbishop Lorenz Jaeger of Paderborn, Germany, observed that "long experience with discussion between Catholics and non-Catholics has made it clear that good will alone is not enough." He urged therefore that "the choice of theologians to take part in such debates must fall on men who not only know their own theology well but are also perfectly familiar with the theology of the others with whom they are engaging in discussion" (op. cit., p. 294).

The Council's text dealing with ecumenism should also include mention of such groups as Buddhists, Confucianists, and Shintoists, said Bishop Vito Chang, former Bishop of Xinyang, China, then living in Germany.

"God provides the means of salvation for every nation and for this reason no nation can feel that the Church is foreign to it. Our treatment of ecumenism should have the widest possible scope" (ibid.).

In summarizing the schema, James C. O'Neill states:

"Chapter IV is a one-page statement on relations between Catholics and non-Christians, especially Jews. It says that principles of Catholic ecumenism are to be applied also to all who worship God or at least try in conscience and good will to observe the moral law.

"Speaking of the Jews, the schema says that the Church, while being a new creation in Christ, 'cannot forget that it is a continuation of that people with whom God in his ineffable mercy once deigned to enter into the Old Testament.'

"The schema says it is unjust to call the Jews an accursed people since the 'Lord by His Passion and Death has atoned for the sins of all men. . . . The death of Christ was not caused by a whole people then living and much less by a people of today' " (*Council Daybook*, Vatican II, Session 2, p. 299).

Priests are warned against saying anything that might bring on hatred or contempt for the Jews. The Church must not forget its "common heritage with the synagogue."

Lastly, it says that mutual understanding and good will are to be fostered and that hatred and persecutions against Jews as well as all injustices to men are to be condemned (ibid.).

Many Council Fathers said that this chapter did not belong specifically in a schema on ecumenism. Some opposed any treatment of the subject by the council; many others favored treatment of the subject, but either in a separate schema or in another schema such as the seventeenth, dealing with the Church in the modern world (ibid.).

In the discussion of the schema on Nov. 25, 1963, Bishop Jean B. Gahamanyi of Butare, Rwanda, asked that the text "give us a stronger statement on the obligation of all Catholics to bring non-Catholics into the fold," which he said should be done with all discretion and mutual respect for another's views (op. cit., p. 302).

On Dec. 2, 1963, just two days before the close of the Second Session, Augustin Cardinal Bea assured the Council Fathers that the last two chapters of the schema on ecumenism are still very much alive and thanked the assembly for casting the votes which passed its first three chapters by a wide margin.

> "There have remained, however, the two final chapters of the draft. . . . I think we should be grateful to . . . the moderators, because they wished to give ample opportunity for speaking on the three fundamental chapters in order to prevent creating the danger that someone might say that a hasty vote was taken on these three chapters and on the two others which treat matters that are sufficiently difficult, present something new, and are of the greatest importance for the life and activity of the Church in our time" (op. cit. p. 319).

The full text of Cardinal Bea's remarks is on pp. 323-324 of the *Council Daybook*, Vatican II, Session 2.

Leo Cardinal Suenens of Malines-Brussels, one of the moderators, on Sunday, Dec. 1, said that it was their intention to bring the two chapters in question to a vote early in the third session.

Whether Chapter V of the schema, dealing with religious liberty, belonged in the document on ecumenism also came under discussion. On Sept. 23, 1964, three American Cardinals expressed strong support for the council's proposed declaration on religious liberty, Cardinal Ritter of St. Louis, arguing for further discussion of the reasoning supporting some of the parts (Vatican II, Session 3, p. 35).

Cardinal Ottaviani, the last cardinal to speak on that day, stated that the proposed declaration goes beyond ecumenism and gives insufficient attention to non-Christian religions. (op. cit, p. 37).

Presenting a report on Sept. 25, 1964, Cardinal Bea dealt with the section on the Jews, then stated that the schema's passages on the Muslims had been "checked and approved by specialists on the Islamic question, both among the Dominican Fathers in Jerusalem and the White Fathers in Tunis. He then emphasized the importance of the section on other non-Christian religions because many of today's non-Christians who believe in God find themselves surrounded by practical irreligion and militant atheism. A statement from the council would encourage them, he said" (op. cit., p. 59, full text of speech on pp. 60-63).

". . . the Coordinating Commission, in a letter dated April 18, decreed that three ideas in particular should be expressed: that God is the Father of all men and that they are His children; that all men are brothers; and that therefore every kind of discrimination, force, and persecution on the basis of nationality or race is to be condemned. . ." (p. 62, #6).

Many requested that the declaration also include Islam.

Bishop Laurentius Satoshi Nagae of Urawa, speaking for all the Japanese Bishops, asked that the declaration's title be changed to include all non-Christians. He warned against a completely negative attitude toward paganism and asked Fathers not to reject all the elements found in pagan culture and to "pay attention to the way in which the Church treats non-Christians" (op. cit. p. 75).

Vietnamese Bishop Nguyen Van Hien of Da Lat "said that the consideration of non-Christians is not only timely but also urgent. He pointed out that a majority of the world is neither Christian nor Jewish. He also said that there should be some reference to Moses, the law giver. Urging the Church to respect good elements in non-Christian religions and countries, Bishop Hien said that many missionary magazines publish pictures and articles reflecting no honor in the countries they are writing about" (ibid.).

Malabar-rite Archbishop Joseph Parecattil of Ernakulam noted that remote longings for Christ can be found in the sacred books of Hinduism which speak of God as director and liberator. The Church, he said, must affiliate to itself whatever is good in every culture.

Archbishop Joseph Attipetty of Verapoly wanted the declaration to state that Christians owe the same charity not only to themselves, but also to all men of all religions according to the spirit and command of Christ.

On Nov. 20, 1964, the final working day of third session of Council, a large majority approved the declaration on the Church's relations with non-Christians, which includes a strong and clear statement on the Jews, but the Fathers did not have enough time to cast the declaration in its final form for promulgation at this session. The vote: 1,651 to 99, 242 voting in favor but with reservations. The commission had to study each of the reservations to determine whether they could significantly add to the final document.

The declaration now had a broader scope than it had in its early forms, since it aimed to take in the whole field of relationships of the Church with non-Christian religions.

Cardinal Bea: "For the first time in the history of ecumenical councils, the principles dealing with non-Christians are set forth in solemn form. The Church has a serious obligation to initiate a dialogue with the one billion men who do not know Christ or His work of redemption, he said. It is the task of the Church to assist them in reaching a full share in the riches of Christ, he concluded" (James C. O'Neill, reporting on Bea, vol. 2, p. 296).

When the fourth and final session of Vatican II convened, the commission had done its work. Reporting on the revised schema on October 15, 1965, Paulist Father Thomas Stransky of the unity secretariat said that the document provides only a starting point for the improvement and development of relations between the Church and non-Christian religions. At present there are few Catholic scholars or institutes devoting research and study to these areas. What is said in the declaration may seem naïve in centuries to come, but at the present, he said, it would be difficult for the council to come up with any more than it has. The Secretariat for Non-Christian Religions must carry on the work which has been sanctioned by the declaration (Vatican II, Session 4, p. 140).

The Declaration on Christian Education, promulgated on October 28, 1965, specifically mentions, within the paragraph on "The Faculties of Sacred Sciences" (#10): "Likewise it is the role of these very faculties to make more penetrating inquiry into the various aspects of the sacred sciences so that an ever deepening understanding of sacred revelation is obtained, the legacy of Christian wisdom handed down by our forefathers is more fully developed, the dialogue with our separated brethren and with non-Christians is fostered, and answers are given to questions arising from the development of doctrine" (op.cit., p. 189).

The final and official vote was cast, and the Declaration on Relation of the Church to Non-Christian Religions was promulgated on October 28, 1965.

In order to avoid misinterpretation, we need to look closely at the remarks of Cardinal Bea and of Father Stransky. Indeed, this was the first time that these principles were set forth in documents of an ecumenical council, but while the principles were clearly and solemnly enunciated, they were not new. The Church does not proclaim "new" teachings, but closely examines what has been *handed down* (that is, *tradition*) and asks new questions in order to better understand what has been revealed. If it is not new, then how old is this issue?

Some of the principles elucidated in *Nostra Aetate* are to be found in the encyclical of Pope Pius XII on Promotion of Catholic Missions, June 2, 1951. Section VII expresses his desire that missionaries should fully understand that "The Church from the beginning down to our own time has always followed this wise practice: Let not the Gospel on being introduced into any new land destroy or extinguish whatever its people possess that is naturally good, just, or beautiful" (#56).

He continues: "Although owing to Adam's fall, human nature is tainted with original sin, yet is has in itself something that is naturally Christian (the reference given for this is Tertullian, *Apologet.*, cap. XVII), and this, if illumined by divine light and nourished by God's grace, can eventually be changed into true and supernatural virtue" (#57).

Pope Pius XII then relates that the Church "has neither scorned nor rejected the pagan philosophies," but after freeing them from error and "contamination" has "perfected and completed them by Christian revelation." The Church has encouraged native art, culture, and traditions. On these points, the Pope quotes from a letter of St. Basil (ca. A.D. 330 — Jan. 1, 379) to his young nephews who are students pursuing their education in pagan schools: ". . .Thus Moses, a man of the greatest renown for his wisdom, is said to have come to the contemplation of Him Who Is only after being trained in Egyptian lore. So later the wise Daniel is said to have been first schooled in Babylon in the wisdom of the Chaldeans, and only then to have come to know Divine Revelation" (#58, quotation from St. Basil, *Ad adolescentes*, 2, MG, XXXI, 567A).

This raises the question: Where is this topic addressed in Scripture?

Three books by Jean Daniélou (named Cardinal with his fellow theologian Father Henri De Lubac by Pope Paul VII during Vatican Council II) treat of this topic: *The Salvation of the Nations*,

University of Notre Dame Press, 1962 (first published by Sheed and Ward, London, 1949); *Advent*, New York, Sheed and Ward, 1951; and *Holy Pagans of the Old Testament*, Baltimore, Helicon Press, 1958 (originally: *Les Saints 'Paiens' de l'Ancien Testament*, 1956).

Daniélou, asking about the attitude of the first Christians to the pagan world around them, writes:

> ". . . Justin Martyr and Clement of Alexandria . . . had the idea that in pagan philosophies there was some sort of presence of the Word, of the Logos, some sort of divine light that enlightened men and gave them whatever of truth was in them. . . . Therefore the Word, who was to communicate Himself in His fullness in Christian Revelation, was already in some way present" (*Advent*, p. 5).

At the same time, those same Church Fathers tell us that an essential part of baptism for a pagan is the renunciation of "the works and pomps of Satan — another way of saying idolatry, that is, pagan religion" (op. cit., p. 10).

The Church Fathers make a distinction — "and we do the same today — between the two elements in the non-Christian world, . . . by recognizing that there were at once real *values*, as a Justin, a Clement, or a Saint Augustine did with Greek philosophy and with Plato, and *acts* — idolatrous worship and magical practices which were literally diabolic. . ." (op. cit., p. 10).

In both *Advent* and *Holy Pagans of the Old Testament* we read about the *first* covenant or promise, that made to Adam, then the later promise made to Noah, neither of whom were of the race or religion of Israel.

The "holy pagans" include Abel, Enoch, Danel (not Daniel), Noah, Job, Melchizedek, Lot, the Queen of Sheba.

> "It is important to note that . . . preparing for Christ is not confined to Israel. The authors concerned [Church Fathers] always make it clear that it is a question of the preparation for Christ as related in the Old Testament; but in the Old Testament Israel does not come into the picture until the eleventh chapter of Genesis. All the preceding chapters are devoted to recounting the religious history of mankind before Israel. . . . To be exact, therefore, it should be said that the Old

Testament describes the preparation for Christ first of all in the cosmic covenant, illustrated by the early chapters in regard to pagan humanity, and after that in the Mosaic covenant" (*Holy Pagans of the Old Testament*, pp. 10-11).

In *The Salvation of the Nations*, Daniélou addresses ". . . the need for a genuinely missionary spirituality, as expressed in Christ's prayer for the peoples still shut out from the Gospel" (op. cit., p. vii).

> "Christianity can, of course, be lived within the narrow limits of the community of which we are a part, whether it be our family or our country. To view Christianity in this light is not to see it in its true perspective.
> "Christianity is catholic by definition, that is, it embraces the world. . ." (ibid., p. 1).
> "Many of us accept as entirely normal that Catholicism is the religion of France, Italy, Spain, and South America, but we also seem to take it as normal that it is *not* the religion of India or China. . . . Let us not imagine that missions consist only in making contact in distant lands with civilizations that are different from our own. The missionary problem is at our very door. . . .
> "It is no longer necessary to go to India or China to seek out these civilizations. They are flowing back toward us. I am referring here particularly to Buddhism and Hinduism. . ." (ibid. p. 2).
> "We find ourselves in the presence not of geographically separated civilizations so much as of a number of universal movements which encompass the entire world . . . each professing to offer the one and only cure for a sick humanity" (ibid., p. 3).

The paragraphs just quoted may shock some persons when we recall that it was first published in 1949. The "flowing back toward us" is no longer a trickle but a flood.

We return to that "new" word, *syncretism*. Daniélou cites it as a grave problem confronting us.

> ". . .Syncretism . . . conceives of a universal religion that is to transcend all particular religions . . . that these latter each possess a part of the truth — Hinduism no less than Islam, Judaism, Catholicism, or

Protestantism. Its task, as it sees it, would consist in dissolving oppositions by rising above them to a superior religion which would embrace all the others. Every soul that would weigh the value of its Catholicism must face this problem and ask itself: Why am I a Catholic rather than a Buddhist or a Muslim? It will not suffice to answer: Because I was born a Catholic. That is tantamount to saying: Had I been born elsewhere, I should have been of another faith. That is to place all religions on the same level" (ibid., p. 3).

In a way, that statement gives greater structure and coherence to syncretism than is literal fact. Daniélou's account of syncretism reads like a description of Bahai. Syncretism as presently known in the United States is not an organization, not a creed, but a way of thinking accepted in varying degrees by many cults, many destructive religious movements, even many individuals who are not connected with or affiliated with any religious movement or church. Sometimes it appears as respect for the beliefs of others, but when respect for other *persons* extends to the point of respecting such *erroneous beliefs* as idolatry, pantheism, or reincarnation, *irenicism* has become *syncretism*.

We read in the Gospel according to St. Matthew (6:24): "No man can serve two masters. He will either hate one and love the other or be attentive to one and despise the other." The rest of that verse and what follows refers to love of money or property, but the verse could refer just as aptly to commingling radically different religious beliefs.

In the earliest days of Christianity, during the lifetimes of the Apostles, Gnosticism was a problem, a compromise between Christianity, Judaism, and whatever happened to be the local paganism. "The Gnostics believed that there existed, above particular religions, a higher truth to which initiates might rise" (op. cit., p. 5).

Nevertheless, every error still retains some portion of the truth. Pagans were not abandoned by God. It was to that small spark that St. Paul appealed when he spoke to the men of Athens who gathered around him at the Areopagus, reminding them of their belief in an Unknown God, Who is the Creator and Source of all life (Acts 17:16-34).

St. Paul appealed to the Athenians to turn from the gods represented by statues to the real Creator God for Whom there was no representation. This was, to put it in terms of this chapter, an appeal to break away from syncretism to the pure original belief which could provide the foundation for Revelation.

An indication of the extent to which syncretist ideas and practices have permeated Christian life can be seen in a document from the Congregation for the Doctrine of the Faith. "Letter to the Bishops of the Catholic Church on Some Aspects of Christian Meditation," issued on October 15, 1989, with the approval of Pope John Paul II, reiterates the caution of Pope Paul VI during his visit to India in 1964 and also repeats in modern form the appeal of the Apostle Paul. The Letter issued by the Congregation for the Doctrine of the Faith addresses the issue of proposals to ". . . *fuse Christian meditation with that which is non-Christian*" (#12).

In #16 of that document, the words from *Nostra aetate* are repeated: ". . . the Catholic Church rejects nothing of what is true and holy in these religions. . . ." Then it adds: ". . .one can take from them what is useful so long as the Christian conception of prayer, its logic and requirements, are never obscured" (#16).

Please note especially all of paragraph 12, in which some important distinctions and cautions are set forth.

One of the latest documents pertaining to the problem of syncretism and one which especially clarifies its multiformity came out of a meeting of the world's cardinals at the Vatican, April 4-7, 1991. One of the two major issues concerning the cardinals was sects and the rise of new religious movements around the world. Outlining the conclusions of the meeting, the communique from the Vatican Press Office stated that the Church was urged to make new efforts to make Catholics more aware of their own identity, to promote knowledge of the Sacred Scriptures, to make their parish communities more welcoming, respecting and involving all members, to draw more members to participate in well-prepared liturgies and devotions, adapted to the culture of the people.

In response to the request of the assembled cardinals that the Vatican address the issue of cults, Cardinal Francis Arinze of Nigeria, President of the Pontifical Council for Interreligious Dialogue, outlined certain challenges posed by the new religious movements.

Is there a common denominator between these groups? That was not entirely clarified.

Cardinal Arinze, however, distinguishes four types, with reference to the knowledge system which is their background:

1. Movements based on Holy Scripture, therefore Christian or derived from Christianity.
2. Movements derived from such religions as Hinduism, Buddhism, or the traditional pagan religions. Some of these assume elements from Christianity in a syncretistic way.
3. Some show signs of a decomposition of the genuine idea of religion and of a return to paganism.
4. Some are gnostic.

Another way of analyzing and categorizing the new religious movements is by their distance from traditional Christianity, if they are located in regions which have been Christian:

1. "Those that reject the Church;
2. those that reject Christ;
3. those that reject the role of God (and yet maintain a generic sense of 'religion');
4. those that reject the role of religion (and maintain a sense of the sacred, but manipulated by man to acquire power over others or the cosmos)" (*Origins*, vol. 20, no. 46, April 25, 1991, p. 750).

The entire analysis of this problem by Cardinal Arinze deserves careful reading, but two matters require repetition here:

"In spite of the diversity of NRMs [New Religious Movements] and of local situations, they all raise one main pastoral problem which is the vulnerability of the faithful to proposals which are contrary to the formation they have received.

"The phenomenon of the sects poses a serious problem of discernment for the pastors of the Church. 'It is not every spirit, my dear people, that you can trust,' says the beloved apostle John. 'Test them, to see if

they come from God; there are many false prophets now in the world'
(I Jn. 4:1)" (*Origins*, op. cit., p. 750).

Syncretism: Suggested Reading

Vatican Council II: The Conciliar and Postconciliar Documents,
General Editor, Austin Flannery, O.P., Northport, N.Y., Costello
Publishing Co., 1975

The Documents of Vatican II, General Editor: Walter M. Abbott,
S.J., Translation Editor: Very Rev. Msgr. Joseph Gallagher, New
York, The America Press, 1966

Pope Pius XII, *Evangelii praecones* (On Promotion of Catholic
Missions), issued June 2, 1951

Pope Paul VI, *Evangelii nuntiandi* (Evangelization in the Modern
World), issued December 8, 1975, in *Vatican Council II*, Vol. 2,
"More Postconciliar Documents, General Editor: Austin Flannery,
O.P., Northport, N.Y., Costello Publishing Co., 1982 (#53 pertains
to relations with non-Christian religions)

The Pope Speaks, Washington, D.C., Vol. 10, #2, 1965, pp. 145-166
on Pope Paul's visit to India

Council Daybook, Vatican II, Session 1, Oct. 11, to Dec. 8, 1962,
Session 2, Sept. 29 to Dec. 4, 1963, Washington, D.C., National
Catholic Welfare Conference, 1965
Session 3, Sept. 14 to Nov. 21, 1964, same publisher, 1965
Session 4, Sept. 14 to Dec. 8, 1965, same publisher, 1966

Pope John Paul II, *Redemptoris missio* (Mission of the Redeemer)
Boston, Mass., St. Paul Books & Media, 1990 (#10, all of Chapter
4, #52 through #57 pertain especially to relations with
non-Christian religions)

Documents of the Congregation for the Doctrine of the Faith, ". . .
And the Truth Will Make You Free," San Francisco, Ignatius
Press, 1990

Daniélou, Jean, S.J., *Advent*, New York, Sheed and Ward, 1951;
Holy Pagans of the Old Testament, Baltimore, Helicon Press,
1958; *The Salvation of the Nations*, Notre Dame, Ind., University
of Notre Dame Press, 1962

Origins, Documentary Service of the Catholic News Service,
Washington, D.C., In particular:

Archbishop Jean Jadot, "The Dialogue of Life," vol. 12, #46 (April 18, 1983)

Archbishop Francis Arinze, "The Urgency of Dialogue with Non-Christians," vol. 14, #39, Mar. 14, 1985

Cardinal Franz König, "Dialogue, A Demanding Struggle," vol. 14, #42, April 4, 1985

Cardinal Francis Arinze, "The Challenge of New Religious Movements," vol. 20, #46, April 25, 1991 [See Appendix IX, below.]

Vatican Paper, signed by Cardinals Francis Arinze and Josef Tomko, "Mission, Interreligious Understanding, Dialogue and Proclamation," vol. 21, #8, July 4, 1991 (very important for understanding the parameters of dialogue with non-Christians)

13.

Discernment

Father Lawrence J. Gesy

SOCRATES' remark that "The unexamined life is not worth living," quoted in Plato's *Apology*, could be the heading for this chapter.

At the present time, one of the greatest obstacles to clear thinking about religious matters is a pervasive attitude that "people should have faith." The quotation marks are deliberate, because many of us have heard that attitude expressed many times in those or in similar words. I have also heard "Everyone needs faith." We could, and should, ask "Faith in what or in whom?" and "What kind of faith?"

St. Augustine says that our hearts are restless until they rest in God. It is that restlessness which impels persons without faith in the God revealed in the holy Scriptures or persons whose faith in that God has been weakened for some reason to seek some new object for their "faith loosened from its moorings."

In the first chapter, we used the image of a yardstick as a standard of measurement in civil society and the need for some standard by which persons can determine what is true or false, valid or worthless, or even dangerous in new religious movements. Here we turn to *how to examine* new religious movements against standards, not only *objectively*, as we do in the other chapters, but *subjectively*, that is in their effects within the spiritual lives of those who become involved, of the families and friends of those who are interested or involved, and those effects as clergy and counselors may observe them.

Each category of destructive religious movements treated in this book appeals to a particular human need or desire, and generally to such a need or desire unchecked to the point where it clouds the mind of the person involved. Some of those needs and desires are not simply neutral. The need for a relationship with God, which sometimes finds expression in desires for many different things and experiences, if understood and heeded, can bring a person to sanctity. On that very topic, St. Augustine said in prayer: "Our hearts are restless until they rest in Thee."

Any curiosity about God, the supernatural, what we can do to grow in our knowledge and love of God and in our prayer life, should be met with respect and cooperation, so that persons may receive guidance and encouragement to seek and to grow along true and health-giving spiritual paths.

Father Thomas Dubay, S.M., says something of importance to us in this regard in *Fire Within* (San Francisco, Ignatius Press, 1989, pp. 243-248):

> ". . . some people would take the view that in the scientific milieu and widespread literacy of contemporary technological societies, the idea of special divine enlightenments and messages merits at best a patronizing smile, at worst, ridicule. . . .
>
> "But there is another group, by no means small in number, who gladly embrace the notion of direct divine communications. Equally citizens of our technological societies and sometimes well educated in their respective secular pursuits, these men and women not only hold to the theoretical possibility that God communes with human beings but also are often enough convinced that He has spoken to them personally or at least that on occasion He sends them an inner light. They readily speak of 'listening to the Spirit.' Some in this group build their spiritual lives more on alleged apparitions and their own presumed inner illuminations than on the word of the Gospel and the proclamation of the teaching Church.
>
> "Within both of these categories, the deniers and the affirmers, there is of course a spectrum of reaction patterns. . . . Among the affirmers there are the absurdly credulous who are convinced that they are constantly privy to divine messages and visions. Others steer clear of these extremes but all the same are not as cautious as they must be in order to avoid different pitfalls. They are insufficiently sensitive to the dangers of illuminism, for instance."

What is this word *Discernment*? What has it to do with *Destructive Religious Movements*?

In theology, the word "discernment" usually is a shortened way of referring to "discernment of spirits," that is, to ascertain the motivating spirit underlying a person's choices or actions. There are many references to this in both the Old and New Testaments, to which we refer later in this chapter. "Discernment" can also refer to making a prudent choice between alternatives, in such matters as state of life or vocation.

Since this chapter, however, refers to "discernment" specifically with reference to destructive religious movements, we must recognize that "discernment" has those meanings for clergy and religious counselors, but perhaps several broader meanings in popular usage. In addition, those who have become involved in destructive religious movements have lost much or all of their ability to think clearly. This chapter, then, is directed primarily to parents, friends, and counselors, whether clergy or lay.

Some of our readers may bring to the chapters of this book a desire to discover more about some of these "new religions" or "cults," especially if they are acquainted with people whose thoughts about life differ considerably from those with which many of us were raised. Can any of these "new ideas" fit into the religion they learned at home, in church, in religious school, and into their presently held belief system?

Some readers may find themselves drawn to one or another aspect of a particular religious movement, attracted, tempted to take a chance. How can they meet the challenge of attempts to recruit them to a new and different religious movement?

Friends and relatives of persons who have become involved in destructive religious movements are often disturbed and saddened, asking: How could my brother or sister do this? We had the same parents; we attended the same church, the same Sunday school. What different experiences caused him or her to turn in this direction? Did I fail to offer love, friendship, even counsel if he or she had a problem? What "went wrong"?

Every person who meets this subject of destructive religious movements, whether in books or in people presently involved as members or as family or friends of members, experiences one or more or all of the above feelings and questions. *How* we deal with those questions and feelings is *a discernment process*.

We can "muddle through," following our thoughts at random, or asking the same questions over and over, taking a roller-coaster ride on our emotions. There are, however, some interesting and very helpful *discernment processes* which knowledgeable and trustworthy persons have worked out over the years.

What Is Discernment?

Let us see how our present use of the word "discernment" can lead us into the process.

"Discernment" is a somewhat strange word in our contemporary language.

We hear it used as a compliment, that a certain person shows great "discernment" in her choice of friends, meaning that she chooses for close friends only persons of good character, and only after becoming well acquainted with the persons, giving herself time to observe them, to learn whether their good qualities are deep or shallow.

"Discern" is used again in discourse by persons who have arrived at a crossroads in their lives: a person may say "I must try to look at all sides of this issue, so that I may discern the best course of action in this situation." Another might say, "I need to make a retreat to discern which path in life I should take next."

The last example reflects the more traditional religious use of the term, "discernment," that process by which a person gradually comes to perceive his or her choice of life work or the direction which his or her or prayer life is taking. The aim of "discernment" in this sense of the word is to enable us to search out the source of those impulses or inspirations which motivate us or move us to serious action.

Each of these uses of the word "discernment" illustrates an aspect of its meaning which we need to examine in order to exercise the discernment process most effectively in our lives.

Let's take them in order:

The first use of "discernment" shows discrimination in choice of friends. It tells us that the discerning, discriminating person has standards, whether they are kept deeply within or openly expressed, against which scale the character of new acquaintance are weighed or compared. Do you remember the yardstick we mentioned in the first chapter? Another element of this illustration is patient reserve for sufficient time to allow careful observation of persons, who seldom show most of their qualities at first or second meeting, preventing hasty judgment. This person is judging a situation by objective standards.

The next two examples of the use of the word "discernment" combine taking "time out" to come to a decision, separating oneself from business or routine obligations and interruptions, in order to concentrate on the pros and cons of a problem. "Making a retreat" in order to come to a decision, to choose a "path in life," is "time out" spent with God, weighing the issues with prayer, trying to reach a conclusion consonant with God's standards, probably examining the situation against objective standards, matters outside oneself, but also weighing his or her own feelings and reactions to the situation, the personal or subjective element affecting decisions.

* * * * *

This brings us to the traditional use of the word "discernment."

Our readers surely fall into one or more of the following categories: clergy or laity; spouses, parents, other relatives or friends of persons interested in or involved with possibly destructive religious movements; or the persons themselves interested in or currently involved with what we may call questionable religious movements. Each will approach the discernment process from a different direction, but the first steps are the same for everyone.

It is of the greatest importance that concerned relatives and friends of anyone interested in or involved in what appears to be some destructive religious movement *also go through a discernment process.* Clergy and counselors also need to go through a discernment process, because while we may have good reasons for believing as we do, it is difficult, if not impossible, to empathize with the difficulties of others and to share with them the grounds of our faith unless and until we have struggled through to deeper understanding of our own beliefs, including that knowledge of ourselves which enables us to understand something about the wellsprings or motivations of our choices.

If people are aware of discernment at all, they seem to think of it as something practiced among priests, religious, and very religious lay persons. And it is true that from the earliest days of the Church discernment was developed by confessors and spiritual directors of persons seeking to grow in the spiritual life of the Church and by the persons they were counseling. The counselors and the counseled alike accepted the major teachings of the Church as basic data. So the literature about discernment grew with little or no deliberate cross-referencing to doctrine, certainly not contrary to doctrine, but parallel to it.

Today, familiarity with fundamental teachings of the Church cannot be assumed. Total breakdown in communication can come about when persons are using similar or even identical words, such as God, spirit, life, thought, even "death" but with quite different meanings. It is essential that all parties to such conversations or consultations assume nothing, but start "from ground zero" by clarifying their understanding of each other's terms.

All discernment starts with God and myself: Who is my God? What do I believe about God? Why do I hold these beliefs?

Everyone is seeking God, whether or not he or she is fully conscious of doing so. By "God" I mean an object or an objective which is so powerful in my life that it motivates me in most or in all of what I do. Some persons seek power. Hitler, Stalin, some Latin-American generals who lead revolutions in order to gain control of their countries; perhaps Saddam Hussein or the late Ayatollah Khomeini would come into that category. Some persons make the pursuit of money their "god." They (men or women) sacrifice time at home with their families to pursue success in business. Other persons make the pursuit of pleasure their "god."

In each of these cases, the persons involved have not practiced the most elementary self-examination. By that I do not mean asking themselves the question: How can I reach my goal? But the more basic questions:

What drives me to seek this particular goal?
Is the goal I have set for myself worth seeking?
Is the goal I seek a kind of blind or curtain masking a different goal which I have not yet identified?

If others have different goals, why? What are they seeking?

All of this leads back to the question: Who or what is *my god*?

Is my "god" that aim which drives everything I do, power, money, personal pleasure, some god I seek without being fully aware that I have a god without a name while there is a God waiting for my acknowledgment?

Before we can begin to answer these questions it is necessary to get some facts. If there is some kind of god "out there" I need to know who and what he/she/it is.

How many different ideas about God exist in the world at this time?

What idea of God did I receive from my parents and relatives, my Church, my religious school? Has my idea of God stayed at the elementary-school level or has it been enriched, enlarged? Has it grown with me?

I have noticed something strange. The same people who would not think of voting without listening to the candidates' speeches, examining their record in previous office, and studying the platforms of the parties, all of which involves a much more adult approach to civil life than can be acquired in high school civics classes, many such people make much more serious choices daily supported only by an elementary-school level of religious education.

I am not blaming those people! The world around us claims our full attention, whether or not it deserves it. All the more reason why we need to draw apart at times to do some basic discernment.

How many gods are there for us to discover and to examine?

It would be worthwhile, if we are Christians, to examine our own Christian God. A good place to start is a little book by J.B. Phillips, *Your God Is Too Small* (New York, Macmillan, 1961). Do not let the date turn you away from this. It is a classic which a great many people have found very helpful. Another book, which deals with more than the Christian teachings about God but also examines the gods of many other peoples, is Peter Kreeft's *Fundamentals of the Faith*, (San Francisco, Ignatius Press, 1991).

A word of caution which cannot be overemphasized: unless we know what we believe about God, *who or what* our God is, and *why we believe* this, we cannot hold any worthwhile discussions with persons who are curious about or involved with destructive religious movements.

Many Christian relatives and friends of persons who become interested in or dabblers in new and possibly destructive religious movements are quite unaware that most of these have *very* different ideas about God, about what Christians call "creation," and inevitably, about human persons, i.e., ourselves. So this is where we start, with the object of our beliefs.

What is the idea of God which I have had until now? Is this God (god?) separate from me, i.e., a Supreme Being, my Creator? Or is this God (god) part of the world around me and including me, that is, is *everything*, including myself, some sort of long-lasting divinity, without "creation" entering into the process by which things are or seem to come to be. That is approximately the belief about divinity (God) of most Eastern religions. The Creator-God Who has given being to the world and its people is the God of Judeo-Christianity and of Islam.

This bring us to the second question:

> Who are we? What is a human being? Have human persons a spiritual dimension — what is generally called a "spiritual soul"?
> And most important of all: What do we mean by "spirit" in relation to ourselves, in relation to others, to life after death?

Notice that I have not even mentioned morality, human acts which can be called good or evil, the "Ten Commandments," doing good for others; nor have I mentioned worship, private (personal) or public (liturgical or "official" Church) prayer. All of that comes later. How we determine what or which moral law we will follow (if any); how we worship a god, or even if we will worship a god; all depends on, follows from, who or what our god is and how we are connected with, related to, that god.

Therefore: Who are we?

Are we created beings, who owe our being to a good God Who has made all things good?

Are we spiritual beings imprisoned in a material body and living in a material world, created so by some capricious evil principle who is fighting against a Good Principle? This is the view of Gnosticism,

Manichaeism, the old religion of Persia/Iran before Islam became the religion of that country.

Or are we waves on an ocean of divinity, divine ourselves? This is what is called "pantheism," that is, that all is god and god is all, admittedly oversimplified.

The "morality" which derives from that last position, if it is logical, is the "morality" of Charles Manson and Son of Sam. Manson states that he is God, and that when he ordered people killed, he was doing them a favor, sending them back into the divinity of which they were a part.

Does this set of *preliminary* questions seem daunting?

No one inherits religious beliefs as we inherit the color of our eyes or our hair. Most of us hope that our children will accept our beliefs, will follow in the religion to which we adhere. Of course we influence them. Children imitate us, or in some instances, because they wish to express their independence, choose to go a different way, or because they see in us a particular trait or action which turns them off, they react against certain traits they see in the adults they know. Young people need to see in the adults around them a desire for God expressed in a committed adult search for better understanding of their belief system.

This brings us to the next step: the subjective, internal part of the discernment process, the examination of ourselves, our feelings, those quirks of personality which affect our thinking and our choices. Does our particular notion of God come out of examined and agreed-to acceptance of the belief system we received from the teachings and examples of the adults among whom we lived while we were growing up?

Is our notion of God a reaction against something we observed in our family which turned us against what they taught? (Was it a case of "don't do as I do, but do as I say"?) One example of this is the adult who cannot call God "Father" because his or her own parent was harsh or abusive. Such a person is limiting the term "Father" to the parent he or she could see instead of realizing that such a parent has not really followed the Father Who is the pattern for all *good* fathers.

A mother who is harsh or too strict in discipline, or a manipulative mother, or a too-meek "clinging vine" of a mother, can turn her children against the particular form of religion she practices.

Does our notion of God come from unexamined acceptance of the ideas of the world around us now?

Can We Find Discernment in the Old Testament?

In the first part of this chapter on *Discernment*, the questions about God with which we were concerned arising from many of the "new" religious movements parallel in many ways the kind of questions and problems about God which we read about in the Old Testament — religious ideas and religious practices which were around and among the Israelites and the Jews. For that reason it is not unusual that we find discernment or its equivalent mentioned in the Old Testament.

When we try to find "discernment" in the Old Testament we discover that tracing that word is no easy undertaking. Translating is never easy, because each language not only has different words for things with which we are familiar, but also different sentence constructions. Complicating translation from the old Hebrew is not only the fact that two to three thousand years separates us from the way of life and the experiences of the people concerned, but words often carry with them associations which enlarge their immediate meaning. We need only think of the word "thanksgiving." To an American, it means not only giving thanks to God for all the good things we enjoy from His Providence over us, it also brings into our memories the pictures of family around the loaded dinner table, perhaps a grandmother bringing a big turkey to place before us. Yet, that word, "thanksgiving," *without the images of turkey, cranberry sauce, and pumpkin pie*, is the exact meaning of the Greek word, "Eucharist" because the Passover was a feast, with a sacrifice, of thanksgiving to God. So, you see, we *cannot* use "thanksgiving" as our English language term for the sacrament. It would be too confusing.

In his three-volume translation with introductions and commentary on the Psalms for the Anchor Bible Series (Doubleday), Father Mitchell Dahood, S.J., elaborates on some of the difficulties in translating from Hebrew to English.

To relate some of that here would require too lengthy a digression, but suffice it to say that there may be more than one Hebrew word which this or that translator has rendered into English as "discern," while another translator will use "intelligent and prudent," and still a third will translate it as "shrewd," or "the power to know," all of which are included in the traditional religious sense of discernment.

In spite of those difficulties, which are not really insurmountable, I think it is evident that "discernment" is being used here in the sense of the act of seeing clearly in a specific instance the issues which a person needs to judge between truth or error, to make a choice between good or evil.

The first biblical instance of discernment is not labeled by any word which could bring it into that category. First Eve and then Adam made bad choices. We are familiar with the consequences of their bad choices.

Also in the Book of Genesis, we come upon words or phrases which are sometimes translated as "discerning." In Ch. 41:33 and 39, the NAB uses that word in connection with Joseph in Egypt: "Therefore, let Pharaoh seek out a wise and discerning man and put him in charge of the land of Egypt. . ."; and later Pharaoh responds: "Since God has made all this known to you, no one can be as wise and discerning as you are. . . ."

One of the most beautiful prayers for the gift of discernment is found in Psalm 119, a "didactic" or teaching Psalm, praising God's Law, elaborately constructed, based on each strophe or section beginning with a letter of the Hebrew alphabet in sequence, and each of the eight verses within the strophes praising the Law using eight different synonyms, e.g law, statutes, commands, ordinances, decrees, words, precepts, promise. Father Dahood uses the word "insight" in each case where the New American Bible uses "discernment," and the Jerusalem Bible translates v. 104, "Your precepts endow me with perception, I hate all deceptive paths."

Let us note the verses in Ps. 119 which speak of the process or act we are examining:

"Give me insight that I may observe your law,
that I may keep it with all my heart" (v. 34)
"Your hands have made me and fashioned me;
give me insight that I may learn your commandments" (v. 73).
"Through your precepts I acquire insight, Most High Honest One,
I hate every false way" (v. 104).

"I am your servant; give me insight,
that I may know your stipulations" (v. 125).
"Into the justice of your stipulations, O Eternal One,
give me insight that I may live" (v. 144).
"May my cry reach your presence, Yahweh,
according to your word, give me insight" (v. 169).

Father Dahood explains in the notes the term "Most High Honest One" in v. 104 (a term not found in the NAB translation. He mentions that the Psalmist uses descriptive names of God which differ in each section, according to the theme of the verses in the section, and in v. 104, a Hebrew word which is sometimes translated as *therefore* "can also be translated as a composite divine name," which would be most appropriate preceding the Psalmist's repudiating "every false way" (*The Anchor Bible, Psalms III*, p. 185).

It is clear from these excerpted verses of Psalm 119 that the Psalmist looks to God as his Creator, who is honest and just, and is asking of God the gift of discernment or insight, to learn and to observe God's law, to reject false ways; and that through observance of God's decrees, the Psalmist expects to live. How the Psalmist hopes to live is expressed in the final verses (174-176):

"I long for your salvation, O LORD,
and your law is my delight.
Let my soul live to praise you,
and may your ordinances help me.
I have gone astray [like a lost sheep]; seek your servant,
because your commands I do not forget" (NAB).
"If I should stray like a lost sheep, seek your servant,
For I have not forgotten your commandments" (Anchor Bible,
Dahood's translation, p. 171).

What is meant by the "precepts" "decrees," "your word," "commands," and "your law"? There were many precepts and decrees for the people of Israel, but basic to and underlying all of them was the recognition that they were "the People of God," to whose father, Abraham, God had revealed Himself, calling them to be His People while He would be their God. And these people had been "brought out of Egypt" and slavery by the power of that God of Abraham, Isaac, and Jacob, led by Moses, to whom He had revealed His Name — Yahweh — and through whom He had revealed His Commandments to that people.

We can see from petitions such as these in the Psalms that the Israelites sought from God the power to discern. One who indeed sought that was King Solomon.

One of the most interesting of the references to discernment in all of Scripture is found in the account of Solomon's famous prayer for wisdom in First Kings. During the night after he had offered sacrifice to God at Gibeon, Solomon asks God, Who had come to him in a dream, for wisdom to lead his people: "Give your servant a heart to understand how to discern between good and evil. . ." (1 Kgs. 3:9, 11, JB). In the New American Bible, the words used are: "Give your servant, therefore, an understanding heart to judge your people and to distinguish right from wrong. . . ." In the verses which follow, Solomon is assured by God that he will be given that wisdom, that "discerning judgment" (1 Kgs. 3:9-15, JB).

The tragedy of the history of Solomon is found in the fact that he used some of his shrewdness not only to surround himself with foreign wives, consolidating his alliances with the nearby kingdoms, but also allowed them to introduce their pagan religions, which included human sacrifice, into his kingdom. He had used his "discerning judgment" to enable him skillfully to seek selfish, worldly goals, becoming the richest ruler of his time.

Solomon well knew that he was asking for discernment or wisdom to judge well from that God whose first Commandment given to His People through Moses stated:

> "I, the LORD, am your God, who brought you out of the land of Egypt, that place of slavery. You shall not have other gods besides me. You shall not carve idols for yourselves in the shape of anything in the sky above or on the earth below or in the waters beneath the earth; you shall not bow down to them or worship them" (Ex. 20:2-5a and Dt. 5:6-9a, NAB).

Throughout Old Testament history, the people who had received such lavish evidence of God's loving providence constantly showed their impatience, their desire for immediate gratification, their curiosity to try forbidden things, by seeking answers through divination; worshiping false gods and goddesses, such as the Canaanite Astarte, even sacrificing their children to Baal or Moloch, to obtain favors such as better crops or victory in war, which they should have known only the one true Creator God could give them.

The kingdom built by David, whose great sin was adultery but not idolatry, lasted just until the death of Solomon. After that, a series of bad kings brought about the subjugation of the entire people to foreign powers, while prophet after prophet tried to call the kings and the people to repentance.

In summary, the terms used in the Old Testament that are translated as "discernment" include the notion of understanding, of being able to distinguish clearly what must be done to know the will of God and to choose rightly, to choose that which has been indicated as fulfilling the Law. In addition, the power to discern appears always as a kind of gift, something which one asks God to bestow.

What Does the New Testament Tell Us About Discernment?

It must be understood that some matters related at length in the Old Testament are hardly mentioned at all in the writings of the Evangelists, St. Paul, and other writers of epistles or letters. This abbreviated information seldom indicates that the matter was unimportant to the New Testament authors, only that they found other matters more urgent, or that they assumed the continued practice of what had been enjoined on the people by the Old Testament writers.

One very important distinction, however, is made very clear in the New Testament. Remember how the verses in the Psalm 119 indicate that the author of the Psalms in question *asks* God for the power or ability to discern, and Solomon *asks* God to give him discernment.

Two kinds of discernment become evident in the New Testament. St. Paul speaks of the variety of gifts of the Spirit, i.e., the Holy Spirit, in 1 Corinthians 12:4-11, among which is listed "the gift of recognizing spirits" (v. 10, Jerusalem Bible, 1966) or "the power to distinguish one spirit from another" (v. 10, NAB). In that passage, he is clearly speaking about what are called "charismatic gifts" or "infused" gifts, that is, gifts or powers given by God beyond the ordinary gifts readily available to all sincere praying Christians, gifts given especially for persons needing them for the good of the Christian community, for a special vocation. This is evident from the next verse:

"All these [preaching, healing, miracles, prophecy, recognizing spirits, tongues, and interpreting tongues] are the work of one and the same spirit, who distributes different gifts to different people just as he chooses" (1 Cor. 12:11, JB).

In 1 John 4:1-6, we find the famous line "put the spirits to a test" in the context: "Beloved, do not trust every spirit, but put the spirits to a test to see if they belong to God, because many false prophets have appeared in the world." In the context of the rest of that passage, it is clear that the author is not writing about some infused gift, but about the gifts of the Holy Spirit which are granted to Christians through the sacraments: wisdom, understanding, counsel (right judgment), fortitude, knowledge, piety, and fear of the Lord (cf. Isa. 11:2-3). Note that "counsel" is often translated as "right judgment," which is precisely what is involved in discernment, the ability to judge rightly.

Father John Hardon, S.J., explains that counsel assists the mind ". . . after the gifts of knowledge and understanding furnish the general principles . . ." and ". . . perfect the virtue of prudence." "Enlightened by the Spirit, a person learns what to do in a specific case and what advice to give when consulted or command to make if . . . in authority" (John A. Hardon, S.J., *The Catholic Catechism,* New York, Doubleday, 1975, p. 202).

With regard to the charismatic gift of discernment, a statement found in the *Dogmatic Constitution on the Church* of Vatican Council II is pertinent:

"Whether these charisms be very remarkable or more simple and widely diffused, they are to be received with thanksgiving and consolation, since they are fitting and useful for the needs of the Church. Extraordinary gifts are not to be rashly desired, nor is it from them that fruits of apostolic labors are to be presumptuously expected.

Those who have charge over the Church should judge the genuineness and proper use of these gifts, through their office not indeed to extinguish the spirit, but to test all things and hold fast to what is good. (1 Thess. 5:12; 19:21)" (L.G. #12).

In St. Matthew's Gospel, Jesus tells us:

"Be on your guard against false prophets, who come to you in sheep's clothing but underneath are wolves on the prowl. You will know them by their deeds. Do you ever pick grapes from thornbushes, or figs from prickly plants? Never! Any sound tree bears good fruit, while a decayed tree bears bad fruit. . . . None of those who cry out, 'Lord, Lord,' will enter the kingdom of God, but only the one who does the will of my Father in heaven. When that day comes, many will plead with me, 'Lord, Lord, have we not prophesied in your name? Have we not exorcised demons by its power? Did we not do many miracles in your name as well?' Then I will declare to them solemnly, 'I never knew you. Out of my sight, you evildoers' "(Mt. 7:15-23, NAB).

That is the famous passage in Scripture which shows us the standard which Jesus uses to discern or to judge whether the spirit which moves us is evil (diabolical, from evil human inclinations), or good: from God, or from our own spirit guided or moved by God. The problem which most of us face is that many destructive religious movements *appear* good. Their fruits are not immediately evident. St. Paul's writings show this, not only the hidden, deceptive quality of many destructive religious movements of his time, but what appears to be a perfect description of New Age and other destructive movements of the present. When you read this, remember that "later times" and "last days" refer to the whole period from the Resurrection of Jesus to the present.

During the week leading to His crucifixion, Jesus spoke to His disciples about the destruction of Jerusalem and the Temple, which would occur in the lifetime of many of them. The disciples asked, "Tell us, when is this going to happen, and what will be the sign of your coming and of the end of the world" (Mt. 24:3 JB), actually, at least two, if not three, separate questions. Many misinterpret that chapter because they fail to distinguish between the questions asked by the disciples which, of course, require separate answers from Jesus.

The first part of Jesus' discourse is a reply relating to the period from that moment (ca. A.D. 33-35) to the period of the Roman War in Palestine, from A.D. 63 until the fall of Jerusalem and the destruction of the Temple in A.D. 70.

". . . Take care that no one deceives you; because many will come in by using my name and saying 'I am the Christ,' and they will deceive many. . . . Many false prophets will arise; they will deceive many, and with the increase of lawlessness, love in most men will grow cold; but the man who stands firm to the end will be saved" (Mt. 24:4-13; see also Mk. 13:5-13, JB).

In that same chapter (24), Jesus is quoted as saying:

"If anyone says to you then, 'Look, here is the Christ' or 'He is there,' do not believe it; for false Christs and false prophets will arise and produce great signs and portents, enough to deceive even the chosen, if that were possible." (Mt. 24:23, 24, cf. Mk. 13, 22-23, JB).

In the two Letters from Paul to Timothy strong words are used with regard to "deceitful spirits":

"The Spirit distinctly says that in later times some will turn away from the faith and will heed deceitful spirits and things taught by demons through plausible liars — men with seared consciences [literally: 'having been branded on their own conscience' as with a hot branding iron] who forbid marriages and require abstinence from foods which God created to be received with thanksgiving by believers who know the truth" (1 Tim. 4:1-3, NAB).

"Do not forget this: there will be terrible times in the last days. Men will be lovers of self and of money, proud, arrogant, abusive, disobedient to their parents, ungrateful, profane, inhuman, implacable, slanderous, licentious, brutal, hating the good. They will be treacherous, reckless, pompous, lovers of pleasure rather than of God as they make a pretense of religion but negate its power. Stay clear of them. It is such as these who worm their way into homes and captivate

261

silly women burdened with sins and driven by desires of many kinds, always learning but never able to reach a knowledge of the truth. Just as Jannes and Jambres opposed Moses, so these men also oppose the truth; with perverted minds they falsify the faith. But they will not get very far; as with those two men, the stupidity of these will be plain for all to see" (2 Tim. 3:1-9, NAB) [Ed. Note: Hebrew tradition attributed these names to the Egyptian magicians who vied with Moses in Ex. 7:11-12, 22].

". . . the time will come when people will not tolerate sound doctrine, but, following their own desires, will surround themselves with teachers who tickle their ears. They will stop listening to the truth and will wander off to fables" (2 Tim. 4:3-4, NAB).

How can we save ourselves from being deceived by the false prophets, drawn into following false Messiahs, become so involved with such movements that we fail to see their poisonous fruits?

From early Christian times until now, "taking time out," "making a retreat," prayer with others who are known to be good, dedicated Christians has been the way.

Probably the most famous of all writings on discernment are the "Rules for the Discernment of Spirits" in *The Spiritual Exercises* of St. Ignatius of Loyola. The idea of drawing apart from everyday life to meditate and pray particularly when some important decision is to be made or in preparation for a change of direction in one's life is not new. It has a long Christian heritage, Jesus going to the desert to fast and pray — and to be tempted by the devil; the Apostles in prayer in the Upper Room as they awaited the coming of the Holy Spirit; and St. Paul after his conversion, spending three years in the desert before starting his missionary work.

With that beginning, the early Church Fathers and later theologians developed what might be called an entire literature on the spiritual life in general and on discernment in particular. St. Ignatius' *Spiritual Exercises*, in which Jesus is presented as the perfect model of God's service calling others to follow him, owes much to that tradition, and includes possibly the best known "Rules for the Discernment of Spirits."

It is important to state "up front" that *The Spiritual Exercises* of St. Ignatius, as he wrote them, is "not a book to be read, and less still a systematic exposition of ascetical principles." says Rev. John A. Hardon, S.J. (*All My Liberty, Theology of the Spiritual Exercises*, Westminster, Md., Newman Press, 1959, p. xiii). It was designed as a set of definite meditations which a retreatant would work through guided by a competent spiritual director.

The "Rules for the Discernment of Spirits" are specifically written as guidelines to help the director enable the retreatant to learn how to understand the dispositions, inclinations, and, it might be, inspirations which provide the motives for choices or decisions.

It is for this reason that we suggest that this chapter should be read carefully by clergy and counselors in particular. Persons attracted to destructive religious movements need to be helped to discern the spirit or spirits which move them. Their family and/or friends need to be guided into clearer discernment of their own feelings and motives before they can effectively relate to the friend or relative interested in or involved in new and different religious movements. In this instance we should remember the advice so often given to attorneys, that the lawyer who acts on his own behalf, pleads his own case, has a fool for a lawyer.

Father Jordan Aumann, O. P., introduces us to what we mean here by "spirits":

> "It is indispensable . . . to be able to distinguish the various spirits under which an individual may act or be acted upon. As used here, the word *spirit* refers to two different types of motivating factors or powers. The spirit of an *individual* refers to the *internal* inclination to do good or evil, and it manifests itself with such regularity that it must be considered a personal trait. Thus, if a person has a propensity to prayer, he or she is said to possess the spirit of prayer; if there is a tendency to arguments and altercations, he or she is said to possess a spirit of contradiction, etc. Understood in this sense, the spirit of a person is usually the result of both temperament and character.
> "But it is also possible for an individual to come under the influence of a spirit that is *extrinsic* to the personality, whether from *God* or the *devil*. For that reason it is the function of the discernment of spirits to judge whether a given act or repetition of acts flows from the spirit of God, the diabolical spirit, or the spirit of the individual" (Jordan

Aumann, O.P., *Spiritual Theology*, Huntington, Ind., Our Sunday Visitor, 1980. p. 399).

It is unfortunate for us that we are generally so familiar with the account of Jesus' forty days in the desert after His baptism in the Jordan that we may find ourselves thinking in clichés. Much is lost in that kind of thinking. So let us start afresh with Matthew 4:1-11.

Jesus is in the desert. The "forty days and forty nights" was a Hebrew and Aramaic way of saying a very long time, somewhat like our old American expression "a country mile," but it was also a definite reference to the desert experience of the Children of Israel, who had to fast and were tempted by the devil after they had escaped from Egypt. The Jews and Jewish Christians (for whom Matthew's Gospel was originally intended) would have recognized that allusion. He had gone into the desert to pray and fast in response to an inspiration or a call of the Holy Spirit in preparation for His coming public ministry. However long a time it was, Jesus was hungry.

Both Matthew and Luke recount the same first temptation. We do not know whether the devil appeared to Jesus in some visible form or whether Jesus was simply aware of a spirit of evil or an evil spirit tempting Him. Because we cannot expect, much less hope, to identify evil so quickly under the guise of good or of legitimacy, it is important for us to analyze this segment of the Gospel.

Hunger is a gift God has implanted in our nature so that we will eat to replenish our bodies as growth and work deplete them. Would it not be right for Jesus to satisfy His hunger, since eating to satisfy honest hunger is not sinful? But notice! Jesus went into the desert in response to the Holy Spirit, and there is no natural food close by. Jesus has the power to turn the stones into bread (later He will turn water into wine and "multiply" loaves and fishes), but in this case He would not be doing it as a sign of the kingdom come into the lives of the people, nor *as a sign* of His love for them, only a use of His power not just for his own convenience but even as a reversal of the purpose of the Incarnation. He came among us to be *truly man*; as man He would share our way of life, even to fatigue, thirst, and hunger.

G. Campbell Morgan states:

". . . the devil's estimate of human life is, that the only reason for man's loyalty to God is that God meets every demand of his need as it arises; and moreover, that man's happiness consists in the satisfaction of his material nature, in a word, that he lives by bread alone. . . .

"The subtlety of the temptation lies within the fact that the devil suggested to Christ that he should satisfy a perfectly legitimate craving. The evil of the temptation lies within the fact that he suggested that a legitimate craving should be satisfied in an illegitimate way" (*The Crises of the Christ*, Grand Rapids, Mich., Kregel Publications, reprint 1989, p. 119).

Acknowledging that human persons have more than animal needs, the devil now approaches Christ on the spiritual level. "Next the devil took him to the holy city, set him on the parapet of the temple, and said, 'If you are the Son of God, throw yourself down. . .' " (Mt. 4:5-6, NAB). It is quite possible that this temptation took place in visions within the mind of Jesus, rather than as the devil transporting Jesus from the desert to the temple in Jerusalem, although that would in no way diminish the force of the diabolical temptation.

". . . throw yourself down. Scripture has it: 'He will bid his angels take care of you; with their hands they will support you that you may never stumble on a stone' " (Mt. 4:6, NAB).

The words quoted by the devil are from Psalm 91, which chants the perfect safety of the person who puts all trust in God. In His answer, Jesus underlines the insufficiency of a single, isolated verse of Scripture. All of Scripture is needed for true knowledge of God's revelation. The temptation here is to make a show of His trust in God, perhaps to gain adherents by an extraordinary spectacle.

The snake-handling Fundamentalists accede to that same temptation to daring trust, for which "presumption" might be a more accurate term. Surely less flamboyant, but in the same category, is the temptation for those persons who join charismatic or Pentecostal movements whose leaders look down upon anyone who does not speak in tongues nor have the more obvious charismatic gifts. Such persons may be drawn to ask for those gifts, which St. Paul clearly tells us are of less value than charity (1 Cor. 12:31-13:13). Each of my readers can find other examples.

The third temptation or testing of Jesus (Mt. 4:8-11) is open and direct. The objective of the devil is not simply to ruin Jesus, but to turn Him from accomplishing His purpose. Was Jesus physically "taken to a very high mountain" and shown all the kingdoms of the world in their magnificence"? St. Luke says that ". . . the devil . . . showed him all the kingdoms of the world in a single instant" (4:5, NAB). Sooner or later, everyone who tries to serve God is tempted to take an easier way out of difficulties incompatible with Christian morality. This only opens a door to envy of the rich and powerful, ultimately to compromise with or even worship of Satan.

Do you ever wonder how anyone can reach the point of turning to Satanism? The devil says to Jesus, "All these I will bestow on you if you will prostrate yourself in homage before me." Note the devil's claim, some right to the kingdoms of this world. Who has given the devil that right if not the people who seek themselves, their own ends instead of God? Later Jesus calls the devil "the prince of this world" (Jn. 12:31).

If we pursue this subject further, we see how discernment could have prevented a terrible end. Many of the Church Fathers interpret the betrayal of Christ by Judas as the result of Judas's seeing Jesus the miracle worker and the powerful teacher as someone who could become a strong king like David. Then when Judas discovered that Jesus would not be such a king, he turned against Jesus to ally himself with the current leaders.

The truth of Jesus' teaching and the evidence of the "signs" He worked, fulfilling the Jewish Scriptures, were external evidence available to Judas. Self-examination in the light of Jesus' teachings, accompanied by prayer, should have enabled him to *discern* his tendency toward greed and desire for the approval of those in power. When Judas discovered at last how he had been deceived by his own inclinations ("I have sinned in betraying innocent blood," Mt. 27:4), he felt keenly the loss of peace and joy which almost surely had accompanied his following of Jesus in the earlier days, bringing him to end in despair and suicide.

Peter's denial of Jesus was a momentary slip. Peter was not sufficiently aware of his impulsive temperament. Note how he asks

Jesus to bid him to come when Jesus appears to the disciples in their fishing boat. That was foolishness rather than an act of courageous faith. When Peter turned from looking at Jesus to look down at his own feet, he became frightened (Mt. 14:22-33). He showed that same impetuosity when he told Jesus that even though the rest of the disciples might be scandalized in Jesus, he would not be. Then he denied Jesus three times (Mt. 26:31-35). Peter, however, learned from his experience, and had sufficient humility to turn back to Jesus in sorrowful repentance.

These examples are given not as patterns to be used indiscriminately by friends and relatives of persons interested in new and possibly destructive religious movements, but as helps to enable us to see when and where discernment was or should have been used, how Scripture can enable us to see into the depths of the human person.

Discernment: Suggested Reading

Almost without exception the literature on discernment is to be found in books or articles in the general category of "Spiritual Theology" or its older designation, "Ascetical and Mystical Theology," or in guides for directors of persons making retreats. Although that is addressed in the chapter itself, it is important to reiterate it here because the books listed here do not deal directly with the issue of discernment with reference to destructive religious movements.

Aumann, Jordan, O.P., *Spiritual Theology*, Huntington, Ind., Our Sunday Visitor, Inc., and London, Sheed and Ward, 1979

St. Ignatius of Loyola, *The Spiritual Exercises* [Any good modern translation is acceptable. The succinct treatment of the "rules for the discernment of spirits" in the *Exercises* can be deceptive unless the reader refers to commentaries.] *The Spiritual Exercises and Selected Works*, edited by George E. Ganss, S.J., in The Classics of Western Spirituality Series, New York, Paulist Press, 1991 [Provides the reader with six pages of invaluable notes and bibliography.] An easily understood and yet quite comprehensive introduction to the Exercises, with an excellent Chapter on

"Discernment of Spirits" is *All My Liberty*, by John A. Hardon, S.J., Westminster, Mo., The Newman Press, 1959.

F. Charmot, S.J., *Ignatius Loyola and Francis de Sales, Two Masters — One Spirituality*, St. Louis and London, B. Herder Book Co., 1965 [Number 32 in the Cross and Crown Series of Spirituality, deals with "Ignatian Spirituality" in Part Two, in six short chapters showing discernment of spirits as practiced in spiritual direction by a master of the art.]

Of particular importance to the adaptation of the basic principles of "discernment of spirits" to the problems connected with destructive religious movements is the teaching of St. John of the Cross.

Faith According to St. John of the Cross, San Francisco, Ignatius Press, 1981, the doctoral dissertation of Karol Wojtyla (now Pope John Paul II) [While it is heavily theological, its profound treatment of the subject can provide a solid foundation for practical applications.]

St. John of the Cross, *Ascent of Mount Carmel* (any good translation) [Treats of the perils of visions in Book II, Chapters XVI through XXXI. The lifetime of St. John of the Cross coincided with a flowering of the occult in Spain, and as a result he became acquainted with both persons who deliberately attempted to counterfeit mystical experiences and with well-disposed persons who were honestly deceived into believing they were experiencing supernatural phenomena.]

Rev. Father Brice, C.P. (no given name), *Journey in the Night* and *Spirit in Darkness*, New York and Cincinnati, Frederick Pustet Co., Inc., 1945 and 1946 respectively [Helpful to those just becoming acquainted with the works of St. John of the Cross, especially Chapters XVI and XXVII in *Spirit in Darkness*. Chapter XXVII, "Manifestation of Hidden Truths," is almost mandatory reading for anyone who is acquainted with or consulted by a person involved to even the slightest degree with destructive religious movements.]

Dubay, Thomas, S.M., *Fire Within*, San Francisco, Ignatius Press, 1989 [Discloses the author's concern regarding spiritual direction, i.e., discernment in practice, in Chapter Sixteen. It is "must" reading for anyone who desires to help persons whose desire for a deeper knowledge of God and of themselves may be taking them into the dangers of unconventional or questionable religious movements. All of the book, which bears the subtitle "St. Teresa of Ávila, St. John of the Cross, and the Gospel — on Prayer," provides teaching for every Christian, not only for contemplatives, fruit of years of study, experience in spiritual direction, and the author's retreat work.]

Refer also to *Visions, Revelations, and the Church*, by Laurent Volken, cited in the bibliography for Chapter 9, "Infestation, Obsession, Possession."

The Difference Between Orthodox Movements and Totalist Groups

1. Churches teach allegiance to God.

Totalist groups demand complete obedience and subservience to one individual who claims to be God, the messiah, a prophet, or some form of deity, who has revelations and gets his instructions directly from God.

2. Churches allow freedom to integrate with society as a whole.

Totalist groups require separation from society. Association with non-members is discouraged, except to gain money or proselytize.

3. Churches teach family love and unity. The family is sacred.

Totalist groups teach that parents are "satanic" or "demonic." Members are programmed to believe they will lose their salvation if they continue to associate with their "flesh" family. Only their new "spiritual family" has meaning in their lives.

4. Churches teach respect for law, government, and society.

Totalist groups teach that they are above the law, and that society's system is to be "worked" to suit their purpose. The law may be broken for a "higher cause."

5. Churches teach honesty and integrity.

Totalist groups teach deceitfulness.

6. Churches teach that the body is a sacred vessel.

Totalist groups have little or no concern for the material body. Only the soul is important. Many cultists have died as the result of self-neglect and poor nutrition.

7. Tithing is done on a voluntary basis in orthodox churches.

Totalist groups take the members' material possessions for their own use or require that most or all of the weekly income be turned over to the cult.

8. Churches encourage autonomy and individual growth.

Totalist groups encourage conformity to the leader's every whim and leaders determine all important life decisions, including marriage.

9. Churches encourage members to think for themselves, to

question and seek answers. Totalist groups discourage, even forbid, any critical analyses, thus creating a sense of utter dependence among their followers.

10. Church members are free to leave a church if they wish.

Totalist groups hold onto their members by using behavior modification techniques that were used on prisoners of war: fear, guilt, isolation from family and friends, low-protein diet, and sleep deprivation. Members face psychic harassment at best, physical threats at worst, if they leave the cult.

11. Churches promote good relations between parents and children.

Many totalist groups practice interference with all communication between parents and children through misrouting of mail and phone calls, by refusing to let parents visit a child, or not letting them be alone together if they are allowed a visit.

12. Churches do not teach methods of self-hypnosis.

Totalist groups do. Members are programmed to believe that any doubt about what the leaders have taught is "satan creeping in." Therefore, all doubts must be stamped out. Methods of "thought stopping" (self-hypnosis), such as chanting, meditation, quoting the same Scripture over and over, and speaking in tongues, become second nature to the cultist. It may take weeks or months to stop this after a person leaves the cult. This is why rational thought is virtually impossible and why parents feel they are facing a "blank wall."

13. Churches do not require members to abandon schools and jobs.

Totalist groups usually require their followers to do this; exceptions being when members are placed in strategic positions to recruit.

14. Churches sponsor hospitals, orphanages, community welfare projects and other programs.

Totalist groups promise to save humanity but generally sponsor no social welfare programs of their own. Money gained is used to enrich the leader, while followers often live in poverty.

(Summary from Michael Royal, Charleston, Va., former member of the Great Commission Church.)

Vatican II Declaration on Religious Liberty

Chapter I
THE GENERAL PRINCIPLE OF RELIGIOUS FREEDOM

2. The Vatican Council declares that the human person has a right to religious freedom. Freedom of this kind means that all men should be immune from coercion on the part of individuals, social groups, and every human power so that, within due limits, nobody is forced to act against his convictions nor is anyone to be restrained from acting in accordance with his convictions in religious matters in private or in public, alone or in associations with others. The Council further declares that the right to religious freedom is based on the very dignity of the human person as known through the revealed word of God and by reason itself. This right of the human person to religious freedom must be given such recognition in the constitutional order of society as will make it a civil right.

It is in accordance with their dignity that all men, because they are persons, that is, beings endowed with reason and free will and therefore bearing personal responsibility, are both impelled by their nature and bound by a moral obligation to seek the truth, especially religious truth. They are also bound to adhere to the truth once they come to know it and direct their whole lives in accordance with the demands of truth. But men cannot satisfy this obligation in a way that is in keeping with their own nature unless they enjoy both psychological freedom and immunity from external coercion. Therefore the right to religious freedom has its foundation not in the subjective attitude of the individual but in his very nature. For this reason the right to this immunity continues to exist even in those who do not live up to their obligation of seeking the truth and adhering to it. The exercise of this right cannot be interfered with as long as the just requirements of public order are observed.

3. This becomes even clearer if one considers that the highest

norm of human life is the divine law itself — eternal, objective, and universal, by which God orders, directs, and governs the whole world and the ways of the human community according to a plan conceived in his wisdom and love. God has enabled man to participate in this law of his so that, under the gentle disposition of divine providence, many may be able to arrive at a deeper and deeper knowledge of unchangeable truth. For this reason everybody has the duty and consequently the right to seek the truth in religious matters so that through the use of appropriate means, he may prudently form judgments of conscience which are sincere and true.

The search for truth, however, must be carried out in a manner that is appropriate to the dignity of the human person and his social nature, namely, by free enquiry with the help of teaching or instruction, communication, and dialogue. It is by these means that men share with each other the truth they have discovered, or think they have discovered, in such a way that they help one another in the search for truth. Moreover, it is by personal assent that men must adhere to the truth they have discovered.

It is through his conscience that man sees and recognizes the demands of the divine law. He is bound to follow this conscience faithfully in all his activity so that he may come to God, who is his last end. Therefore he must not be forced to act contrary to his conscience. Nor must he be prevented from acting according to his conscience, especially in religious matters. The reason is because the practice of religion of its very nature consists primarily of those voluntary and free internal acts by which a man directs himself to God. Acts of this kind cannot be commanded or forbidden by any merely human authority. But his own social nature requires that man give external expression to these internal acts of religion, that he communicate with others on religious matters, and profess his religion in community. Consequently to deny man the free exercise of religion in society, when the just requirements of public order are observed, is to do an injustice to the human person and to the very order established by God for men.

Furthermore, the private and public acts of religion by which men direct themselves to God according to their convictions transcend of their very nature the earthly and temporal order of things. Therefore the civil authority, the purpose of which is the care of the common good in the temporal order, must recognize and look with favor on the religious life of the citizens. But if it presumes to control or restrict religious activity it must be said to have exceeded the limits of its power.

4. The freedom or immunity from coercion in religious matters which is the right of individuals must also be accorded to men when they act in community. Religious communities are a requirement of the nature of man and of religion itself.

Therefore, provided the just requirements of public order are not violated, these groups have a right to immunity so that they may organize themselves according to their own principles. They must be allowed to honor the supreme Godhead with public worship, help their members to practice their religion and strengthen them with religious instruction, and promote institutions in which members may work together to organize their own lives according to their religious principles.

Religious communities also have the right not to be hindered by legislation or administrative action on the part of the civil authority in the selection, training, appointment, and transfer of their own ministers in communicating with religious authorities and communities in other parts of the world, in erecting buildings for religious purposes, and in the acquisition and use of the property they need.

Religious communities have the further right not to be prevented from publicly teaching and bearing witness to their beliefs by the spoken or written word. However, in spreading religious belief and in introducing religious practices everybody must at all times avoid any action which seems to suggest coercion or dishonest or unworthy persuasion especially when dealing with the uneducated or the poor. Such a manner of acting must be considered an abuse of one's own right and an infringement of the rights of others.

Also included in the right to religious freedom is the right of religious groups not to be prevented from freely demonstrating the special value of their teaching for the organization of society and the inspiration of all human activity. Finally, rooted in the social nature of man and in the very nature of religion is the right of men, prompted by their own religious sense, freely to hold meetings or establish educational, cultural, charitable and social organizations.

5. Every family, in that it is a society with its own basic rights, has the right freely to organize its own religious life in the home under control of their parents. These have the right to decide in accordance with their own religious beliefs the form of religious upbringing which is to be given to their children. The civil authority must therefore recognize the right of parents to choose with genuine freedom schools or other means of education. Parents should not be subjected directly or indirectly to unjust burdens because of this freedom of choice. Furthermore, the rights of parents are violated if their children are compelled to attend classes which are not in agreement with the religious beliefs of the parents or if there is but a single compulsory system of education from which all religious instruction is excluded.

6. The common good of society consists in the sum total of those conditions of social life which enable men to achieve a fuller measure of perfection with greater ease. It consists especially in safeguarding the rights and duties of the human person. For this reason the protection of the right to religious freedom is the common responsibility of individual citizens, social groups, civil authorities, the Church, and other religious communities. Each of these has its own special responsibility in the matter according to its particular duty to promote the common good.

The protection and promotion of the inviolable rights of man is an essential duty of every civil authority. The civil authority therefore must undertake to safeguard the religious freedom of all the citizens in an effective manner by just legislation and other appropriate means. It must help to create conditions favorable to the fostering of religious life so that the citizens will be really in a position to exercise their religious rights and fulfill their religious duties and so that society itself may enjoy the benefits of justice and peace, which result from man's faithfulness to God and his holy will.

If because of the circumstances of a particular people special civil recognition is given to one religious community in the constitutional organization of a State, the right of all citizens and religious communities to religious freedom must be recognized and respected as well.

Finally, the civil authority must see to it that the equality of the citizens before the law, which is itself an element of the common good of society, is never, violated either openly or covertly for religious reasons, and that there is no discrimination among citizens.

From this it follows that it is wrong for a public authority to compel its citizens by force or fear or any other means to profess or repudiate any religion or to prevent anyone from joining or leaving a religious body. There is even more serious transgression of God's will and of the sacred rights of the individual person and the family of nations when force is applied to wipe out or repress religion either throughout the whole world or in a single region or in a particular community.

7. The right to freedom in matters of religion is exercised in human society. For this reason its use is subject to certain regulatory norms.

In availing of any freedom men must respect the moral principle of personal and social responsibility: in exercising their rights individual men and social groups are bound by the moral law to have regard for the rights of others, their own duties to others, and the common good of all. All men must be treated with justice and humanity.

Furthermore, since civil society has the right to protect itself against possible abuses committed in the name of religious freedom, the responsibility of providing such protection rests especially with the civil authority. However, this must not be done in an arbitrary manner or by the unfair practice of favoritism but in accordance with legal principles which are in conformity with the objective moral order. These principles are necessary for the effective protection of the rights of all citizens and for peaceful settlement of conflicts of rights. They are also necessary for an adequate protection of that just public peace which is to be found where men live together in good order and true justice. They are required too for the necessary protection of public morality. All these matters are basic to the common good and belong to what is called public order. For the rest, the principle of the integrity of freedom in society should continue to be upheld. According to this principle man's freedom should be given the fullest possible recognition and should not be curtailed except when and in so far as is necessary.

8. Modern man is subjected to a variety of pressures and runs the risk of being prevented from following his own free judgment. On

the other hand, there are many who, under the pretext of freedom, seem inclined to reject all submission to authority and make light of the duty of obedience.

For this reason this Vatican Council urges everyone, especially those responsible for educating others, to try to form men with a respect for the moral order who will obey lawful authority and be lovers of true freedom — men, that is, who will form their own judgments in the light of truth, direct their activities with a sense of responsibility, and strive for what is true and just in willing cooperation with others.

Religious liberty therefore should have this further purpose and aim of enabling men to act with greater responsibility in fulfilling their own obligations in society.

Chapter II
RELIGIOUS FREEDOM IN THE LIGHT OF REVELATION

9. The Declaration of this Vatican Council on man's right to religious freedom is based on the dignity of the person, the demands of which have become more fully known to human reason through centuries of experience. Furthermore, this doctrine of freedom is rooted in divine revelation, and for this reason Christians are bound to respect it all the more conscientiously. Although revelation does not affirm in so many words the right to immunity from external coercion in religious matters, it nevertheless shows forth the dignity of the human person in all its fullness. It shows us Christ's respect for the freedom with which man is to fulfill his duty of believing the word of God, and it teaches us the spirit which disciples of such a Master must acknowledge and follow in all things. All this throws light on the general principles on which the teaching of this Declaration on Religious Freedom is based. Above all, religious freedom in society is in complete harmony with the act of Christian faith.

10. One of the key truths in Catholic teaching, a truth that is contained in the word of God and constantly preached by the Fathers, is that man's response to God by faith ought to be free, and that therefore nobody is to be forced to embrace the faith against his will. The act of faith is of its very nature a free act. Man, redeemed

by Christ the Savior and called through Jesus Christ to be an adopted son of God, cannot give his adherence to God when he reveals himself unless, drawn by the Father, he submits to God with a faith that is reasonable and free. It is therefore fully in accordance with the nature of faith that in religious matters every form of coercion by men should be excluded. Consequently the principle of religious liberty contributes in no small way to the development of a situation in which men can without hindrance be invited to the Christian faith, embrace it of their own free will, and give it practical expression in every sphere of their lives.

11. God calls men to serve him in spirit and in truth. Consequently they are bound to him in conscience but not coerced. God has regard for the dignity of the human person which he himself created; the human person is to be guided by his own judgment and to enjoy freedom. This fact received its fullest manifestation in Christ Jesus in whom God revealed himself and his ways in a perfect manner. For Christ, who is our master and Lord and at the same time is meek and humble of heart, acted patiently in attracting and inviting his disciples. He supported and confirmed his preaching by miracles to arouse the faith of his hearers and give them assurance, but not to coerce them. He did indeed denounce the unbelief of his listeners but he left vengeance to God until the day of judgment. When he sent his apostles into the world he said to them: "He who believes and is baptized will be saved; he who does not believe will be condemned" (Mk. 16:16). He himself recognized that weeds had been sown through the wheat but ordered that both be allowed to grow until the harvest which will come at the end of the world. He did not wish to be a political Messiah who would dominate by force but preferred to call himself the Son of Man who came to serve, and "to give his life as a ransom for many" (Mk. 10:45). He showed himself as the perfect Servant of God who "will not break a bruised reed or quench a smoldering wick" (Mt. 12:20). He recognized civil authority and its rights when he ordered tribute to be paid to Caesar, but he gave clear warning that the higher rights of God must be respected: "Render therefore to Caesar the things that are Caesar's, and to God, the things that are God's" (Mt. 22:21). Finally, he brought his revelation to perfection when he accomplished on the cross the work of redemption by which he achieved salvation and true freedom for

men. For he bore witness to the truth but refused to use force to impose it on those who spoke out against it. His kingdom does not make its claims by blows, but is established by bearing witness to and hearing the truth, and grows by the love with which Christ, lifted up on the cross, draws men to himself.

Taught by Christ's word and example, the apostles followed the same path. From the very beginnings of the Church the disciples of Christ strove to convert men to confess Christ as Lord, not however by applying coercion or with the use of techniques unworthy of the Gospel but, above all, by the power of the word of God. They steadfastly proclaimed to all men the plan of God the Savior, "who desires all men to be saved and to come to the knowledge of the truth" (1 Tim. 2:4). At the same time, however, they showed respect for the weak even though they were in error, and in this way made it clear how "each of us shall give account of himself to God" (Rom. 14:12) and for that reason is bound to obey his conscience. Like Christ, the apostles were constantly bent on bearing witness to the truth of God, and they showed the greatest courage in speaking "the word of God with boldness" (Acts 4.31) before people and rulers. With a firm faith they upheld the truth that the Gospel itself is indeed the power of God for the salvation of all who believe. They therefore despised "all worldly weapons" and followed the example of Christ's meekness and gentleness as they preached the word of God with full confidence in the divine power of that word to destroy those forces hostile to God and lead men to believe in and serve Christ. Like their Master, the apostles too recognized legitimate civil authority: "Let every person be subject to the governing authorities . . . he who resists the authorities resists what God has appointed" (Rom. 13:1-2). At the same time they were not afraid to speak out against public authority when it opposed God's holy will: "We must obey God rather than men" (Acts 5:29). This is the path which innumerable martyrs and faithful have followed through the centuries all over the world.

12. The Church, therefore, faithful to the truth of the Gospel, is following in the path of Christ and the apostles when she recognizes the principle that religious liberty is in keeping with the dignity of man and divine revelation and gives it her support. Throughout the ages she has preserved and handed on the doctrine which she has

received from her Master and the apostles. Although in the life of the people of God in its pilgrimage through the vicissitudes of human history there has at times appeared a form of behavior which was hardly in keeping with the spirit of the Gospel and was even opposed to it, it has always remained the teaching of the Church that no one is to be coerced into believing.

Thus the leaven of the Gospel has long been at work in the minds of men and has contributed greatly to a wider recognition by them in the course of time of their dignity as persons. It has contributed too to the growth of the conviction that in religious matters the human person should be kept free from all manner of coercion in civil society.

13. Among those things which pertain to the good of the Church and indeed to the good of society here on earth, things which must everywhere and at all times be safeguarded and defended from all harm, the most outstanding surely is that the Church enjoy that freedom of action which her responsibility for the salvation of men requires. This is a sacred liberty with which the only-begotten Son of God endowed the Church which he purchased with his blood. Indeed it belongs so intimately to the Church that to attack it is to oppose the will of God. The freedom of the Church is the fundamental principle governing relations between the Church and public authorities and the whole civil order.

As the spiritual authority appointed by Christ the Lord with the duty, imposed by divine command, of going into the whole world and preaching the Gospel to every creature, the Church claims freedom for herself in human society and before every public authority. The Church also claims freedom for herself as a society of men with the right to live in civil society in accordance with the demands of the Christian faith.

When the principle of religious freedom is not just proclaimed in words or incorporated in law but is implemented sincerely in practice, only then does the Church enjoy in law and in fact those stable conditions which give her the independence necessary for fulfilling her divine mission. Ecclesiastical authorities have been insistent in claiming this independence in society. At the same time the Christian faithful, in common with the rest of men, have the civil right of freedom from interference in leading their lives according to their conscience. A harmony exists therefore between the freedom of the Church and that religious freedom which must be recognized as the right of all men and all communities and must be sanctioned by constitutional law.

14. In order to satisfy the divine command: "Make disciples of all nations" (Mt. 28:19), the Catholic Church must spare no effort in striving "that the word of the Lord may speed on and triumph" (2 Thess. 3: 1).

The Church therefore earnestly urges her children first of all that "supplications, prayers, intercessions, and thanksgivings be made for all men. . . . This is good and is acceptable in the sight of God our Savior, who desires all men to be saved and to come to the knowledge of the truth" (1 Tim. 2:14).

However, in forming their consciences the faithful must pay careful attention to the sacred and certain teaching of the Church. For the Catholic Church is by the will of Christ the teacher of truth. It is her duty to proclaim and teach with authority the truth which is Christ and, at the same time, to declare and confirm by her authority the principles of the moral order which spring from human nature itself. In addition, Christians should approach those who are outside wisely, "in the holy Spirit, genuine love, truthful speech" (2 Cor. 6:6-7), and should strive, even to the shedding of their blood, to spread the light of life with all confidence and apostolic courage.

The disciple has a grave obligation to Christ, his Master, to grow daily in his knowledge of the truth he has received from him, to be faithful in announcing it and vigorous in defending it without having recourse to methods which are contrary to the spirit of the Gospel. At the same time the love of Christ urges him to treat with love, prudence, and patience those who are in error or ignorance with regard to the faith. He must take into account his duties toward Christ, the life-giving Word whom he must proclaim, the rights of the human person and the measure of grace which God has given to each man through Christ in calling him freely to accept and profess the faith.

15. It is certain therefore that men of the present day want to profess their religion freely in private and in public. Indeed it is a fact that religious freedom has already been declared a civil right in most

constitutions and has been given solemn recognition in international documents.

But there are forms of government under which, despite constitutional recognition of the freedom of religious worship, the public authorities themselves strive to deter the citizens from professing their religion and make life particularly difficult and dangerous for religious bodies.

This sacred Council gladly welcomes the first of these two facts as a happy sign of the times. In sorrow however it denounces the second as something deplorable. The Council exhorts Catholics and directs an appeal to all men to consider with great care how necessary religious liberty is, especially in the present condition of the human family.

It is clear that with the passage of time all nations are coming into a closer unity, men of different cultures and religions are being bound together by closer links, and there is a growing awareness of individual responsibility. Consequently, to establish and strengthen peaceful relations and harmony in the human race, religious freedom must be given effective constitutional protection everywhere and that highest of man's rights and duties — to lead a religious life with freedom in society — must be respected.

May God, the Father of all, grant that the human family by carefully observing the principles of religious liberty in society may be brought by the grace of Christ and the power of the Holy Spirit to that "glorious freedom of the children of God" (Rom. 8:21) which is sublime and everlasting.

Profile: Spiritual Evaluation of Movements

	<u>Christian</u>	<u>New Age</u>
Whom am I serving? We were created to serve God	God Ezra 10:11, John 1:1-18 Romans 8:1-11	Self, Satan
Source of power? Our power and strength is the Trinity	Trinity 1 John 5:7	Self, Satan
Fruits Produced? Gifts & Fruits are of the Holy Spirit	Love, joy, peace Galatians 5:22-26 1 Corinthians 12	Confusion Despair
Who is God? I Am Who I Am	Creator, Father Exodus 3:14 Job 38-41	Cosmic Consciousness
Who is the Holy Spirit? Spirit of Truth, Wisdom	Sanctifier Matthew 3:11-12	Higher Self
Who is Jesus Christ? He is our Redeemer	Son of God Philippians 2:9-15 John 1	Spiritual Master
Who is man? Created image of God	Sons of God John 1:11-13 Psalm 8	Gods
Source of Salvation? The Name of the Lord	God & Jesus Romans 10:4-17	Self-Divinity
Source of Revelation? Holy Spirit is Truth	Bible, Church John 14	Assorted beliefs Contemporary thought

Ask the following question when discerning any religious movement that is Christian: Does the movement's spirituality agree with Scripture, Tradition, Dogma, Doctrine, and Teachings of the Church? (Profile by Father Lawrence J. Gesy)

Pastoral Statement on Transcendental Meditation

Following is the 1984 Pastoral statement of His Eminence Jaime Cardinal Sin, Archbishop of Manila, on certain doctrinal aspects of the Maharishi Technology of the Unified Field, held after consultation with theological experts.

The Basic Conflict Between Maharishi and Christianity

The Maharishi's doctrine and teaching on (1) God, (2) man, (3) the way to go to God, (4) pain and suffering, and (5) sin is in open contradiction to Christian Doctrine.

1. The "God" of the Maharishi is *impersonal*, as opposed to the God manifested in Christian revelation where God is a personal God who loves each human person in an intimate way.

By denying the Creator as Supreme and teaching that "All is One," Maharishi removes the distinction between the Creator and the creature. This directly leads to, or is an equivalent form of, pantheism.

The "mantras" given to the followers of the Maharishi have been discovered to be invocations, in most of the cases, to deities of the Hindu pantheon, thus in a real sense denying the oneness of God and fostering *polytheism.*

2. *Man* is considered capable of attaining unlimited perfection, of being totally liberated from all pain and suffering through the instrumentality of Transcendental Meditation practiced in the Maharishi way. Similarly through this, TM, man can find solution to all human problems ranging from control of the elements to the attainment of indestructibility and immortality.

Two flaws, among others, appear clearly in this doctrine: (a) It does not accept the *immortality of the soul*, nor life beyond, as belonging to the nature of the soul; (b) ignores completely the existence of *original sin*, a Christian dogma, and the consequences for the realities of life.

3. The way to God is placed by Maharishi in TM as understood by him, his books, and his followers, and it is placed on TM as the exclusive way to God.

Two flaws, again, are hidden in these affirmations: (a) the abuse of the *term TM* which has been appropriated by them as if theirs was "the" TM par excellence, the only authentic one (there is Christian mysticism, even authors speak of Hindu and Buddhist mysticism, and certainly there is also the well-known za-zen method of meditation); and (b) the way to God in the present economy for all is the way of the *Cross* as long as we are pilgrims, as explicitly preached by Christ himself, accepted in Christian doctrine and life. The heroism of Christian faithful suffering with the greatest courage and dignity appears to be absent in the Maharishi way to God.

4. Implicit in the Maharishi approach to the problem of pain and suffering is the rejection of the redemptive value of suffering and of the existence of *Christ as the Redeemer*. In fact, Maharishi in his book, *Meditations of Maharishi Mahesh Yogi* (New York, Bantam Books, 1968, p.23), writes explicitly: "I don't think Christ ever suffered or Christ could suffer." (This statement has been repeated in many places by the Maharishi followers.)

5. *Sin.* Maharishi tries to ignore the existence of sin. In this, Maharishi follows the Vedic doctrine that regards sin as a bodily matter and has nothing to do with the spirit or soul of man. The whole concept of "sin," if implicitly accepted, is considered as something external and legalistic. The real sense of freedom and responsibility is absent, and the "effects" of sin are the object of rituals, mantras, and TM. There is no interior conversion, but a rather manipulative use of TM to attain liberations.

At the basis of this concept and approach is the concept of God, man, the way to God, pain and suffering, described above. From this point of view, one cannot be a Christian and a Maharishi.

6. As for TM, it may be considered as doctrine (content) or as technique (method). From this point of view of *doctrine* it is not acceptable to a Catholic, or a Christian at that. As for TM as technique, in the way the Maharishi group presents it, it is not

acceptable either because of its intrinsic connections with the doctrine (cf. "mantras" and 1 and 2 above).

This kind of TM is to be *distinguished* from various forms of prayer proper to the Oriental religious attitudes, some of which may be acceptable, and even beneficial, if properly scrutinized and used. TM, however, as proposed by Maharishi and as the end-result looked at by the Maharishi doctrine and followers, is, to say the least, quite risky. It becomes not a remedy but an escape. Its unavoidable result, within the Maharishi doctrine context, is the desensitization of conscience by trying to relieve not the guilt and the real disorder but only its symptoms and its accompanying restlessness.

Pope John Paul II on the Devil

In his discourse at the general audience of August 13, 1986, the Holy Father commented at great length on the fall of the angels. This was an eminently pastoral allocution:

"Satan wishes to destroy life lived in accordance with the truth, life in the fullness of good, the supernatural life of grace and love. . . .

"As the result of the sin of our first parents, this fallen angel has acquired dominion over man to a certain extent. This is the doctrine that has been constantly professed and proclaimed by the Church, and which the Council of Trent confirmed in its treatise on original sin (cf. DS, 1511). . . .

"In Sacred Scripture we find various indications of this influence on man and on the dispositions of his spirit (and of his body). In the Bible, Satan is called the 'prince of this world' (cf. Jn. 12:31; 14:30; 16:11) and even the 'god of this world' (2 Cor. 4:4). . . .

"According to Sacred Scripture, and especially the New Testament, the dominion and the influence of Satan and of the other evil spirits embraces all the world. . . . The action of Satan consists primarily in tempting men to evil, by influencing their imaginations and higher faculties, to turn them away from the law of God. . . . It is possible that in certain cases the evil spirit goes so far as to exercise his influence not only on material things, but even on man's body, so that one can speak of 'diabolical possession' (cf. Mk. 5:2-9). It is not always easy to discern the preternatural factor operative in these cases, and the Church does not lightly support the tendency to attribute many things to the direct action of the devil; but in principle it cannot be denied that Satan can go to this extreme manifestation of his superiority in his will to harm and to lead to evil.

"To conclude, we must add that the impressive words of the Apostle John — 'The whole world lies under the power of the evil one' (1 Jn. 5:19) — allude also to the presence of Satan in the history of humanity, a presence which becomes all the more acute when man and society depart from God.

"This 'fall,' which has the character of the rejection of God, with the consequent state of 'damnation,' consists in the free choice of those created spirits who have radically and irrevocably rejected God and his kingdom, usurping his sovereign rights and attempting to subvert the economy of salvation and the very order of the entire universe. We find a reflection of this attitude in the words addressed by the tempter to our first parents: 'You will become like God' or 'like gods' (cf. Gn. 3:5). Thus, the evil spirit tries to transplant into man the attitude of rivalry, insubordination and opposition to God, which has, as it were, become the motivation of all his existence. . . .

"When, by an act of his own free will, he rejected the truth that he knew about God, Satan became the cosmic 'liar and the father of lies' (Jn. 8:44). For this reason, he lives in radical and irreversible denial of God, and seeks to impose on creation — on the other beings created in the image of God, and in particular on people — his own tragic 'lie about the good' that is God. In the Book of Genesis we find a precise description of this lie and falsification of the truth about God, which Satan (under the form of a serpent) tries to transmit to the first representatives of the human race: God is jealous of his own prerogatives and therefore wants to impose limitations on man (cf. Gn. 3:5). Satan invites the man to free himself from the imposition of this yoke by making himself 'like God.'

"On this condition of existential falsehood, Satan — according to St. John — also becomes a 'murderer,' that is, one who destroys the supernatural life which God has made to dwell from the beginning in him and in the creatures made 'in the likeness of God': the other pure spirits and men; the influence of the evil spirit can conceal itself in a more profound and effective way: it is in his interests to make himself 'unknown.' Satan has the skill in the world to induce people to deny his existence in the name of rationalism and of every other system of thought which seeks all possible means to avoid recognizing his activity. This does not, however, signify the elimination of man's free will and responsibility, and even less the frustration of the saving action of Christ. . . .

"The Christian, appealing to the Father and the Spirit of Jesus and invoking the kingdom, cries with the power of faith: Let us not succumb to temptation, free us from evil, from the evil one, O Lord; let us not fall into the infidelity to which we are seduced by the one who has been unfaithful from the beginning" (Pope John Paul II, *L'Osservatore Romano*, August 20, 1986).

The encyclical *Dominum et Vivificantem* was issued on May 18, 1986, and it contains a lengthy section that treats of the devil:

"For in spite of all the witness of creation and of the salvific economy inherent in it, the spirit of darkness (Eph. 6:12; Lk. 22:53) is capable of showing God as an enemy of his own creature, and in the first place as an enemy of man, as a source of danger and threat to man. In this way Satan manages to sow in man's soul the seed of opposition to the one who 'from the beginning' would be considered as man's enemy — and not as Father. Man is challenged to become the adversary of God!

"The analysis of sin in its original dimension indicates that, through the influence of the 'father of lies,' throughout the history of humanity there will be a constant pressure on man to reject God, even to the point of hating him: 'Love of self to the point of contempt for God,' as St. Augustine puts it (cf. *De civitate Dei*, XIV, 28). Man will be inclined to see in God primarily a limitation of himself, and not the source of his own freedom and the fullness of good. We see this confirmed in the modern age, when atheistic ideologies seek to root out religion on the grounds that religion causes the radical 'alienation' of man, as if man were dispossessed of his own humanity when, accepting the idea of God, he attributes to God what belongs to man, and exclusively to man! Hence a process of thought and historico-sociological practice in which the rejection of God has reached the point of declaring his 'death.' An absurdity, both in concept and expression! But the ideology of the 'death of God' is more a threat to man, as the Second Vatican Council indicates when it analyzes the question of the 'independence of earthly affairs' and writes: 'For without the Creator the creature would disappear. . . . When God is forgotten the creature itself grows unintelligible' (GS, 36). The ideology of the 'death of God' easily demonstrates in its effects that on the 'theoretical and practical' levels it is the ideology of the 'death of man' " (*L'Osservatore Romano*, June 9, 1986).

Scriptures Dealing With the Occult

(Have a good commentary and read your footnotes as you look up these passages)

Antichrist
    1 John 2:18,22
    1 John 4:3
    2 John 7

Soothsayers
    Exodus 7:11
    Daniel 1:20
    Daniel 2:27,28
    1 Samuel 28:3,7,8f
    Jeremiah 14:14
    Ezekiel 12:24,25
    Ezekiel 13:6,7,23

Sorcery
    Deuteronomy 18:9-14
    Isaiah 2:6
    2 Kings 17:17
    Isaiah 47:12

Magic
    Genesis 41:8,24
    Exodus 7:11,22
    Exodus 8:7,18
    Exodus 9:11
    Acts 19:19

(Magic)
    Daniel 1:20
    Daniel 2:2,27
    Daniel 4:7,9
    Daniel 5:11
    Acts 8:9f
    Acts 13:6-12

Divination
    Daniel 4:7
    Numbers 22:7
    Numbers 23:23
    2 Kings 17:16, 17

Astrology
    Daniel 5:7, 11
    Isaiah 47:9, 13, 15
    Matthew 2:1-12

Mediums
    Leviticus 20:6

Sabbats and Celebrations

Satanists and witches celebrate eight major Sabbats during the year. Each one holds special significance to them. In addition, Satanists hold a member's birth date in reverence.

> February 2 — Candlemas or Ormelo
> March 21 — Equinoxe (1)
> April 30 — May Eve or Beltane
> June 22 — Solstice (1)
> August 1 — Lammas
> September 21 — Equinoxe (2)
> October 31 — Halloween
> December 22 — Solstice (2)

The most significant of these Sabbats are (in order):

> Halloween
> May Eve
> Summer Solstice
> Winter Solstice

See the following pages for a complete calendar of Occult and Satanic ritual celebrations.

Combination of the Occult

DATE	CELEBRATION	TYPE
January 1st	New Year's Day (Druid feast)	—
January 7th	St. Winebald Day	Blood
January 17th	Satanic Revels	Sexual
January 20th	St. Agnes Eve	—
February 2nd	Satanic Revels *	Sexual
February 2nd	Candlemas	Witches' sabbat
February 25th	St. Walpurgis Day	Blood
Shrovetide	Three days to Ash Wednesday	Witches' sabbat
March 1st	St. Eichstadt	Blood
March 20th	Feast Day (spring equinox) **	Orgies
April 24th	St. Mark's Eve	—
April 21st-26th	Preparation for Sacrifice	
April 26th-May 1st	Grand Climax *	Da Meur
April 30th	Walpurgis Night	Time for one of greatest witches' sabbats
May 1st	Beltane or May Day	Fire Festival
June 21st	Feast Day (summer solstice) **	Orgies
June 23rd	Midsummer's Eve (St. John's Eve)	Fire Festival
July 1st	Demon Revels	Blood
July 25th	St. James Day	—
August 1st	Lammas	—
August 3rd	Satanic Revels *	Sexual
August 24th	St. Bartholomew's Day	Fire
September 7th	Marriage to the Beast Satan	Sexual
September 20th	Midnight Host	Blood
September 22nd	Feast Day (fall equinox) **	Orgies
October 29th	All Hallows' Eve *	Blood
October 31st	Halloween	Fire
November 1st	Halloween	Sexual
November 4th	Satanic Revels	Sexual
December 21st	St. Thomas Day	Fire
December 22nd	Feast Day **	Orgies
December 24th	Demon Revels	Da Meur

* signifies most important holidays (Satanic)

** signifies holidays of lesser importance (Satanic)

and Satanic Ritual Calendars

USAGE	AGE/SEX/SPECIES	RITE
—	—	Occult
Animal or human sacrifice (dismemberment)	13-15 male	Satanic
Oral, anal, vaginal	7-17 female	Satanic
—	—	Occult
Oral, anal, vaginal	7-17 female	Satanic
—	—	Occult
Communion of blood and dismemberment	animal	Satanic
—	—	Occult
Drinking of human blood for strength, homage to demons	any age, male/female	Satanic
Oral, anal, vaginal	any age, m/f	Satanic
—	—	Occult
—	—	Satanic
Corpus De Baahl	1-25, female	Satanic
—	—	
This night or next day (Walpurgis)	—	Occult
Fire Festival	—	Occult
Oral, anal, vaginal	any age, m/f	Satanic
—	—	Occult
Oral, anal, vaginal	any age, m/f, h/a	Satanic
Most important time for practice of magic		Occult
Druids sexual assoc. with demons	any age, female	Satanic
—	—	Occult
Great Sabbat	—	Occult
Sacrifice, dismemberment	infant-21, female	Satanic
Dismemberment, hands planted	infant-21, female	Satanic
Oral, anal, vaginal	any age, m/f, h/a	Satanic
Sexual climax assoc.	any age	Satanic
Great Sabbat: On this night the dead return to earth		Occult
With the demons	male/female	Satanic
Oral, anal, vaginal	7-17, female	Satanic
Great Sabbat	—	Occult
Oral, anal, vaginal	any age, m/f, h/a	Satanic
High Grand Climax	any age, male/female	Satanic

*** A person's birthday on the Occult calendar is the highest of all holidays ***

Satanic and Occult Ritual Symbols

7/6   10/9 12/13

NEMA NATAS   **LIVE-EVIL**   **REDRUM**
AMEN SATAN   **MURDER**

TRAIL MARKERS

There are many forms of directional trail markers which are employed by formal and casual occult groups alike. These markers indicate locations where occult activities may take place and how to get there.

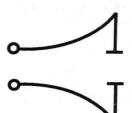

The markers depicted to the right show a small circle or starting place, then a direction to be taken. The rise or fall of the line show hills and valley-type terrain.

Other marker types could be a "pentagram" on the right or left side of a road, trail or even on a house or building.

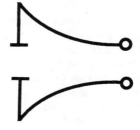

Marker may be very unique and only apply to one group.

SAMPLE ALTAR

The altar may be any flat object where the implements of the ritual are place. The altar will usually be placed within the nine (9) foot circle. This diagram shows a marble or granite slab, 48" x 22" x 2." The pentagram in the center is etched into the slab. Human or animal blood is then poured into the etching. Other symbols may be carved into the slab as characteristic to each group. Implements that would be placed on the altar would include: athame, chalice, candles, parchment, cauldron, book of shadows, and other items as characteristic for each group.

THE INVERTED CROSS OF SATANIC JUSTICE

Often found carved into victim's chest. When used in such a case, victim is usually a traitor. It is also used as a backdrop near a "saphonet" for curse and compassion rituals. The center vertical line indicates man's present. The horizontal line indicates eternity, past and future. The arch indicates the world. The inverted cross appearance symbolized the epitome of anti-Christian theology.

THE SEXUAL RITUAL SYMBOL

This is used to indicate the place and purpose. It is often carved into stone or painted on the side of the road to show present use of the location.

THE BLOOD RITUAL SYMBOL

This symbol represents human and animal sacrifices.

BLACK MASS INDICATOR

Here, the moon goddess "Diana" and the morning star of "Lucifer" are represented. This symbol may be found in both white witchcraft and Satanism. When the moon is turned to face the opposite direction, it is primarily Satanic.

PENTAGRAM

The "pentagram," or without the circle, the "pentacle," may be used in both black and white magic. Generally, the top point represents the spirit, and the other points represent wind, fire, earth, and water.

BAHOMET

The upside-down pentagram, often called the "Baphomet," is strictly Satanic in nature and represents the goat's head.

HEXAGRAM

The "hexagram," also referred to as the "seal of Solomon," is said to be one of the most powerful symbols in the occult.

ANTI-JUSTICE

The Roman symbol of justice was a double-bladed ax in the upright position. The representation of "anti-justice" is inverting the doubled-bladed ax.

TRIANGLE

A "triangle" may vary in size, but is generally inscribed or drawn on the ground and is the place where a demon would appear in conjuration rituals.

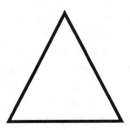

CIRCLE

The "circle" has different meanings — one of which is to symbolize eternity. Another is that of protection from evil without and to contain power within. When used for ritual, it is nine (9) feet in diameter.

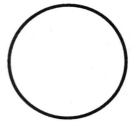

TALISMAN/AMULET

A "talisman" or "amulet" is an object with drawing or writing inscribed in it of a god's name or image of a supernatural power. The majority of these are listed in the "lesser key of Solomon."

ANTI-CHRIST

The "upside-down" cross is a blasphemy of the Christian cross.

CROSS OF NERO

This symbol represented peace in the early '60s; but now, among the heavy metal and occult groups, signifies the "cross of Nero." It shows an "upside down" cross with the cross member broken downward — "the defeat of Christianity."

ANKH

The "ankh" is an ancient Egyptian symbol for life. The top portion represents the female, and the lower portion, the male. This symbol had magical significance.

Ancient Egyptian fertility symbol, symbol of life and worship to Ra, the sun god. To wear this the owners gave up their virginity and practiced orgies as a part of worship.

CROSS OF CONFUSION

The "cross of confusion" is an ancient Roman symbol questioning the existence or validity of Christianity.

"THE MARK OF THE BEAST" (Rev. 13:16-18)

Four different ways which refer to the "mark of the beast" or Satan. Note that the letter "f" is the sixth letter of the alphabet.

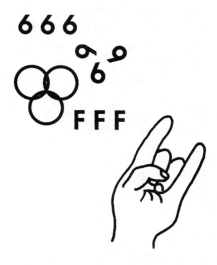

HORNED HAND

The "horned hand" is the sign of recognition between those who are in the occult. It may also innocently be used by those who identify with "heavy metal" music.

SWASTIKA

The "swastika" or "broken cross" is of ancient origin. Originally, it represented the four winds, four seasons, and four points of the compass, At that time, its arms were at 90-degree angles turned the opposite way as depicted here. It turned in a clockwise direction, showing harmony with nature. The "swastika" depicted here shows the elements or forces turning against nature and out of harmony. The Nazis, SWP groups, and occult groups use it in this manner.

ANARCHY

The symbol of "anarchy" represents the abolition of all law. Initially, those into "punk" music used this symbol, but it is now widely used by "heavy metal" followers.

(Symbols from the National Cult Awareness Office)

Appendix IX   (Ch. 1-13) _____

Cardinals Meeting/Cardinal Arinze:

The Challenge of New Religious Movements

The world's new religious movements are a sign "that there are spiritual needs which have not been identified, or which the Church and other religious institutions have either not perceived or not succeeded in meeting," Cardinal Francis Arinze said April 5 [1991] in an address to the April 4-7 consistory at the Vatican of the world's cardinals. The session assessed ways to stem the success of sects in the proselytization of church members. Arinze, prefect of the Vatican Council for Interreligious Dialogue, observed that the success of new religious movements, a worldwide phenomenon, is due partly to their ability to exploit "some weak points in the pastoral ministry and the life of Christian communities." They offer adequate catechesis, satisfying prayer and worship, warm community life, and dynamic lay leadership, and they promise people wisdom, peace, harmony, and self-realization. However, "there should be no blanket condemnation of the new religious movements," he said. In examining what posture the Church should take toward new religious movements, Arinze said, "it should not be an attack" nor should it be "negative against their members." He acknowledged that the Church regards dialogue with every human being and with religious groups as "part of the style of the Church's apostolate," though "the nature of many NRMs and their manner of operation make dialogue with them particularly problematic for the Church." Still, Catholics should always be ready to study and identify "elements or tendencies that are in themselves good or noble and where some collaboration is possible." The new religious movements are defined by Arinze as "more neutral" than sects. "They are called 'new' not only because they showed themselves in their present form after the Second World War, but also because they present themselves as alternatives to the institutional official religions and the prevailing culture." They are "called 'religious' because they profess to offer a vision of the religious or secular world" or of the means to various objectives. A translation by *L'Osservatore Romano* of Arinze's Italian-language text follows.

1. The rise and spread of the sects or new religious movements is a marked phenomenon in the religious history of our times. They operate with considerable vitality. Some of them are of an esoteric nature. Others originate from their own interpretation of the Bible. And many have roots in Asian or African religions, or they combine in a syncretistic way elements from these religions and Christianity.

Bishops are often besieged with requests for information and guidance, or they are asked to take some action regarding this disturbing phenomenon. But in many cases the lack of adequate information can lead either to no pastoral action or to overreaction.

To stimulate reflection and pastoral planning, may I put before you, venerable fathers, reflection on: terminology; typology of the new religious movements; origin of the new religious movements and reasons for their spread; problems posed by the new religious movements; pastoral response, general; pastoral response, specific.

I. TERMINOLOGY

Complex Reality

There is a problem in what terminology to use with reference to the groups under discussion. The reason is that the reality is in itself complex. The groups vary greatly in origin, beliefs, size, means of recruitment, behavior pattern, and attitude toward the Church, other religious groups, and society. It is therefore no surprise that there is as yet no agreed name for them. Here are some terms in use.

Sects

The word *sect* would seem to refer more directly to small groups that broke away from a major religious group, generally Christian, and that hold deviating beliefs or practices.

The word *sect* is not used in the same sense everywhere. In Latin America, for example, there is a tendency to apply the term to all non-Catholic groups, even when these are families of traditional Protestant churches. But even in Latin America, in circles that are more sensitive to ecumenism, the word *sect* is reserved for the more extremist or aggressive groups. In Western Europe the word has a negative connotation, while in Japan the new religions of Shinto or Buddhist origin are freely called sects in a non-derogatory sense.

New Religious Movements

The term *new religious movements* is more neutral than that of sects when referring to these groups. They are called new not only because they showed themselves in their present form after the Second World War, but also because they present themselves as alternatives to the institutional official religions and the prevailing culture. They are called religious because they profess to offer a vision of the religious or sacred world, or means to reach other objectives such as transcendental knowledge, spiritual illumination, or self-realization, or because they offer to members their answers to fundamental questions.

Other Names

These movements or groups are sometimes also called new religions, fringe religions, free religious movements, alternative religious movements, marginal religious groups, or (particularly in English-speaking areas) cults.

What Terminology Should Be Adopted?

Since there is no universally accepted terminology, effort should be made to adopt a term which is as fair and precise as possible.

In this presentation, therefore, I shall generally keep to the term *new religious movements* (abbreviated NRMs) because it is neutral and general enough to include the new movements of Protestant origin, the sects of Christian background, new Eastern or African movements, and those of the gnostic or esoteric type.

II. TYPOLOGY OF THE NEW RELIGIOUS MOVEMENTS

Types With Reference to Christianity

With reference to Christianity we can distinguish new movements coming from the Protestant reform, sects with Christian roots but with considerable doctrinal differences, movements derived from other religions, and movements stemming from humanitarian or so-called "human potential" backgrounds (such as New Age and religious therapeutic groups), or from "divine potential" movements found particularly in Eastern religious traditions.

Different are NRMs which are born through contact between universal religions and primal religious cultures.

Types With Reference to Background Knowledge System

Four types can be distinguished.

There are movements based on holy Scripture. These are therefore Christian or they are derived from Christianity.

A second group of NRMs are those derived from other religions such as Hinduism, Buddhism or traditional religions. Some of them assume in a syncretistic way elements coming from Christianity.

A third group of sects shows signs of a decomposition of the genuine idea of religion and of a return of paganism.

A fourth set of sects are gnostic.

Is There a Common Denominator Among These NRMs?

In an effort to find a common denominator, the sects have been defined as "religious groups with a distinctive world view of their own derived from, but not identical with, the teachings of a major world religion." This definition, of a phenomenological type, is only partially correct. It does not seem to include movements that derive from humanistic, paganizing, or gnostic backgrounds, movements which some sociologists prefer to call "new magical movements."

Moreover, such a definition leaves out any value judgment on the teachings, on the moral behavior of the NRMs' founders and their followers, and on their relationship with society.

From the doctrinal point of view, the NRMs which operate in traditionally Christian regions can be located in four categories insofar as they distance themselves from the Christian vision of the world: Those that reject the Church, those that reject Christ, those that reject the role of God (and yet maintain a generic sense of "religion"), and those that reject the role of religion (and maintain a sense of the sacred, but manipulated by man to acquire power over others or the cosmos).

Social reaction against the NRMs is based in general not so much on their doctrine as on their behavior pattern and their relationship with society.

One, however, should not engage in a blanket condemnation or generalization by applying to all the NRMs the more negative attitudes of some. Nor should the NRMs be judged incapable of evolution in the positive sense.

NRMs of Protestant origin provoke diverse reactions because of their aggressive proselytism which denigrates the Catholic Church, or because of their expansionistic programs and their use of the mass media in a way that looks like commercialization of religion.

In spite of the diversity of the NRMs and of local situations, they all raise one main pastoral problem which is the vulnerability of the faithful to proposals which are contrary to the formation they have received.

The phenomenon of the sects poses a serious problem of discernment for the pastors of the Church. "It is not every spirit, my dear people, that you can trust," says the beloved apostle John. "Test them, to see if they come from God; there are many false prophets now, in the world" (1 Jn. 4:1).

III. ORIGINS OF THE NRMS AND REASONS FOR THEIR SPREAD

Existence of Spiritual Needs

The NRMs indicate that there are spiritual needs which have not been identified, or which the Church and other religious institutions have either not perceived or not succeeded in meeting.

Cultural Identity Search

The NRMs can arise or attract because people are searching for meaning when they are feeling lost in a period of cultural change.

Filling a Void

Many Christians join the sects or NRMs because they feel that in them there is an answer to their thirst for Scripture reading, singing, dancing, emotional satisfaction, and concrete and clear answers.

Seeking Answers to Vital Questions

There are people, for example in Africa, who seek in religion an answer to, and a protection against, witchcraft, failure, suffering, sickness, and death. The NRMs seem to them to confront these existential problems openly and to promise instant remedies, especially physical and psychological healing.

Cashing in on Our Pastoral Weak Points

There are some weak points in the pastoral ministry and the life of Christian communities which the NRMs exploit. Where priests are few and scarce, these movements supply many forceful leaders and "evangelists" who are trained in a relatively short time. Where the Catholic people are rather ignorant in Catholic doctrine, they bring aggressive biblical fundamentalism. Where there is "lukewarmness and indifference of the sons and daughters of the Church who are not up to the level of the evangelizing mission, with the weak witness they bear to consistent Christian living" (John Paul II: Address to Mexican Bishops, 6, on May 12, 1990, in *L'Osservatore Romano*, English edition, May 14, 1990, p.2), the sects bring infectious dynamism and remarkable commitment.

Where genuine Catholic teachings on salvation only in the name of Christ, on the necessity of the Church, and on the urgency of missionary work and conversion are obscured, the sects make alternative offers.

Where parishes are too large and impersonal, they install small communities in which the individual feels known, appreciated, loved and given a meaningful role. Where lay people or women feel marginalized, they assign leadership roles to them. Where the sacred liturgy is celebrated in a cold and routine manner, they celebrate religious services marked by crowd participation, punctuated with shouts of "alleluia" and "Jesus is the Lord," and interspersed with scriptural phrases. Where inculturation is still in its hesitating stages, the NRMs give an appearance of indigenous religious groups which seem to the people to be locally rooted. Where homilies are intellectually above the heads of the people, the NRMs urge personal commitment to Jesus Christ and strict and literal adherence to the Bible. Where the Church seems presented too much as an institution marked by structures and hierarchy, the NRMs stress personal relationship with God.

Not all such methods deserve to be frowned upon. The dynamism of their missionary drive, the evangelistic responsibility assigned to the new "converts," their use of the mass media, and their setting of the objectives to be attained, should make us ask ourselves questions as to how to make more dynamic the missionary activity of the Church.

There are methods used by some NRMs which are contrary to the spirit of the Gospel because these methods do not respect human freedom of conscience sufficiently.

Of course, it is not enough to condemn these methods. It is also necessary to prepare pastoral groups which are to inform and form the faithful, and also to help the young people and the families that find themselves caught up in these tragic situations.

Action of the Devil

We should not exclude, among explanations of the rise and spread of the sects or NRMs, the action of the Devil, even if this action is unknown to the people involved. The Devil is the enemy who sows darnel among the wheat when the people are asleep.

Worldwide Phenomenon

In the United States of America they have flourished from the last century and especially in the last forty years. They come mostly from Protestantism, but also from Eastern religions and from fusion of religious and psychological elements. From the United States they are exported to Latin America, South Africa, the Philippines, and Europe.

In Latin America the NRMs are largely of Christian origin and are generally aggressive and negative toward the Catholic Church, whose apostolate they often denigrate. The same remarks can be made about the Philippines.

In Africa the rise of the NRMs has more to do with the post-colonial political, cultural, and social crisis, and with questions of inculturation and the African desire for healing and help to face life's problems.

In Asia the NRMs of local origin do not seem to be a major menace in countries where Christians are a minority except that they are exported to Europe and the Americas where they attract people, including intellectuals, with their syncretistic and esoteric offers of relaxation, peace, and illumination.

In Europe the crisis of a highly secularized technological society that suffers the fragmentation of a culture that no longer has widely shared values and beliefs favors the sects or NRMs that come from the United States or the East.

IV. PROBLEMS AND CHALLENGES POSED BY THE NRMS

Unity of the Church

The NRMs pull Catholics away from the unity and communion of the Church. This communion is based on the unity of faith, hope, and love received in baptism. It is nourished by the sacraments, the word of God, and Christian service.

Ecumenism

It is important to keep clearly in view the distinction between sects and new religious movements on the one hand, and churches and ecclesial communities on the other.

The distinction between ecumenical relations and dealings between the Catholic Church and the sects must therefore be carefully considered in this context.

Undermining and Denial of the Faith

Some sects or NRMs either undermine major articles of the Catholic faith or practically deny them. They propose a man-made religious community rather than the Church instituted by the Son of God.

Abandonment of the Faith

In more extreme cases, Christians can be led to abandon their faith through the activity of the NRMs. Some movements promote a type of neopaganism, a putting of self instead of God at the center of worship, and a claim to extraordinary knowledge which regards itself as above all religions. Other NRMs engage in occultism, magic, spiritism, and even devil worship.

Atheism and Non-Belief

Some NRMs, especially those that put heavy pressure on the human person, can pave the way for atheism.

Proselytism

Many NRMs use methods that violate the rights of other believers or religious bodies to religious freedom. They say things which are not true of others. They entice vulnerable people like young people, the poor, and the ignorant with money or other material goods, or with heavy bombardments of psychological and other pressures.

Combativeness Toward the Catholic Church

Some NRMs are particularly aggressive toward the Catholic Church. They seem to concentrate on particularly traditional Catholic regions such as Latin America and the Philippines. They strive to pull away as many Catholics as they can from the Church. They do not seem to be as zealous in launching missionary efforts toward people who do not yet believe in Christ. They even misinterpret Catholic efforts to identify with the poor as communism or state subversion.

Psychological Harm to Individuals

There are some NRMS which have done psychological harm to individuals through their methods of recruitment and training and through the harsh measures they adopt to prevent their members from leaving.

Relationship With Society

Some NRMs have created problems for society or the government because of their social posture, their failure to teach their members to be concerned citizens who discharge their duties to others, and the social disorientation of their followers.

Phenomenon to Be Taken Seriously

All this shows that the problems and challenges thrown up by the new religious movements should be taken seriously.

V. PASTORAL RESPONSE: GENERAL

Not a Negative Response

In examining what pastoral posture the Church should adopt toward the NRMs, let us begin by saying what this pastoral approach should not be. It should not be an attack. It should not be negative against their members, although the Church might have to defend herself against the NRMs that attack her unjustly. It should rather be based on light and love.

The Church sees the persons belonging to the NRMs not as enemies to be attacked, but as people redeemed by Christ who are now in error and with whom the Church wants to share the light and love of Christ. The phenomenon of the NRMs is looked upon by the Church as a sign of the times.

The Church, while aware that the NRMs affect only a minority, cannot avoid asking herself such questions as the following: What makes people join the NRMs? What are the legitimate needs of people which these movements promise to answer and which the Church should be meeting? Are there other causes of the rise and spread of these movements? What does God want of the Church in this situation?

Action by Roman Curia

Because individual bishops and many bishops' conferences expressed to the Holy See their pastoral concern over the activities of the sects or NRMs in their dioceses, a questionnaire was sent to the bishops' conferences in 1983 by four dicasteries of the Roman Curia (the Pontifical Councils for Promoting Christian Unity, for Interreligious Dialogue, for Dialogue With Non-Believers and for Culture). The replies received from seventy-five bishops' conferences were analyzed, synthesized, and published by these four dicasteries in May 1986 under the title "Sects or New Religious Movements: Pastoral Challenge."

The document was positively welcomed by both Catholics and other Christians. Within the Catholic Church, it promoted greater communication on the matter between dioceses, bishops' conferences, and the Holy See. It encouraged bishops' pastoral letters and more study at the level of the local churches.

The Holy See has encouraged the International Federation of Catholic Universities to mount a major research project on the NRMs, and this is being carried out. The 1986 document is regarded only as a starting point.

Action at the Level of the Local Church

At the level of dioceses and bishops' conferences, study centers, and commissions on the new religious movements have increased. Books are coming out. Many bishops' conferences are issuing pastoral letters on the phenomenon. Pastoral workers are being informed and trained in an effort to analyze this reality and find adequate answers.

The International Federation of Catholic Universities

As mentioned earlier, four Roman Curia dicasteries requested the International Federation of Catholic Universities to undertake research on the sects, or NRMs. The Center for Coordination of Research of the federation launched the project in 1988. The first project director was Father Remi Hoeckman, O.P. Now it is Father Michael Fuss, professor in the pontifical Gregorian University. More than fifty experts on the five continents are working on the complex project, each in his own discipline, under theological, sociological, psychological, and other aspects.

The results of the federation's research will no doubt be very useful for the pastoral work of the Church. The question of the NRMs does not admit of any quick or easy solution. Scientific and interdisciplinary research and analysis are necessary elements of a well-founded and lasting pastoral approach.

Is Dialogue Possible With the NRMs?

Some people have asked if dialogue with the NRMs is possible. Certainly the nature and the mission of the Church make dialogue with every human being and with religious and cultural groups part of the style of the Church's apostolate. And the Second Vatican Council has called for dialogue with other Christians and with other believers.

The difficulty lies in how to conduct dialogue with the NRMs with due prudence and discernment. The nature of many NRMs and their manner of operation make dialogue with them particularly problematic for the Church. The duty of pastors of the Church to defend the Catholic faithful from erroneous or dangerous associations is a serious one.

There should be no blanket condemnation of the NRMs. Catholics should always be ready to study and identify elements or tendencies that are in themselves good or noble and where some collaboration is possible. They should also keep up study and observation of movements that so far present an unclear image.

There remains the problem of the NRMs which pursue an aggressive strategy against the Church, sometimes with foreign economic and political support. Without refusing to discuss with such groups, the Church has to consider how to defend herself with legitimate means.

VI. PASTORAL RESPONSE: SPECIFIC

Doctrinal Orientation by Bishops

Many NRMs attract Catholics in places where there is doctrinal disorientation or confusion in the Catholic community. Such confusion can in part be due to doubts sown by some Catholic theologians and others who contest some teachings of the magisterium, or because of poor religious instruction, or because of attacks by the sects.

Whatever the cause, the bishops have to remind themselves that they are "preachers of the faith who lead new disciples to Christ. They are authentic teachers, that is, teachers endowed with the authority of Christ, who preach to the people committed to them the faith they must believe and put into practice" (*Lumen Gentium*, 25). Every bishop has to discharge this duty personally and to insist on it "welcome or unwelcome" (2 Tim. 4:1), even when he risks losing the gratitude of the disoriented majority or provoking the attack of the active and agitating minority.

Adequate Catechesis and Bible Initiation

Experience shows that the NRMs exploit situations of religious ignorance among Christians. Adequate catechesis should therefore be attended to as one of the ways to arm the Catholic community against such infections. Such initiation in the faith should give special importance to the Bible.

Catholics should be so schooled in their faith that they always have an answer ready for people who ask them the reason for the hope that they have (cf. 1 Pt. 3:15).

Prayer and Devotional Life

Some NRMs attract people because they promise to offer them satisfying prayer and worship. The Church at the level of the parish should be convinced that her liturgical and devotional tradition adequately responds to the needs of the human soul if properly understood, carried out and lived.

Mysticism, Peace, Harmony

The new religious movements promise people wisdom, peace, harmony, and self-realization. Our presentation of Christianity should be that of good news, of divine wisdom, of unity and harmony with God and all creation, of happiness which is the earthly preparation for heavenly bliss, and of that peace which the world cannot give (cf. Jn. 14:27).

The dimension of religious experience should not be forgotten in our presentation of Christianity. It is not enough to supply people with intellectual information. Christianity is neither a set of doctrines nor an ethical system. It is life in Christ, which can be lived at ever deeper levels.

Due Evaluation of Gestures and Symbols

Many NRMs put the emphasis on the emotional rather than the notional. Without reaching that excess, it will be of help in many parishes and places of worship to take more notice of the body, of gestures, and of material things in liturgical celebrations and popular devotions.

Living Communities

The NRMs often attract Christians because they offer them warm community life. Very large parishes can create problems in this direction unless a deliberate effort is made to seek ways to help each individual to know that he/she is appreciated, loved, and given a role to play. The Church should be seen and personally experienced as a community of love and service, which celebrates and lives the Holy Eucharist.

Build Up Lay Leadership and Participation

Indeed the sects or NRMs flourish more where effective priestly activity is absent or sporadic. But it is also true that the Church needs

313

dynamic lay leadership. Accentuated clericalism can marginalize the lay faithful and make them look on the Church as an institution run by ordained bureaucratic functionaries. The NRMs, on the other hand, display much lay activity.

Discernment

The NRMs often attract people who are hungry for something deeper in their religious lives. The danger is that they offer short-term good but long-term confusion. Thus people can lose their Catholic roots and in spite of temporary growth be left in a worse spiritual situation eventually. This is an important area about which to offer guidelines to pastors and people alike.

Importance of a Diocesan Program

Every diocese or group of dioceses should ask itself searching questions such as the following: What sects or new religious movements actually are present in its territory? What are their methods of operation? What are the weak points in Catholic life in the area which NRMs exploit? What practical helps do the lay faithful receive in spirituality and offering of personal prayer? How does the Church in the diocese and its parishes contribute to the building up of genuine support for Christians in material, social, or other difficulty? Do the Catholics in the diocese live the Gospel in a socially committed way?

What kind of material do the people of the diocese receive from the local or national radio, press, or television, and what is the local church's pastoral social-communications answer?

Does the activity of the NRMs in the area indicate that it would be useful if the bishop issued a document for the guidance of the faithful?

CONCLUSION

Faced by the dynamic activity of the NRMs, the pastors of the Church cannot just go on with "business as usual." The phenomenon of the NRMs is a challenge and an opportunity. The Church should be confident that she has the resources to rise to the occasion. As the Holy Father said to the bishops of Mexico May 12, 1990, "the presence of the so-called 'sects' is a more than sufficient reason to make a deep examination of the local Church's ministerial life, along with a simultaneous search for answers and unified guidelines which allow for preserving and strengthening the unity of God's people. Faced with this challenge, you have opportunely set up pastoral options. These options go beyond a mere response to the present challenge and seek to be channels as well for the new evangelization, so much more pressing in that they are concrete ways to deepen the faith and Christian life of your communities" (addresses in *L'Osservatore Romano*, English edition, May 14, 1990, p. 2).